The Bamboo Paradox:

The limits of human flexibility in a cruel world – and how to protect, defend and strengthen yourself

Finding the Golden Mean that leads to strength and viable flexibility, in order to be happy, healthy and realistically successful

By Dr Jim Byrne.

With contributed chapters by Renata Taylor-Byrne

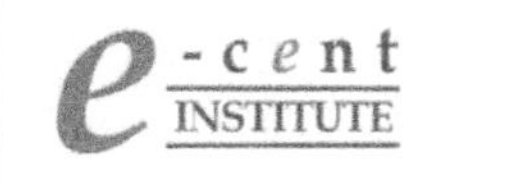

The Institute for E-CENT Publications: 2020

Copyright details

Published by: The Institute for Emotive-Cognitive Embodied-Narrative Therapy, 27 Wood End, Keighley Road, Hebden Bridge, West Yorkshire, HX7 8HJ, UK

Telephone: 01422 843 629

Promoted by the ABC Bookstore Online UK

Distributed by Amazon outlets.

Cover design by Will Sutton

ISBN: 9781708808723

Preface

Waking up to a challenging reality

At the age of thirty-four years, I woke up, for the first time. I became aware of the fact that I was living a life that didn't really work for me – which had never really worked in a remotely satisfactory way.

When I say it had never really worked, you might misunderstand, and think my life lacked excitement; but that is not what I mean at all. I had lived and worked in Bangladesh and Thailand; been to college; been a radical politician; edited a political journal and an alternative newspaper; had three relationships with women; published two books and several significant reports; travelled across Europe on military service; and much more besides. But none of this meant anything to me. None of this had any real, emotional significance.

I woke up because I could not look inside myself and see anything worth considering. I woke up because I found myself writing these words:

> "The valley is empty now.
> Nothing moves on the streets.
> Except people;
> Internal combustion cars;
> Children,
> And every kind of dog.
> I always hate to see it this way,
> Which is all the time!"

~~~

I was depressed by the *emptiness* of my *full* life!

At that point, I began to seek wisdom – to examine my life – and to explore ideas about better ways of living a more meaningful, purposeful, more satisfying life.

Around this time, I came across Thoreau's quotation which claims that: "Most men lead lives of *quiet desperation*".

That felt like a profound truth, but it does not help us to know what to do about it.
~~~

Perhaps you can relate to this situation.

Perhaps your own life does not really work for you, in a fully satisfactory way.

And perhaps it's time to find out why; and what you could do about it.

In this book, I want to share some of the fruits of waking up, and taking responsibility for the direction of my life. What I will tell you about is my journey - shared with my wonderful wife, Renata Taylor-Byrne (who I hardly knew at the point at which I woke up). This was a journey towards wisdom and happiness; physical and mental health; and emotional well-being.

Of course, I had little idea what 'wisdom' meant at that time. I knew the word. Perhaps my thoughts about wisdom went something like this, at that time:

Wisdom may be assumed to be about distinguishing fact from fantasy; though I know how difficult that can be. It should be about being realistic, or practical and logical about life and what it is possible to gain from living well. But it also probably entails knowing where to look, and how to value what we see. (At the age of 34 years I had limited capacity to do any of this).

I also sensed that I had often been foolish in the things I'd said and done; the things I got involved in; and the people I'd allowed to influence me.

I was not good at accepting myself as I was; and often criticized myself for my apparent failings; especially in failing to make enough money for a comfortable life; or to have a group of friends. But I was good at keeping calm. Perhaps, sometimes, I was calm when I should have been angry; but I was often afraid to be angry.

I was aware of the inner conflict in all humans between the desire to be a good, moral individual, and the desire for the fruits of evil (which involve harming others). And I had mainly been able to avoid my evil or immoral urges.

I did not have a developed capacity to laugh and have fun; and I over-worked (because, as I discovered very much later, I am 'a Responsible Workaholic')[1]. I was overly serious; too upset about the mad, unequal world into which I'd been thrown at birth.

And I was not good at feeling grateful for what I actually had in my life; and the many exotic journeys I'd been on.

I was aware of the value of being 'gentlemanly' or polite in my dealings with others, to facilitate the smooth running of social encounters. But I was not self-assertive enough.

I was aware of my limitations as a human and a man; but I had not yet reached the stage of being able to accept my inefficiencies and ineffective behaviours; or my poor general judgements.

I was not good at forgiving others for their unavoidable foolishness; though I was often inappropriately critical of others for their fallible humanness.

I did not often engage in foolish anger; but I did not recognize that I was entitled to take up a full square on the chessboard of life. I tended to live in the cracks between the lives of others.

I had been raised to be very stoical; to 'carry my (Catholic) cross willingly'; to 'turn the other cheek' to insults and injury; to 'roll with the punches'; to ignore the 'arrows of adversity'; and so on.

I had mismanaged my first marriage; and did not (during that six year marriage) wake up to the fact that I had *no idea how to have a happy relationship* - mainly because I came from a family in which my mother and father had an arranged marriage; and they never learned to love each other; and their only love for their children was one driven by *duty*, and not affection. (Of course, it took years for me to understand this aspect of my start point in life!)

~~~

This is my 'progress report' - my book about how to take care of yourself in a difficult world; so you can be happy and healthy, successful and (relatively, realistically) wealthy.

Your physical height, weight, muscle bulk and so on, are not the most important determinants of your ability to be *strong* in the face of life's difficult challenges.

And neither is your IQ, or your academic credentials.

But it is also a book that warns against assuming you are stronger than you could possibly be, given that you are a human being, with a fleshy body, and limited immunity to stress and disease.
~~~

The foundation of your resilience

In many ways, your *ephemeral* mind – supported by a well-rested and nourished body – and a *determination* to be happy and successful - is the best measure of your potential for resilient coping with the unavoidably stressful challenges you inevitably will face. But you also need to learn how to love, and to have nourishing social connections. Physical strength and mental stamina *alone* will not help here. And neither will IQ, academic qualifications or innate cunning!

So what will help?

Today we are bombarded by lots of (good and bad) ideas about 'how to make it in life'. One of these, which needs to be looked at more closely, is the metaphor which says *we should learn to be like a bamboo plant* – supple, pliable, and adapting to the high winds of adversity.

Here are a couple of examples of advice to emulate the bamboo, found on the Internet:

> **Being like bamboo means coming closer to the ancient wisdom of nature itself.** It's understanding that taking care of your soul requires time and patience. In addition, ***it's knowing that it doesn't matter how strong the wind blows or how rough the storm is because you've already learned to be flexible and, above all, resilient.***[2]
>
> ~~~
>
> **Bend but don't break. Be flexible yet firmly rooted** One of the most impressive things about the bamboo in the forest is how they sway with even the slightest breeze. ... A bend-but-don't-break or go-with-the-natural-flow attitude is one of the secrets for success whether we're talking about bamboo trees, (or humans – Ed.) answering tough questions in a Q&A session, or ***just dealing with the everyday vagaries***[1] ***of life.***[3]
>
> ~~~

[1] Definition of vagary: an erratic, unpredictable, or extravagant manifestation, action, or notion. Source: https://www.merriam-webster.com/dictionary/vagary

Are these wise comments? Is this *wise advice - to aim to be more like a bamboo, no matter how strong the wind blows?*

Nobody could deny that the humble bamboo is often the thinnest plant in the forest or jungle when a tropical storm hits; but it is often the only plant left standing when the storm is over.

According to our common 'received wisdom', if you develop some bamboo-like flexibility, you can become as strong and resilient as you need to be, even if you are thin and light and less tall than the average person.

This is how the qualities of bamboo are conceptualized by one business-person:

"Bamboo is flexible, bending with the wind but never breaking, capable of adapting to any circumstance. It suggests resilience, meaning that even in the most difficult times… your ability to thrive depends, in the end, on your attitude to your life circumstances. Like putting forth energy when it is needed, yet always staying calm inwardly". (Ping Fu: 'Bend, Not Break: A life in two worlds').

Being like a bamboo

I will take a closer look at that quotation later. In the meantime, I want to address its implications, *taking it at face value*. Ping Fu seems to suggest that you can learn to bend in strong winds of change or challenge; and to sway in the frequent breezes of trial and tribulation. You can develop a solid foundation, but one which allows you to stay flexible, and to respond to the forces that assail you with a *judo-like yielding* and *returning*. Bend in harmony with the forces around you, without resisting rigidly, and thus avoid being broken. Go with the flow, when the flow is irresistible; but swim against the tide if you need to, when the tide is not too powerful. Eventually, the forces around you may grow tired, and you will be fresh and ready to move forward, when resistance is at its lowest.

Bruce Lee is on record as supporting this kind of perspective:

"Notice that the stiffest tree is most easily cracked" he wrote, "while the bamboo … survives by bending with the wind".

And, beyond what those commentators have said, common sense seems to suggest that, to be like the bamboo, you must not just be well informed about how to use your mind – like an ancient philosopher – but also you must be well fed, well rested, happily related to at least one significant other person; and rooted in some kind of family, social group and/or community. You need to be involved and rooted in your home community, but free to take whatever individual action you need to take, so long as it is moral and legal.

This may be what Jodi Picoult had in mind when she wrote that, "The human capacity for burden is like bamboo – far more flexible than you'd ever believe at first glance".

A flawed metaphor

Of course there are flaws in each of those quotations above – limitations and exaggerations – (which would eventually lead us into *paradox*, or self-contradicting beliefs and actions. I will explore some aspects of that paradox in this Preface; and return to this problem in Chapter 17)[2].

But the common sense argument seems to be that we should *celebrate* the *near perfect* combination of strength and flexibility to be found in bamboo, and that therefore we should *try to emulate* that strength and flexibility in our own difficult lives - when appropriate - as individual human beings.

~~~

The first major limitation of comparing ourselves with bamboo is this: In western science, the world is divided into three major classes: *animal*, *vegetable* and *mineral*. Clearly, bamboo belongs to one of those classes (the *vegetables*) while humans belong to another (the *animals*).

Bamboo is rooted to the spot, while humans, and other animals, move around the world.

To build a bridge from the vegetable world of bamboo, to the animal world of human individuals, let me introduce a transitional entity – a little duck in an endless sea.

[2] The term *paradox* is from the Greek word *paradoxon*, which means "contrary to expectations, existing belief, or perceived opinion."
~~~

Donald C. Babcock has written about a little duck – "something pretty special" - which is out on the ocean; cuddling down in the swells; and riding the waves. Out beyond the surf by one hundred feet[4].

The Atlantic is heaving mightily, producing huge rises and falls; and the little duck is part of that rise and fall.

Indeed, the duck is *resting* while the Atlantic does all the heaving.

Babcock considers that the duck has some physical sense or realization of the *size* of the ocean which is surging up beneath him, and then dropping him down again, many feet each time.

"... the duck reposes in the immediate, as if it were infinity – which (of course) it is", writes Babcock.

Babcock sees this as a profoundly wise attitude on the part of the duck; and he questions whether or not you and I, humans, have as much wisdom in dealing with the great waves that threaten to buffet our own lives!

This little duck is meant to illustrate the 'bamboo qualities' of a little animal. It is meant to illustrate harmony and balance, as well as strength and flexibility – and a certain amount of detachment from unreasonable levels of fear (which bamboo never feels!).

Humans and bamboo plants

But next, we have to make the final migration from bamboo, via the little duck, to a real human individual. To do that, I would like to present a little case study:

About fifteen years ago, I (as a counsellor) was contacted via the telephone system by a young man (let us call him Shami – not his real name!). Shami was an Indian man, working in the US as an IT specialist; and phoning from New York City. He was involved in a relationship with an American woman, and it was not going well; so he wanted couples therapy from me. Shami had been born in India. His parents were well-educated and relatively wealthy. He father was a hospital doctor in Mumbai (not the real location!), where the family lived; and his mother was a research scientist who specialized in the biochemistry of common diseases for a pharmaceutical company.

My initial response was to try to get Shami to work on his beliefs and attitudes towards women in general, and his partner in particular. This seemed to be somewhat helpful, but after three sessions he disappeared.

Months later, he contacted me again. This time his partner had left him, and so I helped him to cope with the grief of losing her; and his shame about not being able to hold down a stable relationship.

Then he disappeared again, for a couple of years. When next he contacted me, he had a new girlfriend, and they were dating a couple of nights per week. They'd met a couple of months back, but already conflict had emerged in their relationship. I tried to dig a bit deeper into Shami's background, to see what was driving his inability to get along with a female partner.

Shami had had an unhappy childhood, because his parents were always working; and he was raised by a nanny and fed by a maid. He hated his father with a vengeance, and he was cold towards his (cold) mother.

This new dating relationship was the fifth or sixth unsuccessful relationship he'd been in, since arriving in America, about eight years earlier. I began to explore his relationship problems more deeply, and traced his problems back to how his mother and father related to each other: which was to say, badly. And also how his mother in particular related to him (coldly). His father had been even more absent (and remote) than his mother.

When Shami was about eighteen years old, he'd decided to study in America, and after graduating, he got a job as a computer programmer. He was what I now know to be 'a Responsible Workaholic' - which is a variety of 'personality adaptation'[5] - and he tended to sit at his computer, in his New York employer's office, from seven o'clock each morning until seven o'clock each evening, wrestling with difficult programming problems.

He popped out of his office and had a burger for lunch; and again for his evening meal, around five o'clock. He worked six days a week, and spent most of Sunday in bed.

He never did any physical exercise; got less than six hours sleep each night, and sometimes a lot less; drank too much alcohol and coffee; and generally was living a very unbalanced life.

I suggested that he clean up his diet, since his junk food diet was making him angry with his female partner. (See Taylor-Byrne and Byrne, 2017)[6]. But he said he'd have to walk six blocks to find any outlet that sold salad or other healthy options; and we wasn't able to spare the time and energy for such a 'long walk'. And, besides, he like burgers, and did not see that diet was a real contributor to his relationship problems.

I tried to get him to do some regular physical exercise, which would reduce his anxiety and jealousy, which seemed to be driving much of his couple-conflict, but he could not be persuaded that it was important to do so.

Shami then disappeared again, and I didn't hear from him for another couple of years.

The next time I heard from him, he had been medically evacuated from New York to Mumbai; was living in his parent's pool house, at the bottom of their garden; and sleeping sixteen hours every day. He had been diagnosed with ME and chronic fatigue syndrome; and with painful myalgia in his neck and right shoulder, which reduced him to tears when it was at its worst. Pain-killing medication only reduced the pain to a small degree.

His parents – a medical doctor and a medical scientist – had failed to find any way to help him. So he phoned me once more.

I tried to help him to get to the bottom of his problems, by focusing on his sedentary lifestyle; his very poor diet; his inadequate amount of regular nightly sleep; and his apparent inability to relax. Plus his childhood relationships with his parents: especially his murderous anger towards his father.

But he didn't want me to play that role. He wanted me simply to help him with his *mental attitude* towards his problems, rather than helping him to *cure* his problems. He wanted me to help him to be *even more Stoical* than he currently was. This caused a falling out between is, because I did not enjoy being used like a verbal or philosophical sticking-plaster. (Some years after I last worked with Shami, I stumbled across the system of Personality Adaptations, refined by Joines and Stewart [2002]. In this system of personality analysis, there are three main 'performing adaptations' – which are adaptations to parents made in early childhood, in order to *make it* with the parents. One of those personality adaptations is called the 'Responsible Workaholic'; and individuals with this adaptation tend to behave in a *perfectionistic* manner; which is perhaps what Shami was trying to do in his work role. They often have problems in their couple relationships, because they apply their perfectionistic standards to their partner, and this causes lots of conflict. So perhaps Shami would have *overworked*, even if the system of capitalism in which he was working was more benign!?!)

Questionable philosophies of life

Shami was a good illustration of what is wrong with some aspects of the three quotes presented above about bamboo. Let me illustrate what I mean:

Jodi Picoult's quote refers to "the human capacity for burden" – and that can be taken to *extremes,* which is what Shami did. The human capacity to tolerate burdens should never be taken to extremes. We need to find *the middle way* between under-working and over-working. (There are, of course, exploitative forces in the world today which would like to persuade you that *over-working is impossible*! My response to that lie is this: "Look at the damage Shami did to himself by overworking!" [But also watch out for your own perfectionist work standards, which may be driven by childhood adaptations to your parents!])

Bruce Lee's quote seems to be beyond reproach. However, note the phrase "bending with the wind". It is important to bend with the wind – *some but not all of the time.* If you, as a human being, encounter a 'wind' that is too strong to be easily or healthily endured, then you have a responsibility to *get out* of that wind – to get the hell out of any such *excessive* wind! This is the beginning of awareness of the bamboo paradox. You can **try** to take flexibility too far, but your body may well break if your mind does not spot the unendurable nature of some of your new burdens!

Many years ago, Charles Handy pointed to the problem of staying in stressful situations for too long, until we become 'cooked', or broken, mentally and/or physically, by stress and strain. He used the analogy of a frog and boiling water. If you place a frog in a pan of cold water, or lukewarm water, it will happily stay there; whereas if the temperature is too high when you drop it in, it will jump out immediately. On the other hand, if you place it in a pan of cool water, and then heat that water slowly, the frog will stay in the pan until it is *cooked to death!* Beware this frog-like capacity to allow yourself to be cooked to death by stress and strain! While you think you are acting like a bamboo, you may, in fact, be acting like ***a dumb frog!***

Ping Fu's quote contains three contentious points, from my perspective:

Number 1: The idea that bamboo - and by extension - human beings, are "...capable of *adapting to **any** circumstance*". This is not true. It is obviously not true of a human, because it did not work for Shami, who is undoubtedly a human. It is not true for a human, because there are legions of burned out teachers spewed out by the education system in the UK (and probably many other countries also; and many other professions, like medicine!). It is not even true of bamboo. If you pour petrol (petroleum gas) over a bamboo tree, and ignite it, the tree will be destroyed. If you pour nitric acid around its roots, you will destroy it! Humans should not try to adapt to "any and every circumstance". Shami should have had more sense. He should have listened to the Hawaiian concept of 'pono', or balance! He wrecked his health by failing to achieve *balance* in his life.

When I teach the concept of *pono* to my clients, I always emphasize that they should seek to base their daily life on 8 hours of work; 8 hours rest; and 8 hours of play, except sometimes. Eight hours in bed each night, in a dark, cool room, with no TVs or computers or mobile phones. And lots of time spent with friends, family, and others, enjoying social connection.

Number 2: Ping Fu asserts that resilience means "...the ability to bounce back *even in **the most** difficult times*." But if you look up a definition of resilience in a popular dictionary, you might get a subtly different meaning, such as this: "the capacity to recover quickly from difficulties; toughness." There is clearly a distinction to be made between Ping Fu's statement ("even in **the most difficult** times"); and my dictionary's definition (of the capacity to recover quickly "from **difficulties**"). And a definition that I found online cited *two examples* of resilient entities:

(a) "...the *often* remarkable resilience of *so many* British institutions". And:

(b) 'Nylon'.

But please note, with regard to example (a) above, the *two qualifiers* in italic typeface: 'often', and 'so many'. This means that it is ***not*** the case that ***all*** British institutions can ***always*** be resilient enough to survive in ***all*** situations. And similarly, ***you*** should not expect to ***always*** be resilient enough to survive in ***all*** the situations that the world may impose upon you. Sometimes you have to beat a sensible retreat! But Ping Fu does not understand these qualifiers, as she implies that we humans have the ability to bounce back "even in ***the most difficult*** circumstances", without exception. But exceptions have to be acknowledged. What Ping Fu should have said is this: "...we humans (often) have the ability to bounce back, even in (very many of) the most difficult circumstances". Remember the exceptions. Remember Shami! Remember the boiled frog!

And then we need to look at example (b) above – ***nylon***. Nylon will *not* bounce back from being burned, or dropped into a vat of acid. And human beings will *not* bounce back from six days a week of sitting on their arses in front of computer screens; and/or eating junk food on a frequent or regular basis; and/or getting insufficient sleep on a regular or frequent basis! And/or being involved in *seriously conflicted* sex-love relationships. Those kinds of lifestyle factors will wreck their health and happiness.

Number 3: Ping Fu is wrong to assert that "...your ability to thrive ***depends, in the end, on your attitude*** to your life circumstances".

This is an expression of the kind of Extreme Stoical philosophy of life which asserts that "people are *not* upset by what happens to them, but rather by *the attitude they adopt* towards what happens to them".

I will show in a later chapter of this book - where I critique *extreme Stoicism* - that this is a *baseless* claim. People *are upset by what happens to them*; and your ability to thrive depends, ultimately, on how well ***rested*** you are, on a regular basis; how ***well-nourished*** you are by a healthy diet; how well your body is ***exercised***; and how well ***connected*** you are to other people; how balanced your life is; how aware you are of the boiled frog phenomenon; in ***addition to*** your *attitude* towards what happens to you; and so on. It is not all in the mind; and it is not all about *attitude.* Attitude is important, but so also is the health of the body; and the point of balance of a multitude of lifestyle factors.

Defending yourself against 'bamboo bullshit'

We live in a world in which there are dark forces that wish us to forget that we are *fleshy bodies*, with physical and mental *needs;* and physical and mental *limitations*; and not mere *cogs* in the wheels of somebody else's financial or technological empire.

Rational Emotive Behaviour Therapy (REBT) has played into this narrative, and given it philosophical support, by promoting a form of Extreme

Stoicism in the name of therapy and wisdom, which it patently is not. (General Cognitive Behaviour Therapy [CBT] also supports this agenda, but to a lesser degree, or in a less obvious way!)

Before Shami had originally contacted me, he had seen an REBT therapist for couples-therapy; and he'd read a few REBT books, by Dr Albert Ellis; and he was strongly committed to being an REBT 'tough guy'! His therapist, and Albert Ellis's books, had taught him to "...stay in uncomfortable situations until you become comfortable with them, and then decide whether or not to leave!" But this was disastrous advice for Shami, which cost him his health, happiness and his very future as an active human being in the social world.

Although I was strongly influence by Albert Ellis's system of REBT, I did not advise my couple-clients to "stay in uncomfortable situations". I told them that my priority was the happiness of both partners, and not the maintenance of the relationship. And, as it happened, my very first client as an REBT coach/counsellor was a forty-five year old man who was on permanent night-shift work in a textile factory. I knew this was bad for his health, and so I helped him to negotiate a way off nights and onto the day shift: (rather than trying to teach him to get rid of his so-called 'irrational beliefs' about night-shift working - which is the REBT approach). I also helped him to negotiate a better wage and conditions with his employers; and I tried my best to help him and his partner to improve their relationship (without putting the continuance of the relationship above the happiness of both partners!)

Albert Ellis's philosophy of life was defective in many ways. (See my critique of REBT)[7]. But one of the worst elements turned out to be his approach to what he called 'high frustration tolerance' – which I would now call 'resilience' in the face of difficulties.

Ellis's solution was to adopt this belief: "I certainly can stand it!" And "it" could be ***anything*** **(meaning everything)**, up to, but not including, one's own death!

(But Shami demonstrated that we humans ***cannot stand everything***, up to, but not including, our own death!)

And the *unaddressed questions* in Ellis's Extreme Stoical philosophy of life are these:

1. "Is it <u>*safe*</u> to *try* to stand it, or to *go on* enduring it?"

2. "Is it *sensible* to try to stand it?"

3. "Do I *have to* stand it, or could I get out?" And:

4. "Should I stay, or should I get out?"

It was not *safe* for Shami to stay in his *rotten job*!

It was not *sensible* for Shami to stay in his *oppressive employment*!

He *did* <u>*not*</u> have to stand it, since he could have got into something less oppressive (at least in theory)!

And, with the benefit of hindsight, he must be able to see that *he* <u>*should*</u> *have got out when he could!*

About this book

In this book, I will review the research that we have done on the *limits* of human endurance, and the *determinants* of that endurance, as well as our philosophy of life, which will help you to *optimize* your strength and flexibility, while at the same time taking care of your health and happiness.

I will look at effective approaches and ineffective approaches to:

- diet,
- exercise,
- sleep,
- relaxation,
- and philosophies of life.

I will teach you *the middle way* between extremes in all five of those areas of lifestyle self-management

Initially, I will introduce some key concepts and skills from *moderate* Stoic philosophy. This is intended to help you to know how to be 'reasonably flexible', as opposed to being 'unrealistically flexible'.

Then I will outline some of the ways in which you could get fooled by some of the *extreme* elements of Stoicism, and/or Buddhism, which are reminiscent of some of the errors in the three quotations about bamboo, shown above.

(That is to say, Extreme Stoicism encourages its adherents to behave as if they were blocks of wood, which cannot be hurt or harmed by anybody or anything. But Shami and the boiled frogs of this world demonstrate that that is not achievable. Even Albert Ellis failed to operate like an indifferent block of wood when he was dismissed by his Institute in 2004/2005).

Then I will outline my own ***Nine Windows** model,* which shows nine ways of reframing adversities, so that you can remain calm and centred and grounded in many of the difficult situations that you will most likely face in the future. These nine windows are strongly influenced by ***moderate** ideas* from Stoicism and Buddhism.

I will also summarize your needs for the right kind of nutrition, and effective approaches to sleep, exercise and relaxation.

And then I will return to the human-bamboo paradox, and link it to western stress management research.

Without this kind of information, how can you hope to achieve balance (*pono*) in your life?

And without this information, you may well fall foul of the *bamboo paradox*, and end your life like Shami - broken, bedridden and weighed down by physical pain and emotional gloom, because of trying to be *too flexible in a madly cruel world!*

~~~

Jim Byrne, Doctor of Counselling, Hebden Bridge,

March 2020

~~~

Contents

Part 1: An introduction to Moderate Stoicism:

Or how to create a flexible mind

In Part 1, I want to present you with a good, general introduction to some of the most powerful, moderate, mind-management techniques that were created by Stoic philosophers in ancient Rome.

These approaches to life are designed to help you to develop a realistic and sustainable level of flexibility in the management of your mental processes (which include thinking, feeling and perceiving). Instead of trying to teach you to be like a bamboo, or a block of wood, they will teach you how to be a *wisely flexible* human being.

Part 1 will not contain any references to the ways in which you should also try to build up your physical strength, flexibility and resilient. That work will be presented in Part 4, below. (Part 2 will present some criticisms of some *extreme elements* of Stoicism, *which should be avoided.* And Part 3 will present my own fusion of moderate Stoicism and moderate Buddhism, to provide nine ways to re-frame any problem).

~~~
~~~

Chapter 1: Learning how to be more philosophical about life's difficulties

Introduction

Life is difficult and frustrating. It will grind us down unless we learn to manage the way we *apprehend it* in our minds; (and - as I will show in Part 3 – we also need to take care of our bodily strength and resilience – because the body and mind are *not* separate).

The insight that life is difficult is one of the key messages left to us by the Buddha Gautama. It is also a strong strand within European Stoicism, which originated in ancient Greece, and reached its full flowering in ancient Rome.

I have been studying these approaches to life for almost forty years.

As a counsellor for more than twenty years, I have taught elements of this philosophy – derived from *moderate elements* of Stoicism and Buddhism – to most of my clients who were struggling with a range of serious life difficulties.

I have also sought to include elements of this kind of philosophical approach in my books for self-help enthusiasts.

This current book is intended for the general reader who wants to become more wisely flexible (as appropriate) in the face of the strong winds, the storms, of the post-2008 *world economic crash*. It should also be of interest to counsellors and self-help enthusiasts.

We are all philosophers of sorts

Philosophy is as natural for a human being as grazing is for a cow. We are natural philosophers, and the dark arts of those who wish to control us for their own benefit is to *feed us **false** philosophies* (like feeding polluted food to a cow).

If you take your philosophy from the mass media, or state funded education systems, how do you know that your ideas are even reasonably valid, or the best way to promote a thriving society?

If you work in counselling and therapy, or use counselling and therapy services, or self-help resources, then you need to beware of being enrolled into philosophies that work against you. And you need to beware of passing on *defective philosophies* that you do not fully understand.

Over the past twenty years or more, I have read the *Enchiridion* by Epictetus, at least three times; the *Meditations* of Marcus Aurelius, at least twice; and the REBT version of Stoic philosophy many times. Does that mean I now understand Stoicism? And can I be sure that Stoicism is a philosophy that will serve me well?

Initially, I swallowed Stoicism whole; and then later I developed a more balanced view of its strengths and weaknesses. In this and subsequent chapters of Part 1, I will concentrate on *some important* ***strengths*** *of Stoicism,* which will be helpful for anybody who wants to develop the qualities of wise and appropriate flexibility (as opposed to trying to be like a *bamboo plant, which is impossible for a human*). Part 1 will be particularly helpful to counsellors, psychotherapists, coaches, psychologists, social workers, and students of those disciplines; and self-help enthusiasts.

The origins of Stoicism

Firstly, it seems the Stoic ideas of Epictetus and Marcus Aurelius are expression of the 'third stage' in the evolution of Stoic philosophy. (See William Irvine's book, *A Guide to the Good Life: The ancient art of Stoic joy;* Oxford University Press, 2009). Irvine traces the history of the development of Stoicism from Zeno of Citium, in ancient Greece, through to the end of the Roman Empire. In the process he describes three phases in its development, two within Greece, and one of adaptation to Rome. Zeno, it seems, began as a shipwreck (which he later described as 'a great good fortune') which led him to explore the philosophies being taught in public places in Athens - and later at training schools – in an effort to come to terms with his great losses at sea, where, it seems, he lost all of his wealth and fortune.

He first became a Cynic – which is a form of anti-materialistic asceticism – and later fused cynicism and Plato's philosophy, by attending Plato's Academy.

Under Zeno's guidance, Stoicism thrived in Athens; but after his death it went into decline; and had to be reformulated to make it more appealing to the public.

The basic theory

The basic Stoic philosophy is *to live in accordance with nature.* If we do this, they say, we will be living a virtuous life, and a good one (meaning an enjoyable, happy life). However, there is an immediate problem.

*What does it **mean** to "live in accordance with nature"?*

Well, for the Stoics it meant performing the functions of a human with excellence; and their idea of what was uniquely human was this: Being Rational; the use of Rationality. Which can also be thought of as being logical, reasonable and realistic.

But, today, we know that 'emotional intelligence' is an important aspect of what it means to be fully human, and emotional intelligence cannot be reduced to 'reason', 'rationality' or 'logic'. Emotional intelligence involves being able to read our own emotions, and the emotions of others; and being able to manage our own emotions, and to communicate about our emotions with others.

In Part 3 of this book, I will introduce you to my own synthesis of Buddhist and Stoic perspectives on life's problems – as a way to help you to *re-frame* (or to re-think/feel/perceive) your problems, so they do not seem so distressing.

Furthermore, for a Stoic, to live the good life is to live *an ethical life,* and this also means to live in accordance with nature; which also means to live a rational life; a life dictated by reason/rationality. (And this will sometimes mean that a Stoic [adopting *an extreme tolerance* of the intolerable] will be *blind* to human emotions, which should not be discounted!)

There is a further complication with the Stoic perspective. This results from the fact that, it could be objected that both Conservatives and Social

Democrats (or Republicans and Democrats) believe they are living a life dictated by reason/rationality; as do fascists and communists; and Catholics and Protestants. And yet none of these polarized viewpoints can agree on anything.

- So how is it possible to pin down the answer to the question: "How should I live?"

- Or: "What must I do in order to live in accordance with nature?"

There are, I think, no easy answers! So if somebody tells you they are advocates of Stoicism, and they think you should do X and not-Y, ask them this:

- "How did you work this out?"

- "What are the principles upon which this conclusion is based?"

If their conclusion is "You should do X, but not-Y"; ask them:

- "What are the *premises* that support that conclusion?" (See Bowell and Kemp's book on *Critical Thinking Skills*)[8].

Philosophy is a very tricky discipline. Irvine actually suggests that people should *choose* their philosophies according to their natures, or personalities (which seems a little too pragmatic and risky, in my view). But he also thinks that Stoicism would be *a suitable* philosophy of life for many people. Therefore in this and subsequent chapters, I will introduce some key philosophic ideas from Stoicism, which I judge to be *moderate, achievable* and *helpful* for most people.

The E-CENT refinement of Stoicism

It is not perfectly effortless to work out what your personality is, and what kind of philosophy of life would suit you. For a start, your 'Good Wolf' side – to borrow a concept from the Native American Cherokee people - may want to live one way; and your 'Bad Wolf' side may want to live another way. I think there is an objective case that can be made that ***you should live according to the dictates of your Good Wolf*** – assuming it has been well trained by your parents and teachers. *Social morality is important!*

To live according to the dictates of your Good Wolf means:

1. ***To develop admirable and pro-social virtues***, like: love, gratitude, compassion, charity, tolerance, patience, forbearance, generosity, and so on; and to avoid engaging in inappropriate anger, rage, hostility, greed, meanness, vainglory, and so on.

> The best way to develop your virtuous side is through daily practice; and the best way to establish such a daily practice is through awareness raising; and the best way to raise you awareness in this area is to *prioritize* three or four of the virtues listed above, in the form of a daily affirmation which you read at the start and end of each day. For example:
>
> > "I am now committed to being more loving, grateful, compassionate and charitable, in all my dealings with other people". (Repeat this to yourself ten times every morning, and ten times each evening. Examine your conscious at the end of the day, to see how well you performed; and if you fell short of your gaol, recommit to doing better tomorrow!)

2. ***To follow the Golden Rule:*** In other words, do not harm anybody in any way; Treat others as you would like them to treat you. (This is the basis for defending greater equality, and the case against inequality). Again, you could have this as a written goal, which you review every morning and evening:

> "I will treat other people as I would like them to treat me, if our roles were reversed. I will never treat anybody in ways that I would not wish to be treated by them".

3. ***To actively strive to maximize happiness*** and minimize suffering in your dealings with others. One way to proceed to is to live with this question every day of your life:

> "How can I (morally and legally) maximize the happiness of those people with who I am related, at home and in work? And how can I minimize the suffering that I cause to others?

The art of living in accordance with the dictates of your *Good Wolf* is the art of blending the guidelines in 1, 2 and 3 above, from one situation to another.

Of course, some neo-liberals will doubtless tell you that 'morality is relative to the individual', and that 'greed is okay for greedy people', and poverty for poor people. I suggest you begin to develop arguments against this kind of *absolute relativism.* (Cultural variations exist, but there is *widespread agreement* from society to society about the need to respect human life, personal dignity, and so on). One place you can begin is with Philippa Foot's ideas on ***Goodness***. (See, to begin with, Chapter 10 of a book titled, *What More Philosophers Think;* edited by Baggini and Strangroom; pages 103-114)[9].

Philippa Foot is a very interesting philosopher who spent decades thinking through her ideas on *Goodness* before she published anything; and she has now published three books on the subject. She is very impressive if only for this reason: She has finally invalidated David Hume's claim that ***you can never derive an 'ought' from an 'is'.*** That is to say, she can demonstrate that ***we must be moral when a logical case for being moral is made.*** This is, after all, an example of *living in accordance with nature: living morally in line with our reasons for doing so!*

Philosophy is slippery and difficult to do; but it is, in the end, all we have got when we want to reason our way through our lives.

*Don't let other people tell you **what** to think,* unless you are sure they are moral beings, who have your best interests at heart. (Even then you should subject their ideas to the most stringent tests you can devise!) Learn how to think for yourself - or should I say, learn how to *perceive/feel/think* for yourself - and ***learn how to live in accordance with the wishes of your Good Wolf.*** You will have mastered your philosophy of life when you understand that this makes sense.

Furthermore, as will be shown in a later chapter, in Part 2, below, Stoicism has *an Extreme element* as well as *a Moderate element*; and the extreme element is *counterproductive* and *destructive,* as well as being *totally unrealistic* as a guide to action for a normal human being.

So, to begin with, make a commitment to keep your mind calm by reasoning about your problems. (And by exercising your body; getting eight to nine hours sleep each night; and eating a healthy diet). The most effective strategy for reasoning about your life is to ***keep a daily journal,*** and write at the start and/or end of the day about what you set out to achieve; what you achieved; what went well; and what went badly. In this journal, examine your conscience: Did I live today according to *the Golden Rule*? Did I try to live in accordance with nature? With reason and rationality? In accordance with positive emotions; and emotional intelligence?

Make a commitment to be a moral person; to shun manipulation or exploitation of others. Avoid becoming lazy, greedy, egotistically ambitious, selfish (as distinct from self-caring), ignorant or vain.

In the next chapter I will begin to introduce some insights and practical strategies that were developed by the Stoics.

~~~
~~~

Chapter 2: William Irvine's account of Stoicism

Preamble

Earlier, I mentioned William B. Irvine's book – *A Guide to the Good Life: the ancient art of stoic joy* – which I want to return to now.

The blurb on the dust jacket begins like this: "One of the great fears that many of us face is that, despite all our efforts and striving, we will discover at the end (of our life) that we have wasted our life. In (this book), William B. Irvine plumbs the wisdom of Stoic philosophy, one of the most popular and successful schools of thought in ancient Rome, and shows how its insight and advice are still remarkably applicable to modern lives".

While *some people* might fear wasting their lives on the wrong kinds of goals, others may just be unclear as to what is the best way to set about creating a "good life". Or how to give up creating "a bad life".

In Part 2 of his book, Professor Irvine presents five "Stoic psychological techniques"; and I will present two of those five in this chapter. The first of these is called "Negative Visualization".

Familiarity breeds contempt

One of the biggest problems we humans face is this: When we desire something we do not have, we value it highly. (This could be a new car; a new watch; new clothing; a new house; a job promotion; etc.) But once we get it, and have it for a while, we get used to it; take it for granted; and no longer value it highly.

The Stoics developed a way to counteract this human weakness, which is called 'negative visualization'.

Negative visualization was developed to cope with the very human problem of "hedonic adaptation" – which is the way humans quickly adapt to whatever we get or have, and then ask the world, "What else have you got for me?" The more familiar we become with things that we possess, the less we value them. We take them for granted. And this causes lots of problems.

Before we get something we value, we *long* for it, and *desire* it intensely. (Think of a new sex-love relationship, for example). Once we get it, we may enjoy it for a while. However, eventually *we adapt to having it,* and begin to *take it for granted.* It does not matter what it is. It could be a fancy car, a big house, a great relationship, a new baby, or whatever. The human mind – in its "hungry ghost" manifestation (which is how most of us are most of the time) – adapts to what it's got, and wants more.

Werner Erhard had a humorous way of illustrating this, in his Relationships Course. He would talk about a couple getting together, and falling in love, and thinking to themselves, "Isn't this wonderful! This is so great!"

Then Werner would say:

"And you know how it goes. Don't you? He says 'I love'. And she says 'I love you'. And he says 'I love'. And she says 'I love you'. Then, after a while, that wears out. Suddenly one of them says: 'What else ya got?'"

This is a good example of 'hedonic adaptation'; of coming to take for granted something that was once valued.

Enter the Hungry Ghost

The 'hungry ghost' (which is a function of the Bad Wolf side of human nature) is never satisfied. Just look at the recent example of the Chief Executive of a major multinational corporation who was earning more than GBP £1.7 million per year – yes, PER YEAR. Then he went to a board meeting and said: "Gentlemen. My remuneration package is not sufficient to motivate me to **get out of bed** in the morning. You should ***double*** my gross earnings per year".

But it's not just a few greedy capitalists who are like this. (And by the way, where do you think greedy capitalists came from? The same place greedy feudal lords came from. And the same place greedy Phoenicians came from. And the same place greedy slave owners and slave traders came from. And the same place sexist husbands of all social classes came from. And the same place sexist wives come from. And the same place oppressive parenting came from. THE HUMAN HEART – THE BAD SIDE: THE BAD WOLF INSIDE EACH AND EVERY ONE OF US). This is an example of the way the Bad Wolf performs in each and every one of us, some but (hopefully!) not all of the time.

Even "I" have a Hungry Ghost

Am I saying I am "holier than thou"? No way. Back in 1980 I got a letter from the tax authorities who had determined that I had been overpaying my taxes, and telling me I was due for a "substantial rebate". So immediately the "monkey mind" which runs my "hungry ghost" got to work. This is how it went:

"Great. I need some new bedding, so about £200 would be enough to pay for that. So I hope my rebate is at least GBP £200. But the bedding won't look right unless I decorate this room. So I really need four or five hundred pounds. Let's double that to be on the same side, which means I need £1,000. But the new decoration will make the furniture look old, and so I'd better replace that. Which means I ***need*** about three to six thousand pounds. But actually my living space is too small, so I really need to buy a new place, which I could probably get for about £12,000. But I also need a new office, so more like £25,000. But there are running costs to meet, and my business needs quite a bit of investment, so I really need about £250,000. But it's always good to have a savings account as a backup. So let's hope my rebate is at least £500,000. And then I have to get my new home redecorated and furnished properly. And then I will be so tired I will have to take a holiday. But a holiday on my own would not be great, so I need to hire a villa in France, and invite everybody I know, and have a big party, and a two week holiday. Total **need:** £750,000!"

The Hungry Ghost is a Delusional "Thing Addict"

It was at that moment, as I heard myself say: "I ***need*** £750,000 back from the tax office, otherwise it just won't be enough" that I knew of the existence of the "hungry ghost". The hungry ghost is that insatiable part of us that always wants more: More things; more of everything, except what it does not like.

We can see it all over the Western world today. Almost nobody is happy with their lot; whether they have £5; £50; £500; £5,000; £5 million pounds; or £5 billion pounds; or even £5 trillion pounds. Nothing can fill the hole in the belly and heart of the "hungry ghost", because it is itself unreal; a phantasm; a fundamentally self-doubting, self-damning, self-important ***non-self!*** It is the untrammelled ego – *King Baby* and *Queen Baby*, straddling the world of materialism with an appetite that will fall away immediately the individual ***chooses*** to operate from the ***Good Wolf side of their nature***: the pro-social, loving, caring, contributing self. The one who is willing to be the source of love in the world. The one who is willing to make a contribution to others as their driving motivation. The hungry ghost falls away when the individual chooses to operate from Good Wolf, because the Hungry Ghost is a delusional part of the Bad Wolf - the selfish, insecure, hateful, angry, rage-full, resistance to reality.

The reality that the Hungry Ghost is attempting to deny is that ***the world that works best is fundamentally social, relational, and loving***; that the individual is ***secondary*** to the social relationships that gave birth to it. Even if an embryo came out of a test-tube, it could not exist today ***without the relationships of care that went into parenting it, nurturing it, and sustaining it***, until such time as it could move out into the wider world, where it is *sustained by the division of labour between countless numbers of social individuals* who make the life of each of us possible.

But how can we tame this hungry ghost; the Bad Wolf; and how can we get beyond hedonic adaptation? The stoic solution was to engage in something they called 'Negative Visualization'

Negative Visualization

What is negative visualization? Negative visualization is almost the reverse of the Hungry Ghost. When I engage in negative visualization I tell myself:

"It could happen that not only will I only get £5 from the tax office; but I could also experience business failure, and all of my income could disappear. I could lose my current (poorly decorated) home, and have to live in a night shelter. I could fall and experience brain damage (as happened to a friend of mine recently). I could lose my eyesight (in a sudden accident, or through progressive degeneration). The same goes for my hearing, my ability to walk, my ability to talk. I could lose my wife. I could fall out with my friends and lose all of them".

This is a very different approach to that advocated by the Positive Mental Attitude (PMA) movement, which encourages you to *think positively* about everything, all of the time.

You have to be careful with Negative Visualization that you do not depress yourself or make yourself anxious. *This will only happen if you* ***insist*** *that the negative possibilities of the future* ***have to be avoided****, and that you would not be able to cope if they materialized in your life.*

So what are the benefits of Negative Visualization?

I have experimented with it recently and found that afterwards I am extremely grateful to life for my eyesight, my hearing, my wonderful marriage, my home, my work, and on and on. I have no difficulty finding things to be grateful for.

If you want to experiment with Negative Visualization, I suggest you try to do it a couple of times per day, and to follow it immediately with the Gratitude List, which is described in a postscript below. (Basically the Gratitude List is a list of three things you can be grateful for, at the end of each day, which you write down before going to bed). Seneca, Epictetus and Marcus Aurelius – three of the most famous Roman Stoics - all used the Negative Visualization technique in their Stoic practice.

The Stoics held the belief that everything in our lives is "merely on loan to us" for our short time on earth. For example, Epictetus suggests that: "In the very act of kissing (our) child (goodnight), we should silently reflect on the possibility that she will die tomorrow." (Irvine, 2009, page 69)[10]. In this way we come to appreciate the child more; to value our time with her or him; and treat her or him with the respect and dignity that is appropriate to this valued but ephemeral relationship which time will erase, as surely as the desert winds erase the footprints of camels.

But we must beware of depressing ourselves by focusing *in a bad way* on the temporary nature of life. For this purpose, *Moderate Buddhism* is a balancing philosophy, which helps us to stay focussed in the present moment. The death of your child is just a *concept*, which relates to an *unknowable* future. Of course we will all die, but not in this present moment. So, learn to live your life in day-tight compartments – without losing sight of the ultimate fact that life is temporary – and you will have the best of both worlds.

Try experimenting with Negative Visualization, followed by the Gratitude List, and see what effects it has in your life.

For example, suppose you are in a highly competitive work situation, where there is a constant struggle for promotion; and you are not doing well in this 'rat race'.

Sit down, and instead of focussing on the promotions you cannot seem to get, try instead to focus on all those things which currently have, which you could lose at some point in the future; and which you will most definitely lose at the point of your death.

The list - which you should write out - could include your eyesight; your ability to walk and talk; your job, which provides an income of sorts; your general good heath; your capacity for happiness (as in laughing at a comedy film; or enjoying a good book; your relationships at home and in work).

Next, focus your attention upon the fact that you have not lost any of those things; that you can see, and hear, and stand up, and walk, and talk; and so on.

Now write down three things you can be grateful for. These could include anything you like, such as your job, or your home, or your partner, or your children (or the fact that you do not have any children!); and so on.

Then try meditating on the present moment. Sit quietly, and focus your attention on some object in your field of vision, like a mark on the wall, or an object on your desk or table. Allow your breathing to slow down, and begin to count your breaths in and out. Counting 'One', on the in-breath; 'Two', on the out-breath; 'Three' on the in-breath; and 'Four' on the out-breath. Repeat this process over and over again. Sit quietly for a few minutes, and then get up and move around.

Doesn't life seem much better, more acceptable, less stressful than it did when you were in your 'Hungry Ghost' state; craving promotions or more money, or whatever?

Find out for yourself if this approach could be helpful for you, and the people in your life. It could help you to enjoy your life much more than a non-philosophical approach to life.

~~~

"Negative visualization", has the beneficial effect of helping us to appreciate what we have got, instead of whining about what we have not been able to acquire: (*Things*, again! The problem of *desire*, again!)
~~~

Now I want to write about ***the problem of control.***

What we can and can't control

In the opening of his famous handbook on how to live a Stoic life - the *Enchiridion* - Epictetus said, in archaic language, that some things are within our control and some are not.

Within our control are our own thoughts and actions (he said). Almost everything else is outside of our control, or in the control of others, who may wish to thwart our desire to acquire them.

According to Epictetus, it is a huge mistake to confuse what is within our control and what is not, because then we make the very serious mistake of trying to control what cannot be controlled, which is a source of great frustration; and this spoils our tranquillity. Furthermore, since ***tranquillity is the core of happiness*** in Stoic philosophy, we also destroy our happiness.

My treatment of "negative visualization" above came from Professor William Irvine's book - *A Guide to the Good Life: the ancient art of stoic joy* - in which it appears as one the "five Stoic psychological techniques". The second of those five techniques is personal management of "the dichotomy of control". The dichotomy of control refers back to the description of Epictetus's view that some things can be controlled and some things cannot be controlled - by you, the individual - and that much of your misery comes from trying to control the uncontrollable.

Irvine begins by quoting Epictetus to the effect that "It is impossible that happiness, and yearning for what is not present, should ever be united". What does this mean? It means what the Buddha meant when he said that "the source of all suffering is desire". And it is also equivalent to the Buddhist principle that, if you create one hair's breadth difference between what you have got and what you want, heaven and earth are set apart!

We do not (normally) *desire* those things that are *present.* We tend to desire what is not currently available to us. And that sets up a tension: *I want it and I cannot have it. Isn't this unbearable; frustrating; and depressing? Why does the world have to be so nasty towards me? What a miserable life I have to lead!*

But the solution is not to depress or kill yourself, or to make yourself miserable about the things you cannot acquire. "A better strategy for getting what you want … is to make it your goal to want only those things that are easy to obtain – and ideally to want only those things that you can be certain of obtaining", according to Irvine's rendering of Epictetus's insight.

What this boils down to is as follows:

You most often cannot change the world around you, but you ***can*** change your desires and goals in relation to the world (with some effort). So give up desiring those things which are too far out of your reach. Aim only for goals which are realistic and probably achievable. And if you fail to achieve them, you can try again, but if you repeatedly fail, then you should set a new goal of not desiring that thing which you have failed to acquire.

According to Irvine's reading of Epictetus, by giving up desiring what is beyond your reach, you will thereby avoid all the frustrations and anxieties associated with trying to control the uncontrollable. And, according to Epictetus, you will thus become invincible!

"If you refuse to enter contests that you are capable of losing, you will never lose a contest". (Irvine, page 86).

If you want to be happy, you could also follow the advice of Teddy Roosevelt, who famously said:

"Do what you can, where you are, with what you have!"

~~~

Epictetus's thesis on control says that ***some things are within our control and some things are not.*** This is referred to as his 'dichotomy of control'.[11] The more important element of his thesis, however, was that ***it is only after we learn to distinguish what we can from what we cannot control, and then restrict ourselves to <u>only trying to control the controllable</u>, that inner harmony and outer effectiveness become possible.***

Here's a refinement of Epictetus's Dichotomy of Control: Professor Irvine's ***Trichotomy*** of Control:

1. *What we can control* ***completely,***

2. *What we can control* ***partially****, and*

3. *What we* ***cannot*** *control.*

I will also outline my own therapeutic process for working on control issues, which I call the '<u>Conditional</u> Dichotomy' model:
~~~

Some things can be controlled…IF…;

and some things cannot be controlled…UNLESS…

~~~

The Trichotomy of Control

In reviewing Epictetus's dichotomy of control, William Irvine reformulates it thus:

There are certain things over which we have complete control, and certain things over which we do not have complete control.

He then goes on to divide the latter branch of this dichotomy into two:

Those things over which we do not have ***complete*** *control;* and:

Those things over which ***we do not have any*** *control.*

From this conclusion it would follow that it is reasonable for us to try to control those things which are ***completely*** within our control, and those things over which we may have ***some control***. And we should avoid trying to control those things which are beyond our control.

This strikes me as clearly an 'academic presentation', which is not unreasonable for an academic. However, my own experience of working with these ideas has produced a much more practical, pragmatic modification of Epictetus's thesis.

My Conditional Dichotomy Model

When I first came across Epictetus's thesis on giving up control of the uncontrollable, I began to experiment with trying to operationalize it in my life. I set up a matrix on an A4 writing pad, as follows:

1. What I can control ☑	2. What I cannot control ☒
1. xxxxxxxxxxxxxxxxx 2. xxxxxxxxxxxxxxxxxx	1. xxxxxxxxxxxxxxxxx 2. xxxxxxxxxxxxxxxx

I then tried to list those things I can control and those that were beyond my control, but I quickly ran into a problem: the problem of ***belief!***
~~~

If I 'believe' something is beyond my control, is it therefore the case that it is definitely beyond my control? No, clearly not. I can be mistaken about such judgements.

I also realized that the 'weight of experience' would prejudice me to list as uncontrollable all those things that I have not been able to control ***thus far!***

So then I had to make a judgement. How can I preserve what is valuable in Epictetus's dichotomy, and how can I render it more user-friendly?

This is what I came up with:

1. Begin by assuming that anything that cannot be ruled out as very obviously beyond my control - such as flying through the air by flapping my arms; or withdrawing thousands of pounds from my empty bank account - should be listed in column No.1 above.

2. Then, against each item in column 1, put a conditional clause, as follows:

1. What I can control ☑	**2. What I cannot control ☒**
1. I can increase my bank balance by 50%, **IF...** 2. I can improve my relationship with person Y, **PROVIDED...** 3. I can improve my physical health, **AS LONG AS...**	1. xxxxxxxxxxxxxxxxx 2. xxxxxxxxxxxxxxxx

The contents of column 1 are subjected to an analysis of what it is I would have to do to keep each item in that column. Those necessary actions by me then become what I call "if clauses" - "If..."; "Provided..."; "As long as..."

But there was still something missing - a quantifier of each goal, as follows:

1. What I can control ☑	2. What I cannot control ☒
1. I can increase my bank balance by 50% **BY THE END OF JUNE,** IF… 2. I can improve my relationship with person Y **(SO THE RATIO OF POSITIVE TO NEGATIVE MOMENTS REACHES 5:1) (BY THE END OF DECEMBER),** PROVIDED… 3. I can improve my physical health **(SUFFICIENT TO ELIMINATE MY ACHING JOINTS, BY EASTER NEXT YEAR),** AS LONG AS…	1. xxxxxxxxxxxxxxxxx 2. xxxxxxxxxxxxxxxx

If I fail to achieve these goals in column 1, by the due dates, then I can revise those goals and try again. I still do not know if they will ultimately prove to be controllable. That is to say, I still do not know if these are goals which are

1. Completely *within* my control
2. Completely *beyond* my control; Or
3. *Partially* within my control.

The answer to that question has to be resolved in practice, and not in the kind of theoretical discussion presented by Professor Irvine. And why is that? Because an outcome could be 'theoretically' within my control, either completely or partially, but prove ***in practice*** to be beyond my (achievable/achieved) control.

Let us now assume I have failed to achieve all three goals listed in column 1 above. The matrix now looks like this:

1. What I can control ☑	2. What I cannot control ☒
	1. Increasing my bank balance by 50% **BY THE END OF JUNE,** 2. Improving my relationship with person Y **(SO THE RATIO OF POSITIVE TO NEGATIVE MOMENTS REACHES 5:1)(BY THE END OF DECEMBER),** 3. Improving my physical health **(SUFFICIENT TO ELIMINATE MY ACHING JOINTS, BY EASTER NEXT YEAR),** AS LONG AS...

However, this is still not the whole story. I can still work on column 2, by modifying the targeted goals, and adding a new kind of conditional clause, which I call an "unless clause", as follows:

1. What I can control ☑	2. What I cannot control ☒
	1. Increasing my bank balance by 30% **BY THE END OF DECEMBER, ...UNLESS...** 2. Improving my relationship with person Y **(SO THE RATIO OF POSITIVE TO NEGATIVE MOMENTS REACHES 4:1) (BY THE END OF NEXT JUNE)** ...UNLESS... 3. Improving my physical health **(SUFFICIENT TO ELIMINATE *MOST OF* MY ACHING JOINTS, BY NEXT SUMMER)** ...UNLESS...

So now I have an 'unless' clause, and I can begin to try to work on the contents of those 'unless' clauses. Some examples of 'unless' clauses for the three goals above could be:

1. Unless I get a second job...

2. Unless I go on a communications skills course...

3. Unless I research and discover a new diet or supplement...

What becomes clear from this reflective process is that it is not at all easy for an individual to distinguish between what they can and cannot control.

Some things are clearly beyond our control, such as the colour of our eyes; our baldness; or lack of physical height; etc.

Some things are clearly within our control, such as picking up the phone and calling a friend.

But the territory in between is very grey and obscure. It requires a lot of hard work to determine which of those grey areas in my life might eventually prove to be within my control.

However, the bottom line of the stoic philosophy is this: So long as I do not demand that I should be able to control something that appears to be, for all intents and purposes, beyond my control, then I will not overly upset myself.

And to the degree that I want to set goals, I should set them in such a way that my reach does not exceed my grasp! Be realistic! A goal that stretches you 5% or 10% beyond where you are now is much more realistic than one that assumes you can change some feature of your environment by 100% in a relatively brief period of time.

> *"You can't have everything.*
>
> *Where would you put it?"*
>
> Ann Landers
>
> ~~~
>
> *"Nothing will content those who are not content with a little".*
>
> Greek proverb
>
> ~~~

~~~
~~~

Chapter 3: Some additional Stoic attitudes

Introductory recapitulation

Let us briefly restate some of the psychological attitudes and techniques of the Stoic philosophers – Marcus Aurelius, Seneca, Epictetus and Musonius Rufus – as reviewed by William Irvine in his book, *'A Guide to the Good Life: the ancient art of Stoic joy'*, before we move on to look at the concepts of 'fatalism', and self-denial.

So far I have looked at Negative Visualization and the Dichotomy/ Trichotomy of Control, and in the process touched on Hedonic Adaptation.

Hedonic adaptation means that whatever we get from life, we quickly adjust to it, and move on to ask: 'What else ya got?' We do not remain *grateful* for long, no matter how fortunate we may prove to be. In Buddhism this is a manifestation of the 'hungry ghost', or the empty, 'insatiable ego'. In E-CENT theory - (created by me, with the support of Renata Taylor-Byrne) - this is a manifestation of *the Bad Wolf*, (which is the evil side of human nature, as opposed to *the Good Wolf*, which is the virtuous side of human nature).

Negative Visualization involves imagining that everything we have today will be lost in the future, through misfortune, aging, or death. Having thus reminded ourselves of what is going to be lost at some point, we also in the process remind ourselves of *what we still have, and should be grateful for* in the present moment, and thus we overcome our innate tendency towards hedonic adaptation.

The Dichotomy of Control was expressed in the statement by Epictetus to the effect that, freedom and happiness result from understanding one principle: *There are certain things we can control and certain things we cannot control. And it is only after we have learned to distinguish between what we can and cannot control, that inner harmony and outer effectiveness become possible.* I also discussed my refinement of this psychological principle, with the two-column technique, listing what we can and cannot control, and then adding "if clauses" and "unless clauses" on each item.

Let us now move on to look at the Stoic concepts of Fatalism, and Self-Denial:

Fatalism and Non-attachment

The Stoic concept of 'fatalism' is comparable to the Buddhist concept of 'non-attachment'. The Stoic view is that the Fates have already decided the outcome of every action and every life. Everything is pre-determined. This is also the 'thrownness' of Existentialism. Humans are borne into a particular family history, in a particular historic epoch, and the currents of life are already carrying their family along at the point of birth. There is thus a huge kinetic momentum at the very core of every life, which carries it into a particular future. This, of course, seems to rule out any place for free will, which is unacceptable to me - but I do not exaggerate the degree of free will that we may have. (See my paper on Free Will and Determinism)[12].

William Irvine's book is very helpful in the way he clarifies the Stoic concept of fatalism: in that he believes that the Stoics were advocating *fatalism with regard to the past and the present*, but <u>not</u> the future.

With regard to the past, they were saying we cannot change anything about the past, so we had better fatalistically accept it. This is similar to the Buddhist concept of acceptance of what is so.

With regard to the present moment - by which is meant this very instant in time, and not this "whole day", or "whole hour" - the Stoics were saying that this cannot be changed right now. It is what it is right now - even if it proves possible to change it five minutes from now, or tomorrow, or next week. So we should practice *fatalism towards the present moment*.

However, with regard to the future, Stoicism does not rule out the setting of goals and then functioning intelligently towards them. But if we collect evidence tomorrow that we have failed, *we should fatalistically accept that outcome*. In the next moment we may, if we wish, *reassert that goal*, or a similar one, or a different one, and try to bring that into existence *in the future*. And if we fail, *we accept our failure fatalistically*.

Thus fatalism is a fatalism of the past and the present, but not of the future. We may be able to change some aspects of our future. We may be able to steer our lives from the path of our 'thrownness'.

<u>**One refinement**</u>: When we set a goal for change in the future, we should not be attached to the outcome, because if we are we will spoil our

tranquillity. We should *prefer* to achieve the outcome, but be willing to countenance failure (often repeated failure).

It is preferable to set a goal, with the knowledge that *it might not succeed* this time, or for a long time, or, indeed, ever. So we set the goal, and then we *monitor the outcome*. When we see that the goal has not been achieved by our expected 'deadline', we can accept that that is 'reality', and set the goal again, for a later date, without getting upset about the fact that it did not happen. After all, 'we are actors in a play that the manager (Providence) directs', and we do not *control* the script or the enactment of it.

It is much better, in the Stoic view, to make a commitment to make our contribution to our society than it is to ***wish*** for something for ourselves. If we work hard to make our social contributions to our family, our community, our culture, the sick and needy, and so on, we may in the process gain some rewards for ourselves. But the aim should not be to gain rewards. For, just as in Buddhism, *to the degree that you want **anything** that you do not already have, to that degree you **wreck** your own mental and emotional tranquillity.* So commit to ***want*** *what you* ***have,*** and to live a good life of social contribution, and accept (fatalistically) whatever life delivers to you.

It ***should*** all be exactly the way it is, in the past, and in the present! (But watch this point: We do not want to suggest to a counselling client, or self-help enthusiast that they should accept the immoral behaviour of others; that they should kowtow to sadistic or unfair treatment! It is important to hold the world to reasonable standards of morality and fairness. See my paper on justice and fairness for counsellors and therapists)[13].

Self-denial

I now want to focus upon Stoic psychological technique No.4, which is about self-denial. However, this is not a concept that makes much sense to most of the hedonistic consumers of modern materialist society.

The mantra of the modern materialist is this: ***Gorge yourself on whatever pleasures you can acquire, even if you have to sign away your future to get them. Big houses, fast cars, rich food, exotic wines and spirits, fancy clothes, exotic holidays, expensive education for children, expensive toys and gadgets and gimmicks, gold watches, diamonds and pearls, dinner***

parties, furs and finery, musical events, films, the theatre, and on and on. ('Consuming' is the only role offered to most people in the West today!) Like hungry ghosts, trying to fill up an empty void within, they gorge on the material and overlook the beauty of the sunset, the local river, or the trees in the local park, which cost nothing. They have forgotten the blissful sensation of slaking a genuine thirst with clean, cool water. They have forgotten the simple pleasures of sitting chatting with a dear friend in simple surroundings.

Defining self-denial

Self-denial is often understood to mean 'abstinence', or refraining from excessive indulgence in physical pleasures, such as sex, food, drink - especially alcohol. One common form of self-denial, or abstinence, is the practice of ***fasting,*** in some religions. Self-denying abstinence is an act which has been entered into *voluntarily, and consciously,* with some *self-development goal in mind.*

Abstinence can also refer to giving up a drug, such as alcohol or marijuana or heroin, etc.

It is probably widely agreed that total abstinence from pleasure or leisure is a physical impossibility for a human, and so abstinence is normally temporary, as in occasional fasting; or selective, as in giving up alcohol, but *not* all enjoyable drinks.

But what are we to make of the Stoic advocacy of partial and occasional expressions of 'self-denial'?

Self-denial in E-CENT

E-CENT is unlike any other modern philosophy or therapy, in that we do not admit of the possibility of a 'unitary self'. In E-CENT, the self is split in several different ways:

We are each split, by our nature, into good and bad urges and tendencies, which we call the 'Good Wolf' and the 'Bad Wolf'. We are also split into Parent, Adult and Child ego states. Thus, it is very important to deny any urges which come from the Bad Wolf side of the self.

I have given considerable thought to the Stoic concept of self-denial, and this is what I think. Stoics deny themselves certain pleasures in order not to become *addicted* to pleasures. Since we often cannot control the availability of pleasures in our lives, it is not self-supporting to allow ourselves to become dependent upon something that may disappear! It is also the case that, because of the problem of Hedonic Adaptation, we will adapt to whatever level of pleasure we have in our lives, and thus we need more and more pleasure in order to achieve equanimity, much less happiness. Thus, a good Stoic should discipline him/herself with:

(a) **Negative Visualization** - or imagining we have lost something pleasurable from our lives, so that we will appreciate it the more when the visualization is over; and:

(b) **Actual self-denial** - such as not eating cake just because it is available, and learning to take pleasure from the eating of smaller portions of plainer foods.

If our economic circumstances change for the worst, we will know that we can handle the resulting deprivations. It is also the case that we are likely to feel less anxious about the future if we have 'imagined the worst' and figured out how to cope with it, minimize it, and optimize our response.

~~~
~~~

Chapter 4: Is there a problem with Hedonic Adaptation and Negative Visualization?

When I first wrote about these subjects, they seemed to me to be quite straightforward:

1. Hedonic adaptation means that **we get used to the goodies we acquire**, and we want more, and bigger, and better goodies to replace them. ('Much wants more', as people say in Yorkshire!) We take them for granted; we tire of them; we get bored with them; we want some new 'excitement'!

2. Negative Visualization means that we **imagine** that we have lost some of our goodies – really feel what that would be like. **Then remind ourselves – "Oh. Look. I haven't lost it after all!** What joy!" And we can thus learn to re-appreciate what we have already got – instead of becoming 'hedonically adapted' (or accustomed) to them.

However, when I first posted some of my writings about Stoicism on the internet, I then made a video clip referring back to this article. One person who saw the video clip (but did not read any of my articles or papers – as far as I can tell) raised a concern. Let us call her Miss X.

Negative visualization and anxiety

Miss X pointed out that she was prone to anxiety, and she wanted to know – I think – whether I would agree that Negative Visualization is likely to induce anxiety in those who practiced it?

This is a very important question. It is an ethical question. I am aware of the concept of 'ontic dumping', which means dumping a new or contrived 'reality' into the mind of somebody who is then disadvantaged by that dumping.

To illustrate 'ontic dumping', we could say somebody, called Person A, is quite happy, watching the sunset, for example, and Person B comes along and reminds them that ***there is a vicious war going on in Country X.*** This is an example of 'ontic dumping', where 'ontic' refers to 'what is', or 'what exists', and dumping means 'dropping a thought into the mind of another'.

Person B in this example may go from feeling relaxed and happy to feeling a sense of dread about that tragic war.

If I advocate Negative Visualization - which is about thinking into the future and imaging that some current valuables or assets, relationships or states of being (such as health) have been lost - am I not teaching individuals how to 'ontically dump' on themselves: to dump negative expectations into their present consciousness?

If the answer to that question is an unequivocal 'Yes', then I should disavow the use of Negative Visualization at once, and apologise for ever suggesting it.

However, I do not advocate Negative Visualization as a ***stand-alone*** approach to developing happiness. This recommendation must be seen in the context of a long list of my recommendations.

There is a joke about the idiosyncratic perceptions of some Irish people, in which a British tourist is driving through Ireland. He stops his car and asks a local farmer, sitting on a wooden gate: "Could you tell me the way to get to Mullingar?" The farmer pushes his cap back to the back of his head, scratches his forehead vigorously, and replies: "If I was going to Mullingar, I would not start from here!" (Boom, boom!)

And, in a less jocular vein, I must say that, if I was teaching somebody how to be happy, starting from scratch, I would not start with Negative Visualization. It's the wrong place to begin. A better place to begin is described the paper is co-authored with Renata Taylor-Byrne, entitled: Zen Tigers and Strawberry Moments. (See ***Appendix A***, below). This is about learning to live in the present moment - in 'day-tight' compartments. The three elements of that advice are:

1. Regarding the past: There is no use crying (endlessly or excessively) over spilled milk. (But it is important to engage in appropriate levels of grief!)

2. Regarding the future: I'll cross that bridge when I come to it.

3. And regarding the present moment: By staying inside my day-tight compartments, I can enjoy the ('strawberry flavoured!') present moment.

I think this would be a better place for Miss X to begin working on her mind control. Negative Visualization would be a long way down the road.

Once she has got a good grasp of the Zen Tigers model; I would want to teach her to meditate, as described in ***Appendix B: How to Meditate***.

Then I would refer her back to the beginning of this book, where I begin to build up a set of insights into how to be happy.

~~~

Having said all that, it might be that Miss X just failed to do the complete activity. This is how it is supposed to go:

Negative Visualization means that we ***imagine*** that we have lost some of our goodies - really feel what that would be like. ***Then remind ourselves - Oh. Look. I haven't lost it after all!*** What joy!" And we can thus learn to re-appreciate what we have already got - instead of becoming 'hedonically adapted' (or accustomed) to them.

Perhaps she forgot to remind herself of this fact: "It ***hasn't*** really happened. ***No real loss has occurred!"***

But perhaps her problem is that she is now more aware that it either could happen in the future (e.g. the loss of her job), or that it will definitely happen in the future (e.g. the loss of her life, at the point of inevitable death!), and she is now ***anxious about that***. If so, she needs to understand anxiety better, and so I wrote to her to suggest that negative visualization might not be her cup of tea, and that she should not feel obliged to use any process that might seem to harm her in any way. And I suggested that she should use Rational Emotive Imagery (REI) if ever she feels anxious about anything in the future.

Rational Emotive Imagery (REI)

REI was created by Dr Maxie Maultsby, and adapted by Dr Albert Ellis in a more emotive form. Basically, REI calls on a therapy client to "imagine the worst", meaning the worst outcome they might get in their problematic situation. Then get in touch with their feelings about what they are *imagining*, without resisting any feelings that come up: ("Feel it; feel it; feel it"). Then, without changing anything about the bad thing being visualized, the client is told, "Now change your feeling about it so that it is less intense, less strong". This usually means, for example, feeling anger, and trying to reduce it until it is mere irritation and annoyance; feeling depressed, and
~~~

reducing it so it is just sadness; feeling anxiety (which was Miss X's feeling) and reducing it to concern.

The method of reducing these emotions, taught in Rational Emotive Behaviour Therapy (REBT), is to give up *unrealistic demands* and *exaggerated-awfuls* about the 'bad thing' being visualized; and to stick to only *preferring* that it not exist, and recognizing that *it is not 100% bad.* (I teach a slightly different approach, as shown in Chapter 11, on the Nine Windows Model).

Miss X might be making the mistake of telling herself: "If something could be frightening, or anxiety-inducing, I ***absolutely must*** avoid it, because bad feelings are not nice experiences". If she is, then this would constitute 'repression' of her thoughts/feelings, which in the psychodynamic perspective is very bad, because "Whatever you resist persists". And once you repress a fear, it become far more damaging, as it now 'rattles around in the subconscious mind' causing all kinds of 'free floating anxiety'.

So it might be better for Miss X to use the Rational Emotive Imagery approach outlined above.

Cognitive Emotive Imagery (CEI)

CEI is simply the process of applying the Nine Windows model (from Chapter 11) to an imagined or anticipated future noxious event, which might be a source of anxiety; or a past noxious event, which could be a source of traumatic memory.

Imagine the worst, while looking through the nine windows, one after the other, and you thus effectively reframe your problems.

Once you have reframed your problems, they 'show up' differently. They no longer have the same 'meaning', or emotional affect.

Using "what if" visualization

Humans typically treat their past as a ***fixed entity***. "It was the way it was", they might believe, "and it could not have been otherwise". This feeds into hedonic adaptation. We take it for granted, become complacent about it, and thus our valuation of it drops.

In "what if" thinking or visualization, we assume that our past was different from how we normally think of it. For example, we could imagine that we never met our marriage partner, and we try to think/feel what that would have been like. Afterwards we might find that our appreciation of our marriage partner may have gone up, as hedonic adaptation is broken down.

It seems some psychologists and scientific researchers are beginning to take an interest in this kind of 'what if' visualization. According to an article by Wray Herbert, in the January/February 2011 issue of *Scientific American Mind*[14], "Some scientists are beginning to think that imagining an alternative reality might have ironic and tonic effects. Indeed, it might be a practical tool for strengthening commitment to country, workplace and relationships".

Needless to say, of those three areas for improvement, I am only interested in improving relationships. "One of the first studies to explore this effect looked at people's satisfaction with their romantic partnerships. Social psychologist Minkyung Koo[15], then at the University of Virginia, and her colleagues asked individuals in committed relationships to write for 15 to 20 minutes about how they might have never met or gotten to know their partners. Others wrote the story of how their meeting really happened, and still more people wrote about a typical day's activities or a friendship. After the exercise, the people who had imagined not knowing their partner displayed the biggest increase in relationship satisfaction…" Herbert, 2011, page 66.

Herbert (2011) points out that the scientists who have investigated this process "…were curious about the 'near loss' experience - specifically the feelings of poignancy that occur when what we cherish disappears. When we feel we are losing something – that time is becoming scarce, for example – the bittersweet mix of happy and sad emotions ***can reinforce our appreciation of what we have".***

Herbert fails to link this phenomenon back to the Stoic technique of negative visualization, which is essentially what it is. The **'what if' process** simply asks the participant to imagine losing something from their past, while **the Stoic technique of negative visualization** ask the participant to image losing something in their future.

~~~
~~~

Dale Carnegie on Imagining the Worst

In Chapter 2 of his wonderful book on ***How to Stop Worrying and Start Living,*** Dale Carnegie (1988)[16] presents a formula which is relevant here. It is a way to quickly handle any kind of worry, such as worrying about the fact that you have been told you are soon to die, or you have discovered your company is collapsing, or you are about to be made redundant - or your partner is about to leave you. The formula goes like this:

1. Analyze the situation fearlessly and honestly and figure out what is ***the worst*** that could happen here. (Imagine the worst case scenario).

2. Reconcile yourself to ***accepting*** the worst case scenario, if you have to. (At this point, relaxation and a sense of peace are likely to emerge!)

3. Now devote your time and energy to ***trying to improve on*** the situation which you have already accepted mentally.

Face up to your fears. Face up to your problems. Do not try to run away from them. Just because they might involve discomfort, this is not a good reason to run away from them. You can handle feeling worry and anxiety. It is only by looking your worries in the face that you can figure out

(1) what it is you had better accept; and

(2) what you should now try to improve upon.

Imagining the worst is a very helpful process, and imagining loss can be very beneficial. ***But don't overdo it.*** *Little and often* is probably best, and go back to focusing on the positive for the rest of the time. (For example, immediately after negative visualization, write out a list of three to six things in your life for which you can be truly happy - such as your eyesight, your home, your job, your partner, your intelligent brain, and so on).

~~~
~~~

Chapter 5: The Stoic perspective on anger

> *"Say to yourself in the early morning: I shall meet today inquisitive, ungrateful, violent, treacherous, envious, uncharitable (wo)men. All these things have come upon them through ignorance of real good and ill".*
>
> ***Marcus Aurelius**, Meditations.*

Preamble

The philosophy of Stoicism has much to teach us about anger, especially Seneca's essay 'On Anger'.[17] But Stoicism has strengths and weaknesses in its explanation of anger.

Stoicism (in its moderate form) is an empowering philosophy of life - including a system of logic and a unique ***cosmology*** (or ***science*** of the origin of the world), combined with a *compensatory philosophy* for coping with the undoubted difficulties of life. The cosmology of Stoicism does not contain a transcendent deity, or god/gods, but rather it posits an indwelling rational principle of a 'fiery substance' of which each of our souls is seen to be a part. (Aurelius, 1992[18]; Epictetus, 1991[19]; Irvine, 2009[20].)

Stoicism was created by Zeno of Citium, in ancient Greece, about 300 BCE[21]. Zeno had studied Cynicism with Crates, plus some of Plato's philosophy at the Academy (Irvine, 2009, pages 32-33). His own life had been seriously disadvantaged by a shipwreck at sea, in which he lost all his material assets, and his philosophy partly constitutes a coming to terms with the harshness of life as he experienced it. Stoicism survived for at least 400 years, in Greece, and, in slightly modified form, in ancient Rome.

Anger as 'passion'

According to the Stoic view of life, anger is one of the 'passions'. Seddon (2000)[22] tells us that: "In Stoic theory there are four primary passions: **desire** ... is an impulse towards some anticipated thing regarded as good; **fear** ... is an impulse away from some anticipated things regarded as bad. The other two (passions) are: **delight** ..., an impulse towards some present thing regarded as good, and **distress** ..., an impulse away from some present thing regarded as bad... **Anger**, sexual desire and love of riches for instances, are types of **desire** ... The Stoics explain the passions in terms of the judgements we make regarding the circumstances we find ourselves in". (Seddon, 2000, page 2).

This taxonomy of passions has its appeal, and it seems in many respects to be intuitively right. However, it is probably better to see *anger as a* ***response*** *to the blocking of some important desire*, rather than an *expression* of a desire. (In E-CENT, we see *inappropriate or excessive anger* as being pretty central to the emotional state called the Bad Wolf. While the Good Wolf is driven by love, the Bad Wolf is driven by hatred, and inappropriate or excessive anger is a manifestation of hatred. [Of course we do need appropriate levels of anger to fuel our self-defence capacities in a difficult world; including fuelling our assertive communications).

Returning to the pure Stoic perspective, anger for a Stoic is a *passion*, induced by a *judgement* that something bad is being done to us, and we have to retaliate:

"...the passions have an essential cognitive (or thinking) component without which they would not be able to serve, as they do, as ways for us to relate to what goes on in the world. Passions are grounded in *how we find the world*, in how we *judge matters*; this being so, the passions can be evaluated as appropriate or inappropriate, justified or unjustified". (Seddon, 2000, page 3).

This is what Epictetus meant, in the Enchiridion, when he said: "(Wo)men are disturbed not by the things which happen, but by the opinions[23] about the things. ... When, then, we are impeded or disturbed or grieved, let us never blame others, but ourselves, that is, our opinions". (The *Enchiridion*, page 14).

The E-CENT objection to Epictetus

We do not accept *this extreme perspective* in my system of Emotive-Cognitive Embodied Narrative Therapy (E-CENT). Why not? Because, if I become angry when a man punches me in the face, then I am angry...

(a) Because of the punch; and:

(b) The precise intensity of my anger is a result of the nature of my (socially shaped, and habit-based) opinion (judgement). (And this 'opinion' or 'judgement' is better thought of as my habitual perception/ feeling/ thinking).

(c) So what is really happening, in the moment of the punch being struck, is what can be called 'pattern matching', in which my non-conscious mind automatically matches this experience to a previous experience, and emits whatever response I used (successfully) in the past, to deal with such an assault. (And this, of course, is also an example of Stimulus-Response-No-Choice, because it is totally automatic and habit-based!)

I am angry because of the punch in the same way that any animal will respond with a fight or flight reaction if you strike it, or threaten it. And the more unrealistic are my expectations, such as that "nobody will ever punch me", and the more insistent I am that "it's impossible to come to terms with such an assault", the more intense will be my anger. So the correct equation here is this:

The EVENT ***multiplied by*** my INTERPRETATION/JUDGEMENT causes the response of the (habit-based, socially-shaped) EMOTION: (which may be mild or intense anger; or irritation versus rage).

I can reduce the intensity of my anger (*in the **future*** – but not in the present moment) by making my judgements (interpretations/opinions/beliefs) less extreme. But it would not be sensible/appropriate for me to be *completely unmoved* by (or completely indifferent to) this unjustified physical assault upon my vulnerable body, because my body can and will feel unpleasant, aversive pain.

Practice Detachment

Stoicism, like Buddhism, would teach me to practice detachment from 'angering actions' by other people. However, there is a problem here. Initially, I do not *choose* my own way of responding to other humans.

Why not?

Because we are born into a culture, we imbibe the values and attitudes of that culture: and I imbibed the habits and values of my particular family, schools and community - including particular attitudes about anger. This has both advantages and disadvantages.

It is advantageous because we imbibe the moral rules of our family and community by *osmosis*. They simply seep into us over time. And if our family and community is relatively moral, we will also be relatively moral agents, which is important for the smooth running of the world. However, we will also tend to imbibe all the *inanities* and *absurdities* of our family and community, and behave as if they are laudable ways of being; and that is the downside of non-conscious habit-formation, based on socialization.

Furthermore, we also seem to have innate ***needs***, which are not just *preferential attitudes*. And it is not a good idea to practice detaching from our needs! Human needs were most famously described by Abraham Maslow in his Hierarchy of Needs. Those needs are then elaborated - and either delivered or non-delivered - by our community and family culture.

It seems we ***need*** a sense of security; a sense of autonomy; opportunities to receive and give attention; friendship, love, intimacy; etc.[24] However, these are not ***absolute*** needs, once we get beyond childhood. *We need to be loved if we are to thrive*, but we can *survive*, after a fashion, without much love, once we are grown up. (But it's much better if you can learn to love and be loved throughout your lifespan, for optimum happiness and health).

However, we don't, for example, need to be loved and approved by **everybody,** and certainly not **all of the time,** or even **most of the time**.[25] As long as there are people who love us and care about us – one or two, perhaps – we can live quite well despite the slings and arrows of outrageous fortune, which often includes being insulted and put down by associates and work colleagues, etc. (If we can *control that,* then we should aim to do so. But if their behaviour is beyond our control, then we have to accept that this is not controllable at this time. [It helps to know how to assert yourself – to know how to ask for what you want, and to say no to what you do not want – in such situations].)

It is arguable that some people, some of the time, show signs of anger when insulted or frustrated by others, because they want to be loved, accepted or respected all of the time, and cannot seem to *defer that need* to specific times and specific relationships. If that is your problem, then you need to recognize that *you cannot control* being loved and approved, or even respected, by everybody, and so you'd better stop expecting that. You'd better recognize that *you live in a difficult world,* and that 'into every life a little rain must fall'. Accept that you are bound to run into difficult people and difficult situations from time to time, and then roll with those difficulties, in order to avoid becoming angry about them.

Your culture may also have something to say about insults, such as: "Sticks and stones may break your bones, but names will never hurt you". This is going to be meaningful for an individual in a context in which they do receive ***some love and affection,*** but also some insults and put downs. It is **not** going to be helpful to say this to an individual who does not receive any significant degree of love and affection from their family, for example. A cold and harsh mother who tells her son that "sticks and stones" may break his bones but "names" will never hurt him is missing the point. If a substantial part of his needs were being met, he might not be so sensitive about some name-calling.

So, clearly, I am not advocating simplistic indifference to insults; to verbal bullying. We do need to get some of our needs met; and we may need to tackle verbal bullying in the workplace, and in schools, etc. (This can be done on an organizational basis, or by individuals learning to assert themselves).

However, when we get beyond having some ***reasonable*** level of need satisfaction, and have some reasonable rules of behaviour protecting us in work or in school, we may still have outstanding problems with insults. In this context, it is necessary to go beyond merely seeking to get more 'needs met', or more 'administrative protection'. This is where we may need to *practice indifference* to the verbal jibes of others. (It is initially very difficult to practice indifference to verbal jibes and insults; so it helps if you are willing to 'fake it till you make it'!)

One way to do this is to practice indifference to ***all evaluations*** of your 'selfhood', whether positive or negative. If somebody says to you: "You're a great person", try translating this into what it really is, which is either:

(1) a comment on your behaviour or traits. Or:

(2) a statement like this: "I really like you or admire you",

Respond by saying:

(1) "You're right, I do ***behave*** well (in this respect)"; or "That's right, I do ***have*** (that impressive trait)". Or:

(2) "I'm glad you like me!"

But do not allow this to ***inflate your ego*** – to persuade yourself that you are "a better person" just because somebody likes your traits or behaviours; or that they admire or respect you.

Over time, you will learn to distance your **sense of self** - your *aliveness,* and your *capacity to be aware* – from the **evaluations** other people make of your traits and behaviours. (You might make an exception with one or two people who are very close to you, and who you trust to be on your side, and not to deliberately or consciously put you down!)

Then, one day, when somebody decides they dislike one or more of your traits and/or behaviours, and they tell you, "You are a big tish!", you will also tend to be *indifferent* to **that** evaluation, because you will recognize that it is ***a comment (an evaluative comment, and interpretation) of one or more of your traits and/or behaviours.*** Or that this particular person does not happen to 'warm towards you'!

So tell yourself: "I am **not** that trait or behaviour. I own it. I am responsible for it. But I am not it!" That is to say, I do have a roman nose, and a balding head, but I am not my roman nose or my balding head. Or I do act inefficiently in relation to Activity X, but I am not my inefficient actions!

This will allow you to feel detached from the label that is thrown at you. This is a form of ***indifference*** to the false (or mistaken, or ill informed) evaluations others make of your essence. It is **false** to say I am (wholly) good (in my essence) because I have one or more admirable traits and/or behaviours. And it is equally **false** to say I am (wholly) bad (in my essence) because I have one or more negative traits and/or behaviours.

So it has nothing to do with **sticks** and **stones**. It has to do with *perceiving/feeling/thinking straight.*

~~~

From my study of anger in the literature of Stoicism, Buddhism, and evolutionary psychology and neuroscience, I have evolved ten principles of anger management, as follows:

~~~

Ten principles of anger management (in E-CENT counselling

Introduction

Anger is one of the main emotions that humans feel in certain kinds of stressful situations. The other two are anxiety and depression.

Anger is the emotion that corresponds to the 'fight response' when an animal or human feels threatened, or (in the case of humans), seriously frustrated by another person, or insulted by somebody, or confronted by the bad behaviour of others.

In civilized societies, anger can be either ***appropriate*** to the circumstances surrounding the angry individual; or ***excessive*** and ***aggressive***. (Or sometimes, as with passive individuals, their anger maybe ***lacking***, and too ***weak***!)

In order to teach our clients how to manage their anger appropriately, we have evolved a set of principles which can help to summarize coping self-talk, and coping actions.

Here are the first ten such principles:

Principle 1: Anger is natural, normal and innate, or inborn into each of us. So you should not try to get rid of *all traces* of your anger.

Anger can keep us safe in a dangerous world. But it can also lead us to engage in conflict that is *against our best interests*; and harmful to others (which is at least immoral, and sometimes illegal!) (So anger can be constructive or destructive).

Anger can help us to know when we are being threatened, exploited or exposed to danger, and help us to fight our way out. And it is good to learn a system of self-defence which will reduce your aggression, and keep your powder dry until you absolutely have to use it!

It is often the case that what is required is a *moderate level of anger*, directed in the form of assertive actions or assertive communications (which are not aggressive or hostile or harmful or hurtful of others).

~~~
~~~

Principle 2: Because anger is natural and normal, that does not justify anybody discharging their anger in an ***unthinking*** or ***uncontrolled*** way. Just as the elimination of waste products from the body is natural and normal, and that we have ***socialized ways*** of doing that decorously - (meaning, politely and with restraint) - so also do civilized individuals have decorous (or polite and restrained) ways of managing their anger.

Furthermore, in a family that knows how to manage its emotions well, the children learn to control their anger so that they feel reasonable levels of anger, and avoid excessive, destructive anger.

If your family did not teach you to control your anger to reasonable, assertive levels – and to avoid aggressive and destructive anger outbursts; and to avoid passive 'wimping out' – you can still learn how to do that ***today***. It is never too late to learn new approaches to emotional self-management.

~~~

Principle 3: An angry reaction to frustration or insult is a manifestation of the **fight response** which is innate in all animals. But you cannot fight a traffic jam, or too many emails, or a clever insult; or even a sense of being neglected. Therefore, you have to rewire yourself to respond with something other than anger in those situations where anger will not guide you into the right course of action. The first piece of rewiring that you could benefit from is this:

Teach yourself, over and over again, to accept the things you cannot change and to only try to change the things which are fairly clearly changeable.

For example, remember that we can (often – with much difficulty!) change aspects of our selves (some of our behaviours, values, beliefs, etcetera). But we cannot reliably change other people; and certainly not often; or routinely. But we do have the right to try to influence our partners and significant others, to the degree that we allow them to influence us. So use influencing strategies instead of anger to try to change your partner or a significant other.

And teach yourself to *laugh off insults and affronts!* This will rob your adversaries of the victory of seeing how much they have upset you!

~~~

Principle 4: Anger is very often a 'false friend'.

In a life threatening situation, you have to act first and think later. But most of the situations in which you become angry are (most likely) far from being life threatening!

Anger whispers in your ear that you are right and the other person is wrong; that you are being taken advantage of or abused; and that the other person must be punished for this transgression. Very often, ***this is not the only way to look at the situation***. And this is often ***a false statement!***

The other person may be ***unaware*** of the fact that they are causing you a problem. And/or: The problem they are causing you may be of a kind that you also, in your turn, ***unavoidably*** cause to other people - and you would not want them to get angry with you for this act.

So don't automatically trust ***the voice of anger-inducement*** in your ear. Challenge it. Ask yourself:

Is this true?

Is there a better way of looking at the situation?

Will getting angry really **help me** *in any significant way?*

Or will it actually make matters worse?

~~~

Principle 5: ***Inappropriate anger*** is like picking up a hot coal with the intention of throwing it at the person who insulted or frustrated you, or broke your personal rules.

When you pick up that hot coal, **you** are the one who gets burned; just as, when you swallow *the poison of resentment*, **you** are the one who is going to be made ill by it. The person you resent or hate is not going to die because of your resentment or hatred.

Resentment ***attaches us*** to the resented person.

Hatred ***attaches us*** to the hated person.

We get **stuck** to those people and situations against which we respond angrily.

Instead of picking up a hot coal to throw at those who seem to rile us, we need to learn to ***respond appropriately***. And **sometimes**, responding
~~~

appropriately means *doing nothing!* Letting it go! (One way to do this is to persuade yourself that, very often, the 'winning formula' is to accept that *life will frustrate and harry you* – but you have ***the power*** to let that wash over you, and not to get stuck!)

At other times, responding appropriately might mean using a well thought out **assertive** communication message. (Such as: "I am ***angry*** that you did [X], because it has [negative effect Y] on my life. And I would ***prefer it*** if you would not do that again!" Or: "I am angry that you would not do Y for me; and I really think it was unfair, given what I do for you!"

(Search for online information on how to assert yourself).

~~~

Principle 6: Avoid developing automatic, habitual anger triggers – because some situations that look like they justify anger actually do no such thing. You may often feel affronted in situations where no affront exists and nothing needs to be done by you. Some contexts in which doing nothing is called for – in which case you should let it go - include:

(1) *Situations of* ***chaos***, in which **nobody** could be expected to have prevented the frustration or difficulty – for example, a busy motorway (Highway, autobahn), or a crowded pavement, and somebody 'gets in your way!'

(2) *Lack of* ***intent*** to offend on the part of the offending party. Imagine you are boating on a foggy river. A big white boat comes out of the fog. It is heading straight towards your boat, and likely to cause a collision and some damage to your hull. You become very angry. Then you notice that the boat has nobody on board – it is adrift!

Many people are just like that boat. Nobody (conscious) is on board! Non-consciousness abounds. Humans are creatures of habit! Do not assume ***intentional*** *offence* as your default position.

~~~

Principle 7: Distinguish between what you can control and what you cannot control.

If you **can *control*** some frustration or insult, or unfairness, or the offending behaviour of another person, then you should ***take appropriate action*** to do that; (unless you decide that it is not important enough to justify the energy you would have to expend to control or change it - in which case you should accept it or laugh it off.)

If you **cannot** ***control*** some frustration or insult, or bad behaviour of another person, then ***you must come to terms with it*** - and **accept** it - if you are to avoid angering yourself ***unnecessarily*** and to no good end!

Teach yourself this mantra: "I accept the things I cannot change, and only try to change the things I think I probably can". Repeat this mantra several times every morning and evening, until it becomes part of your core philosophy of life.

~~~

Principle 8: Distinguish between passive, aggressive and assertive options. (***Inappropriate anger*** means always going for the ***aggressive*** option).

Sometimes an individual may put up with a lot of injustice, unfairness, or frustration, or insults: and then, finally, they flip over into rageful anger. This is often called 'the passive-aggressive modality'. The individual is ***too passive for too long***, and then they become ***too aggressive***.

In Transactional Analysis (TA), the passive phase is called "Collecting Brown Stamps" - because the passive-aggressive individual is collecting a stamp (or record of offence; or negative experience recording) each time they are offended against; and one day they intend (consciously or non-consciously) ***to cash in their book of stamps*** (when it is 'full') for ***an explosive outburst of aggressive anger***.

The passive-aggressive individual flips from passivity to aggression, and does not have a middle gear - just top and bottom: too little or too much.

Passive-aggressive behaviour can also involve an individual who is angry, but who operates indirectly, covertly; and denies that they are angry; but they put an 'untraceable spanner' in the works of those people with whom they are angry. (These people often engage in sabotage of others).

The passive-aggressive flip, and the indirect passive-aggression approach, are both unhelpful, destructive in the longer term, and counter-productive. They will not get you what you want - if what you want is better human relations, and a chance to get more of your wishes granted.
~~~

The solution to both of these passive-aggressive approaches is to ***learn to be assertive***; which means: asking for what you want, and saying 'no' to what you do not want – and doing it in a non-aggressive manner.

~~~

Principle 9: In Rational Emotive therapy, the main target for anger-reduction is this:

Give up **demanding** that you ABSOLUTELY must not be frustrated, insulted or wronged.

It may often, or even normally, be the case that *you MORALLY should not* have to face particular forms of frustration by others; and you certainly should not be insulted by them, or wronged by them.

But we live in a world of *imperfect* fellow humans, and each of us has a **good** side and a **bad** side. So, as Marcus Aurelius used to teach, you should tell yourself each morning:

"Today I am going to run into all kinds of difficult, offensive, challenging, frustrating, insulting, malicious, untrustworthy and overbearing individuals. All of these states have been visited upon them because they (often) lack clarity about the nature of real Good and Evil!"

If you are thus forewarned; forearmed; you will not be surprised when a sleep-deprived individual - who still has too much alcohol washing around in their brain; and who had a big conflict with their partner before leaving home – pops up in front of you in a way that frustrates or insults you.

Let it go! You already knew you would run into him or her! Do you want to demonstrate that you are just as stupid, uncivilized and evil as they are proving to be?

~~~

Principle 10: In your intimate relationships it is important to maintain a 5:1 ratio of positive to negative moments. Therefore, you cannot resort to anger very often, and most often you will have to learn how to be ***reasonably assertive***, instead of either passive or aggressive.

You must learn how to communicate and negotiate, instead of blustering and browbeating; or shouting and name-calling; all of which is aggressive and offensive, and damaging to your relationships.

Also, in close relationships, you should remember Dale Carnegie's rule: ***Do not kick over the beehive, if you want to collect honey. If you offend your nearest and dearest, they will resent that, hold it against you, and you will not 'collect any honey' from them!***

~~~
~~~

50.

Chapter 6: Managing grief

If you want to be happy, one of the skills you need to learn is how to manage your negative emotions: anger, anxiety, depression, etc.

One of the inevitable emotions you will have to face is grief. Grief is the feeling of deep sorrow, brought about by a serious loss, especially the loss of a loved person.

A pertinent question is this: Is grief inevitable, and what can we say about the extent of grief?

Should we indulge in it, or try to minimize it?

Accept grief as natural

According to Professor William Irvine, the Stoics saw grief as a *reflex* action, just like the startle reflex we experience in response to a sudden loud noise, or a sudden unexpected movement. Thus, for Seneca, grief was seen as an emotional reflex. Therefore:

"..in his consolation to Polybius, who was grieving the death of his brother, Seneca writes: 'Nature requires from us some sorrow, while more than this is the result of vanity. But never will I demand of you that you should not grieve at all". (Page 153)[26].

When you experience a loss, and especially the loss of a loved one, it is inevitable that you will feel grief. This may begin with numbness, or disbelief. This may be followed by anger, which is intended to bring the loved one back. These responses seem to be wired into us by nature. (Bowlby, 2005)[27]. Next, we may realize that the lost person will never come back; never be found again; and then we may begin to weep and to feel deep sadness. At this point, it is necessary to express your sadness and sense of loss in words, to other people, or in writing:

"It is now generally agreed among psychiatrists, that, if mourning is to lead to a more rather than a less favourable outcome, it is necessary for a bereaved person – sooner or later - to ***express*** his (her) feelings. 'Give sorrow words,' wrote Shakespeare, 'the grief that does not speak knits up the overwrought (or overly-upset) heart and bids it break'." (Bowlby, 2005, page 113).

Express your grief

Shakespeare's comment is very apt. If you do not express your grief, you will get stuck with it inside of you, in a very painful way. Thus, it is important to act on Freud's advice, and do not suppress your grief; do not deny that you are in pain.

Be willing to feel the pain completely. (It won't kill you!)

Be willing to talk about your loss to significant others; and:

Be willing to cry and express the pain non-verbally.

However, the moderate version of Stoic philosophy would warn against over-indulging in grief. This reservation can be expressed in four points, which are discussed in Professor Irvine's book. Here they are:

1. Although **we must grieve**, we should aim to **minimize our grief**, without denying or repressing it. Grief is a major pain, a significantly 'sore emotion'. It drains our coping resources, and renders almost everything and every moment of our lives miserable. However, if we try to deny our grief, to cover it up with alcohol and prescription medicines, then it will be pushed into the non-conscious parts of the mind, where it will do more damage than it was doing in our conscious mind; and it will go on interminably, whereas it would most often burn itself out in time if left to its own devices, like a forest fire. (Interestingly, American psychiatry, in the form of the Diagnostic and Statistical Manual (DSM) - which is *not* based on any kind of statistics, in practice - now *denies that grief is normal,* and tries to pathologize our normal sense of loss! This is a denial of our humanity and our normal, natural, *helpful* and *healthy* emotions.)

2. We can **minimize** our ***future grief*** by using a process that I described above: *Negative Visualization*. How does this work? Well, if you recognize that everybody who is currently in your life will one day die, and that you also will die - and if you spend some time dwelling on the inevitability every single day, without becoming morbid about it - then you will not be taken by surprise when somebody in your life dies. Recognize that nothing lasts forever. Nobody lives forever. "Life ***and death*** are the life of the Buddha!" (Where 'Buddha' simply means "an enlightened human being" – or

someone who is "awake [to the present moment]"). In this way you will minimize your grief, but you *will not*, and *should not*, try to get rid of it completely.

3. ***Negative visualization*** can also be used to **bring to an end** excessively protracted grief. William Irvine gives an example of Seneca, the Roman Stoic, using this form of 'retrospective negative visualization' with a woman (Marcia) "who, three years after the death of her son, was as grief-stricken as on the day she buried him. Rather than spending her days thinking bitterly about the happiness she has been deprived of by the death of her son, Marcia should, says Seneca, think about how much worse off she would be today if she had never been able to enjoy his company. In other words, rather than mourning the end of his life, she should be thankful the he lived at all". (Page 155). More realistically, she could mourn the end of his life, while recognizing that there are things she can be grateful for in her life today, and happy memories of her son that she can keep for the rest of her own life.

It is not easy to come to terms with our mortality. But we should try to develop the following attitudes. Teach yourself that:

You are a temporary phenomenon; a transitory being;

so am I;

and so are all your loved ones.

Get used to it. Anticipate it. Recognize that death is inevitable; and that if death robs you of some pleasures, it also *robs you of all pains*! Forever!

Do the Negative Visualization exercise (imagining the death of all your loved ones), and then write out this Gratitude list every day of your life:

> "I am grateful (for this person)..."
>
> "I am grateful for (that person)..."
>
> "I am grateful for my own life".
>
> "I am grateful for my own health".

Then go out and have a ball with the people you love. *Make hay while the sun shines! Life is short, so wear your party pants!*

~~~
~~~

54.

Chapter 7: Stoicism and Happiness/Unhappiness

Over many years, I have written about the Stoic approach to social relationships. In particular, I have written about the statement from Marcus Aurelius' book, ***'Meditations'***, to this effect:

> *Every morning, before setting out to take up your social role, you should remind yourself that today you will meet with all kinds of frustrations and difficulties at the hands of your fellow humans.*

Marcus and other Stoic philosophers do not consider that this reality - of how difficult our fellow humans tend to be - allows us to opt out of our social responsibilities. They believe we have a duty to cooperate with our fellow humans for the common good. I normally add the idea that, in order to deal with these difficulties of social relationships, you should study assertiveness training and Transactional Analysis (TA), as well as my Nine Windows Model (described in Chapter 11), to help you to deal effectively with the difficulties that your fellow humans will throw at you on a daily basis.

I also tend to point out that the Stoics distinguish between your social relationships which are based on *social duty*, on the one hand, and your *friendships*, on the other. With regard to friendships, they say you can indeed be highly selective as to who you choose, and how you relate to them. You **don't** have a duty to have friends, or to indulge them if you do. In particular, the Stoics warn us of two things:

1. We need to maintain our **tranquillity**, as that is a big part of the basis of our happiness (eudaimonia). Therefore, we should avoid loud and aggressive persons, and whiners and moaners.

2. We also need to preserve our *moral character*, as that is the biggest part of the basis of our happiness (eudaimonia). Therefore, we should not form friendships with people who are morally degenerate, decadent or evil, as moral degeneracy is like a disease which is passed along by contact.

So, let us go back to those occasions when we are doing our duty, and have to associate with people who threaten to spoil our tranquillity. I have already suggested that TA, Assertiveness Training and the Nine Windows model have strategies for dealing with those kinds of situations. But what did the Stoics suggest? According to Professor Irvine, they had various strategies, and I will mention just three here:

1. When somebody behaves in an annoying manner with you, remind yourself that many people may also be annoyed by some of your own values, attitudes or behaviours. This should teach you tolerance and acceptance of their way of being, for the duration of that time when you *have to* associate with them. And we can also remind ourselves that if we allow ourselves to be annoyed by him or her, then we are allowing our tranquillity to be spoiled. This could help us to feel *detached* from the annoyance.

2. The second thing that Marcus recommends is that we give up the habit of speculating about what those difficult people are doing, thinking, saying or planning. We should also *hunt down and eliminate* any emotions of jealousy or envy, or paranoid suspicions, etc. This should enhance our sense of detachment from those difficult people with whom we *must* associate for the social good.

3. The third point made by Marcus is that impudent and ignorant individuals exist; and we cannot 'un-exist them'. They are part of the natural order of life. To expect that annoying people will not annoy us is like expecting that the sun will always shine, and the rain will stay away, because we find it so difficult. Life doesn't work like that. Into every life a little rain must fall. And into every social life, a little annoyance and irritation and frustration and difficulty must also fall. We should, in short, expect boorish people to behave boorishly. This should help us to be more accepting of the difficulties and frustrations of working and cooperating with others for the greater social good.

~~~
~~~

Chapter 8: Quick review

The goal of stoicism is *to promote tranquillity* in its followers. To this end, Stoic philosophers teach the four psychological techniques that I have covered in Chapters 2 and 3, above. These are:

(1) Distinguishing between what you can and cannot control;

(2) Imagining you have lost your present 'possessions', in order to combat your complacency about your ownership of them (described as *using negative visualization* to overcome *hedonic adaptation*);

(3) *Fatalism* about the past and the present (which means that our goals have to be *for the future,* and not for the past; [and they have to be flexible goals, which *may not* be achieved!])

(4) Self-denial, which means refraining from seeking our own maximum comfort (in order to harden ourselves against future adversity and deprivation; and to develop immediate confidence that we could cope with future deprivations).

And:

In addition, Stoic philosophers teach the following requirement:

- *Observing ourselves to determine that we stick to our Stoic practices* (which is called 'meditating on our Stoicism').

Furthermore, I have described the Stoic approach to managing anger and managing grief; and also their approach to happiness and unhappiness.

~~~

In addition to those psychological techniques, Stoic philosophers also offer advice on how to conduct ourselves in our daily lives. I would like to add a mention of their advice to not seek fame or fortune for two reasons:

(1) Fame and fortune are *beyond your control;* and:

(2) Because they are beyond your control, and will involve a lot of effort, they are likely to *destroy your tranquillity.*

Additionally, Stoics point to the problem of choosing friends who may shatter our peace of mind, and so we should be careful who we befriend.
~~~

In his section on 'Duty', subtitled 'Loving Mankind', Professor Irvine looks at the Stoic advice on establishing and preserving social relationships.

To have love and friendship in our lives depends upon other people, which can imply that other people are a boon to us. However, other people were also described as 'hell' by Jean Paul Sartre. Think about rude individuals who cut in front of us in lines and queues of all sorts, and in traffic lanes. We may have noisy neighbours who are insensitive to our need for quiet sleep time. Family members may bring us their problems and thus burden us. Your boss might insult you and thus trigger a bad mood in you. Work colleagues may engage in political manoeuvring against you, or act in incompetent ways that negatively impact you. And sometimes friends cause us to feel slighted by forgetting our birthdays, failing to attend our parties, or failing to invite us to theirs.

Because other people exist, as neighbours, friends and members of the public, we feel obliged to perform in ways that will maintain our status amongst them. This involves dressing in a particular way; having an impressive motor car, the right kind of house, in the right part of town, and so on. We thus tend to feel anxious in case we get it wrong, don't look the part, and thus "lose social status"!

But paying for all those desirable props – the clothes, cars, houses, etc. – requires a lot of money, for which you have to work, and thus you will most likely feel constant anxiety about losing your job, for then how can you maintain your so-called 'social status'? And even as we succeed, we feel the pain of being envied by those who are less successful than ourselves, who now do not like us! And we also probably feel unpleasant pains of envy about the lives of those who are more materially successful than ourselves. Where then is our tranquillity: or our peace of mind?

Despite the pain that can be caused by other humans, Stoics do not live in caves on their own. Stoicism asserts that, "… man (and woman) are by nature ... social animal(s) and therefore ... we have a duty to form and maintain relationships with other people, despite the trouble they might cause us". (Irvine, 2009, page 129).

Following a tradition – the *teleological* tradition – established by Aristotle, the Stoics thought that everything 'in creation' exists for a reason. This is a system of faith rather than science, and to render it scientific we must ask instead, what are the primary qualities of human existence. The most obvious of these is social living, and this was divined by the Stoics, coming at it from a different philosophical tradition. Humans have no choice, if they are born at all, but to be born into a social group of at least two or three individuals, and normally many more, in the form of a community. Implicit in this situation is the idea that "we are designed to live among other people and to interact with them in a manner which is mutually advantageous". (Irvine, 2009, page 129). Thus the Stoics concluded that humans are a lot like bees: social, collective beings, mutually interdependent. From this they inferred that our highest form of expression is to be *rational* and *social*, and to treat being rational and social as our duty. (But they overlooked the fact that we are, by nature, 'irrational', meaning emotional, feeling beings - and our emotions have their own validity and importance; and should not be discounted. And they also overlooked the fact that we are ***bodies*** as well as minds, and as such, we have to take care of our bodies if they are to be as flexible and resilient as our enlightened minds).

~~~
~~~

Part 2: The Problem of Extreme Stoicism

In Part 1, we looked at various aspects of *Moderate* Stoicism, which we think of as being good and helpful. But now we want to present a critical evaluation of *Extreme* Stoicism, which we see as being bad and unhelpful.

Extreme Stoicism is characterized, most obviously, by two unrealistic and unreasonable assertions by major Stoic philosophers.

Firstly, Epictetus famously said that people are *not upset by what happens to them*, but rather by the *attitude* that they adopt towards the things that happen to them. This is extreme because, most human beings will *predictably* respond with negative emotional states to being subjected to harsh treatment, whether physical or psychological.

And secondly, Marcus Aurelius asserted that "nobody can harm us", which is patent nonsense, in a world of murder, rape and economic violence.

~~~
~~~

Chapter 9: My critique of extreme Stoicism

By Dr Jim Byrne, Copyright (c) 2014/2019/2020

~~~

This chapter first appeared as Chapter 4 of my critique of Rational Emotive Behaviour Therapy (REBT).

Introduction

In this chapter I will focus upon looking at the *nature* of *extreme* Stoicism, which will entail attempting to *distinguish it* from *moderate* Stoicism. And I will include some examples of REBT positions which constitute expressions of extreme Stoicism.

The main theorists I will have to review include:

(1) Zeno of Citium - (which is modern Cyprus) - who created this system of *philosophical thought and practice.*

(2) Epictetus, who was a Greek slave, who studied Stoicism and got his freedom because of his high achievement in learning and practicing Stoical approaches to life. And:

(3) Marcus Aurelius, a Roman emperor who applied Stoicism diligently to his daily life and wrote up his reflections in a journal which he called his *Meditations.*

So let us begin by looking at the life and contribution of Zeno.

Zeno and me

Human memory is very fragile, but I think it was somewhere in the late 1980's that I first heard about Stoicism: probably sometime after 1989, but possibly up to five years earlier. Initially, I (and/or Renata, my wife) came across a couple of random quotations from Marcus Aurelius and Epictetus.

Furthermore, if my memory serves me well, it was about two years after my introduction to REBT (in 1992) that I first heard the story of Zeno of Citium,
~~~

the founder of the school of Stoicism. I can't recall where or how I heard the story, but I can distinctly recall how I *construed* the story, and how I tried to pass it on to others.

This is *my* story of Zeno:

"About 300 years before the current era (BCE), a wealthy merchant called Zeno of Citium was sailing his ship around the Aegean sea when it ran aground and was wrecked. He lost all his possessions, which can be assumed to have been considerable wealth, and perhaps some family members. Walking ashore near Athens, and making his way to that city, he began, immediately, to expound a philosophy of life in which it mattered not at all whether one was shipwrecked, on the one hand, or ennobled and enriched, on the other; or completely ignored by life. The point of life was to *live in mental tranquillity.*"

I told this story to others (especially my therapy clients), drawing the following lesson from it: "If Zeno can walk ashore and accept the loss of *everything*, surely you can cope with the *relatively small loss* that you have just described to me!" - (which could have been a redundancy; or the end of a marital relationship, for examples.)

I now assume that I had to tell myself this story first. I had to buy into this kind of *extreme* form of endurance of deprivation, before I could consider selling this idea to others. And it never occurred to me that this might be an *extreme reading* of the life of Zeno. (I had been raised in conditions of harsh deprivation, both economic, social and emotional; by parents who were extreme stoics; victims of enormous economic hardship; and my expectations of life were consequently very low!)

When Professor William Irvine (2009) begins the story of Zeno's life, he has a somewhat different emphasis:

"Zeno's father was a merchant of purple dye and used to come home from his travels with books for Zeno to read. Among them were philosophy books purchased in Athens. These books aroused Zeno's interest in both philosophy and Athens."

"As a result of shipwreck, Zeno found himself in Athens, and while there, he decided to take advantage of the philosophical resources the city had to offer. He went to a bookseller's shop and asked where men like Socrates could be found. Just then, Crates the Cynic was walking by. The bookseller pointed to him and said, 'Follow yonder man'. And so it was, we are told, that Zeno became Crates' pupil. *Looking back on this time in his life,* Zeno commented, 'I made a prosperous voyage when I suffered shipwreck' [Footnote: Diogenes Laertius, 'Prologue', I, 13-14]." (Irvine, 2009).

This story produces a very different interpretation of Zeno's adaptation to his loss through shipwreck. In my version of the story, which now seems extreme, Zeno *loses everything!* (But in William Irvine's version, he probably lost *one* ship; perhaps it was not *totally* lost, but needed repair; perhaps his cargo was *totally* lost, or *partially* lost?!? We don't seem to know.)

In my version, Zeno *immediately* accepts his loss. But in Professor Irvine's story, Zeno is *looking back on this time* of his life, with the benefit of *some distance*, some *considerable hindsight*, and he can <u>now</u> see that his loss was also a gain - after the lapse of *considerable* time!

But what I was preaching was this: "We (humans) should be able to *immediately* adapt to any and all losses; right now, immediately. With no time spent 'crying over spilled milk!'" Some of this might have come from my family of origin. But I suspect most of it came from my study of Albert Ellis's philosophy of psychotherapy and life.

My parents lived lives of quiet desperation; poverty stricken; and in a loveless marriage; in a pre-welfare society; they had little choice but to become extremely Stoical, with the help of the Catholic Church. Their focus was on getting to Heaven, to escape this *vale of tears*.

When I was a little boy, if I cried about anything, my mother would get her face in close to mine, with an angry expression, and a raised hand, and announce, angrily: "I'll give you *something* to cry about, if you don't stop crying right now!" Then: "Do you want me to give you something to cry about?"

To which I must have indicated, "No!"

"Then stop crying right now!" she'd insist. And I did. And so I learned to *ignore* my feelings, and to be *extremely* Stoical about my life of suffering. (See ***Daniel O'Beeve's Amazing Journey,*** which is my fictionalized autobiography, or 'personal mythology', for details of my early life [Byrne, 2018b][28]).

However, I think it is beyond doubt that some of my harshness with my clients probably also came from Albert Ellis: "Why the f*** *must you* be able to escape from other people's unfairness?" he frequently demanded to know of volunteer 'clients', in public demonstrations of REBT.

When facing up to his fear of flying, and having to take a flight in the early 1960's, Ellis declared: "If I die, I die!"

This is clearly an *extreme* philosophy of *unquestioning endurance* of the most outrageous misfortune, on a par with the Judaeo-Christian surrender: "God's will be done!"

A more normal human response

However, there are *no humans* who are capable of such *immediate adjustment* to painful adversity. It most often *takes time* to process our losses and failures; our traumas and adversities. We know this from a lot of studies of attachment, and studies of innate emotions. Grief is the common, innate emotional response to serious losses or failures. In Byrne (2016)[29] I took a close look at grief, which I described like this:

"**Grief**: Feelings of intense loss when I lose a significant 'attachment figure', like mother, father, partner, etc. (I attach myself to significant others [especially mother {or my main carer}], by innate urging. This maximizes my chances of survival, so I can reproduce, and pass on to my offspring this same urge to attach to me and their other carers. But the downside of my strong attachment is that when my attachment figures die, or become unavailable to me, I experience an intense sense of loss [grief]). This is also the foundation of sadness and depression.")

Of course, I also feel grief when I lose something which is a significant part of my personal domain, such as a job, or my current home, etc. Or, in Zeno's case, his ship. And because these feelings are innate in all animals, we have *no choice* but to feel them. We cannot (and probably *should* not) try to turn ourselves into logs of wood, or lumps of rock, with *no feelings* about our difficult life circumstances

When I came to look at depression, in Byrne (2016) I could clearly see that depression is a form of grief. This is how I described it:

Depression: The E-CENT theory of depression says we have to distinguish between *transient grief* and *stuck depression*.

Grief is 'depression' which is *appropriate* to some significant loss or failure in the recent past. While *depression* is stuck-'grief' which is *inappropriate* to loss or failure in the more distant past. Inappropriate depression could also come from *exaggerating* the degree of badness of a current or recent loss or failure; or refusing to accept its inevitability; or trying (in your mind) to reverse an *irreversible* loss or failure.

This distinction (between grief and depression) is equivalent to saying that there is *appropriate depression* (called 'grief', which *gradually* heals itself) and *inappropriate depression* (called 'depression', which *gets stuck* and needs some kind of psychological intervention).

Grief and depression are intense forms of sadness about real or symbolic losses (or failures), combined with a sense of hopelessness and helplessness.

Grief is a helpful emotion which has enhanced human survival; while there is also a kind of *inappropriate-depression* which indicates a grief process that is stuck, and which is not being processed over time; or an *exaggerated sense* of recent loss.

When clients present with grief about a recent (significant) loss or failure, E-CENT counsellors offer *sympathy* and *understanding*, and *sensitive attunement* to their emotional state. Over time, we encourage the client to cry, to grieve, and to heal. There is only so much crying that a person can do about a loss (or failure), if they are gradually *completing their experience* of that loss (or failure).[30]

Stuck-depression is an unhelpful emotion: When client grief goes on for more than about eighteen months or two years, we consider that the process is stuck and needs to be moved forwards. Sometimes that stuckness is caused by *trauma* – arising out of the fact that the client was already overly stressed when they experienced the loss or failure in question. So we assist this client by suggesting that we help them to work through the desensitization process outlined in Appendix C of Byrne (2016). Or we guide them through a process of getting in touch with their depressed feelings, naming them, describing them in words, and reflecting upon their growing understanding of ***what it means*** (to them) to have these feelings (about their loss [or failure]).

On the other hand, sometimes the process of grieving is stuck because of temperament/character problems within the client. This normally takes the form of *excessively strong demands or expectations that the loss or failure must be reversed*, somehow - even if somebody has died, or the lost thing no longer exists.

In this latter kind of stuck-depression, we might use the ***Nine Windows Model*** to teach the client to *reframe* their depressing loss or failure. (See Chapter 11 below). And/or we might recommend that they write out a ***Gratitude List***, every night, for thirty or sixty nights, containing five or six items for which they can be *grateful*. Thus, they learn to focus upon what they've got, for which they can be grateful, instead of what they have lost.

And we would tend to refer depressed clients to see a nutritionist to make sure they are on a diet which supports their emotional wellbeing; and/or to point them towards certain forms of (educational) dietary advice, which might include this: Try the Mediterranean or Paleo diets. Eat oily fish, like salmon and sardines, for the omega-3 fatty acids, which are good for you brain. Avoid sugary foods, but do have complex carbohydrates, from vegetables, fruit and (some experts say) whole grains. (The Paleo diet promoters and others do not like grains. But some say rice and millet are okay!) Gluten-free oats might be a good compromise. It seems almonds stabilize moods, and Ayurvedic medicine practitioners recommend that we eat ten almonds every day. Some theorists recommend Brazil nuts (e.g. Dr John Briffa)[31], two per day, to help with the production of serotonin. (See Chapter 5 and Appendix E of Byrne, 2016).

We normally, also, recommend that depressed clients pay particular attention to their need for regular physical exercise. (See Taylor-Byrne, 2016a)[32].

~~~

This approach to grief/ depression, which we have developed in E-CENT counselling, is much more holistic than the REBT approach of trying to whip the client out of their perfectly natural upset about a *recent* loss or failure.

I now regret every instance where I told my story of Zeno as if he would not have needed *a long time* to recover from his shipwreck experience. (A long time to *integrate* this very difficult experience into his lived life-story!) I implied that he *adjusted immediately, and so must you and I!* I now see that piece of 'teaching', in which I frequently engaged, as a form of completely *unjustified*, and *unhelpful*, *extreme* Stoicism.
~~~

Time heals all wounds (under normal circumstances), and time has to be allowed for the grieving process. If the individual gets stuck in the grieving process beyond eighteen months or two years, there probably is a case for *rethinking* what is sticking them. But we must not *rush* them, or push them, or try to *hurry* them along. And we certainly should not imply that *they should be able to withstand any and every kind of trauma*, and take it in their stride, without experiencing any stress or strain.

~~~

My extremism, illustrated above, links back to my family background, and not just to Albert Ellis. My parents had to be very stoical in the face of their very harsh lives. And I learned from their harshness to have very low expectations of my own life. (See my fictionalized autobiography: Byrne, 2017)[33].

Something similar could be said of Albert Ellis. He learned to be very stoical in the face of his extreme parental neglect, and this personal experience biased him (like me) towards being attracted to the more extreme elements of Stoic philosophy, when we eventually encountered them. (Byrne, 2013)[34]. And this kind of extremist thinking, which is a *denying* of our *reasonable* emotions, is unhelpful, and has no place in psychotherapy. As shown above, I have evolved away from this kind of harsh denial of the emotional nature of human beings.

Let us now move on to look at Epictetus.

Epictetus

The extremist tendency within Stoicism - the desire to learn how to be as unfeeling as a stone - actually originates in an ancient Greek philosophical tradition called Cynicism. Zeno was influenced by Cynicism, but was said to have moved away from its harshness under the influence of more Platonic ideas (from Plato's followers).

Epictetus, who was said to be one of the more loyal followers of Zeno in the later Roman period of Stoicism, knew the philosophy of Cynicism very well, but was supposed to be practising something less extreme. Nevertheless, it may be that he had more than a little attachment to the aims of Cynicism.
~~~

This is discussed in Professor William Irvine's book on Stoicism (Irvine, 2009):

"When someone told Epictetus – who, although himself a Stoic, was familiar with Cynicism – that he was contemplating joining the Cynic school, Epictetus explained what becoming a Cynic would entail: 'You must utterly put away the will to get, and must will to avoid only what lies within the sphere of your will: you must harbour no anger, wrath, envy, pity; a fair maid, a fair name, favourites, or sweet cakes, must mean nothing to you'. A Cynic, he explained, 'must have the spirit of patience in such measure as to seem to the multitude as unfeeling as a stone. (Being reviled [or hated]), or blows, or insults are nothing to him'." (Irvine, 2009: page 30).

Zeno had studied with Crates, the Cynic teacher, in Athens; and Epictetus seems to strongly admire both Zeno and Crates. Indeed, in Epictetus's description of Cynicism above, I see more than a little of my definition of Epictetus's extreme Stoicism. And, we know that the Cynic movement continued right into the second century AD, and "...found a warm admirer in the Stoic Epictetus". (Rees, 1960)[35].

Albert Ellis was influenced by Epictetus. Ellis and Beck and other key figures in the Cognitive-Behavioural Therapy tradition have tended to use one or two of Epictetus's more extreme Stoical statements to characterize their own approach to helping clients to re-think or re-frame their problems. The most famous such statement is normally rendered like this:

People are not upset by what happens to them, but rather by the attitudes they adopt towards the things that happen to them.

The full statement from Epictetus is this:

"Men (and women) are disturbed *not by the things* which happen, but *by the opinions* about the things: for example, death is nothing terrible, for if it were, it would have seemed so to Socrates" - (who went willingly to his own death – JB) – (F)or the opinion about death, that it is terrible, is the terrible thing. When, then, we are impeded or disturbed or grieved, let us never blame others, but ourselves, that is, our opinions. It is the act of an ill-instructed man (or woman) to blame others for his (or her) own bad condition; it is the act of one who has begun to be instructed, to lay the blame on himself; and of one whose instruction is completed, neither to blame another, nor himself". (Page 14, Section V, the *Enchiridion*)[36].

But this is a *false view* of human emotion - which was adopted by Albert Ellis and Aaron Beck - to the effect that cognitions cause emotions. In my book on ***Holistic Counselling*** (Byrne, 2016), I have this to say on this subject:

"People ***are*** affected by their environments, and especially their social environments (which contradicts the extremist view expressed by Epictetus in his most famous dictum: where he states, in the ***Enchiridion***, that "people are not disturbed by what happens to them, but rather by the attitude they adopt towards what happens to them"). Most often, our emotional reactions are automatic, very fast, and non-conscious (Goleman)[37]. The emotional arousal occurs in a fraction of a second, which is far too fast for any thinking to take place. And very often, the strong emotional reaction is 'self-preserving' or *self-protective*, or *survival oriented*, and not at all 'irrational'."

Furthermore, according to the extensive research project of Jaak Panksepp[38], human cognitive processes – including attention, perception, memory, languaging and thinking – are all *regulated* by our innate emotions, and not vice versa! However, Daniel Siegel (2015)[39] clarifies that our emotions are both *regulating* and *regulated*. And Daniel Hill (2015)[40], summarizing the work of Allan Schore and Peter Fonagy, suggests that *regulation of non-conscious primary affects (or simple innate emotions, JB) is more fundamental than the conscious insights of mentalizing (or thinking in language).*

~~~

As I became aware of the problem (in myself and others) of extreme Stoical attitudes, I began to try to distinguish them from more moderate elements of Stoicism. I thought I had found some archetypal examples of the two tendencies some years ago when I considered them like this:

1. An example of an *extreme* Stoic position: *People are not upset by what happens to them, but rather by their attitude towards what happens to them.*

2. And an example of a *moderate* Stoic position: *There are certain things we can control and certain things we cannot control, and freedom and happiness are determined by making this distinction and acting upon it.*

And for a while, this distinction stood up to my own scrutiny. For example, I developed a moderate Stoical approach to teaching my clients how to distinguish between what they could and could not control, and to only try to control what seems likely to be controllable.
~~~

This is how I described it in one of my blogs: "We teach our clients to draw two columns on a sheet of paper, and to head one of them 'Can control', and the other 'Cannot control'. They are then advised to put most things which could at least theoretically be possible to control, given the right amount and kind of effort, in the left-hand column (Can control), and everything else in the right (Cannot control) column. We then teach them to add conditional clauses on their top priorities in those columns. For examples: *'Can control, IF...'*, in the left-hand column; and, *'Cannot control UNLESS...'*, in the right-hand column. So this is about empirical enquiry into what seems, in practice, to be controllable."

It seemed to me, at that point, that I had found a clearly *moderate* strand of Stoicism, until I read Irvine (2009), and found that Epictetus is not interested in empirical investigation of what *may* be controllable. Instead, he assumes ***he knows*** *what is controllable in advance!* This is what Irvine writes:

Part 1: "Epictetus says we have *complete control* over our opinions, impulses, desires, and aversions. I (William Irvine) agree with Epictetus that we have complete control over our opinions", if (continues Irvine) by opinions he means our opinions about which goals and values to choose.

And I (Jim Byrne) will return to this point later.

Part 2: Irvine then continues: "I have qualms, though, about including our impulses, desires and aversion in the category of things over which we have complete control. I would instead place them in the category of things over which *we have some but not complete control*, or, in some cases, into the category of things over which we have *no control* at all." (Page 90).

Irvine then gives an example (in the form of thought experiments) in which he shows that impulses, desires and aversions *arise within us, automatically*, and we have some degree of control over *whether or not we act upon them*, but not whether or not they *arise*! (Pages 90-91).

Thus, Epictetus is *clearly wrong* to say we have control over our impulses, desires and aversions. We can *try* to *train ourselves* to give up desiring things that are bad for us, or to bravely face up to some of our aversions; and we can (often) stop our impulses before we act upon them. But we are, as argued in E-CENT theory (Byrne, 2016) largely non-conscious, automatic, habit-based creatures, who have *some capacity* to begin to reshape ourselves in the present moment, for enactments in the *future*, through significant commitment and effort; but we are *stuck with being the way we are* in the present moment! And in this present moment, we have whatever desires, aversions and impulses that were shaped within us by our previous social and *socializing* (or conditioning) experiences!

So much for Part 2 of Irvine's statement. Now back to Part 1.

This is what Irvine said: "I agree with Epictetus that we have complete control over our opinions", if by opinions he means our opinions about which goals and values to choose.

However, I (JB) would take issue with this conclusion by Professor Irvine. In principle, a human being can *often* choose their own goals and values. But, in practice, this has to be seen in the context that we are all *socialized* by our family of origin, our schooling, our wider culture, our exposure to the mass media, and influential peers, and so on. In the context of all of this shaping, how much space is actually left, for most people, most of the time, to form their own goals and values? I suspect it is very little indeed. But we can never rule out *the possibility* that Person X might be able to *decide*, today, to set a particular goal; or to abandon one value, and to adopt its opposite, for example. So much for the *possibility*, in practice. What about the *probability*? I would say it is *not very high*, for *most* people, *most* of the time!

People are shaped by their personal histories!

~~~

To repeat the most important point from above:

Epictetus is *clearly wrong* to say we have *control* over our impulses, desires and aversions.

We are innately emotional beings. We are born with a set of innate feelings. (Panksepp, 1998; Darwin, 1872/1965). And those feeling states are *shaped* by our interactions with our mothers/main carers, and other social relationships. (Siegel, 2015).

People *are* upset by what happens to them. And the *nature* and *degree* of their upset is a function of *their socialized 'affect regulation mechanism' – which comes from experiences of being socialized, educated, and shaped in our family of origin and our schooling, etc.* This (socialized affect regulation mechanism) is stored in the upper region of their orbitofrontal cortex (OFC) – overlapping the prefrontal cortex and the limbic system - and its job is to damp down the *emotional surges* which come up from the limbic system (or emotional centres of the brain), via the lower region of the OFC.
~~~

People are upset by what happens to them, *as interpreted* by their socialized schemas/stories/pictures[41], which are emotive-cognitive-experiential structures in long-term memory. (Siegel, 2015; Hill, 2015).

We can learn to improve our 'affect regulation' abilities, especially through interactions with a good attachment counsellor; or even a good rational/cognitive therapist. But the CBT therapist will think that they have "...helped the client to get rid of their irrational belief, or their negative automatic thought", which they assume was the source of the upset.

The attachment counsellor, on the other hand, will think that they have "...helped the client to rewire the upper region of their OFC, so they are better able to damp down their limbic surges of innate emotional response to environmental stressors". I am convinced that the attachment counsellor is right and the REBT/CBT therapist is wrong.

And I dislike the fact that the REBT/CBT therapist will get to their destination by *blaming the client* for "upsetting themselves". And that they will persuade the client to *jump over their emotions* in the future, while the attachment counsellor will teach the client to read their own emotions, and those of their significant others; to learn to manage their own emotions; and to learn to communicate with others about emotional matters in general. That is to say, the attachment counsellor will promote *emotional intelligence;* while the REBT/CBT therapist will promote *discounting of emotions,* plus the development of *an extreme Stoical detachment* (which ultimately will not work, because, in practice, we humans are not at all like the lump of wood, or inanimate stone, that a good Stoic strives to be!)

Let us now move on to look at Marcus Aurelius.

Marcus Aurelius

My research and reflections led me to believe that Marcus Aurelius and Epictetus show signs of having both a *moderate* tendency - (for example, *dedication to reality*) - and an *extremist* tendency - (illustrated by *trying to tolerate the intolerable* – and *advocating* toleration of the intolerable to their followers).

Here is an example from my counselling practice which should help to illustrate the distinction between *moderate* and *extreme* Stoicism. I think I can still sustain this distinction (at the moment):

Over a period of more than ten years, up to 2008-9, under the influence of Albert Ellis's system of rational therapy, (which I have now abandoned), I've used bits and pieces of Stoic philosophy with my counselling clients. Even after abandoning REBT, I have continued to use some (moderate) elements of Stoic philosophy with my E-CENT clients.

In recent years, (roughly 2012 to 2017), I've had three clients who had great difficulty handling difficult people in public places, such as workplaces, commercial offices, and educational settings. Those individuals would come to me, week after week, complaining about having (once again!) run into people who insulted them, used sarcasm with them, or hooked them into nasty *psychological games* (of conflict). Eventually, I developed the habit, with those three particular clients, of *always* reaching for my copy of Marcus Aurelius' book of ***Meditations***, turning to Book II, Verse 1, and reading out this (moderate) statement:

1. An example of moderate stoicism

"1. Say to yourself in the early morning: I shall meet today inquisitive, ungrateful, violent, treacherous, envious, uncharitable men (and women). All these things have come upon them through ignorance of real good and ill (or evil). …"

And, after several such experiences, each of these clients ***eventually*** made a commitment to *teach themselves* this lesson, so they could avoid being upset when they (inevitably!) ran into difficult people in the future. Indeed, each of them wrote down this statement from Marcus, and carried it with them, and eventually they each came to terms with *the reality* that there are Good and Bad 'Wolves' out there – and that the Good and Bad Wolf lives inside each of us. (This is an old Cherokee insight. It's a metaphor for good and evil tendencies within individual humans - which I also taught to my three clients – alongside some assertiveness skills! See my paper on this subject[42].)

But if you have Book II of the *Meditations*, by Marcus Aurelius, in front of you, then you will notice something significant. I have not quoted Verse 1 *in full*; and the reason is that the second part of Verse 1 is an example of *extreme* Stoicism:

2. *An example of extremist thinking*

This is what the second part of Verse 1 says:

"But I, because I have seen that the nature of the good is the right, and of ill the wrong, and that the nature of man himself who does wrong is akin to my own (not of the same blood and seed, but partaking with me in mind, that is, in a portion of divinity), *I can neither be harmed by any of them*, for no man will involve me in wrong, nor can I be angry with my kinsman or hate him; for we have come into the world to work together, like feet, like hands, like eyelids, like the rows of upper and lower teeth. To work against one another therefore is to oppose Nature, and to be vexed with another or to turn away from him is to tend to antagonism". (Page 7)[43].

I could not offer this second part of Verse 1 to my three clients as *sound advice*. Why not? For the following three reasons:

1. Because of the *foolish* claim that "I can (not) be *harmed* by any of them…" (Of course I can – physically and mentally - and so can you!)

2. Because of the *untenable* idea that my clients *cannot* be angry with their tormentors. (Yes they can – and if they are emotionally healthy, then they will often be *appropriately angry* with their tormentors! That is to say, assertively angry.) And, finally:

3. Because of the *strange* idea that to work against one another is to oppose Nature. (I will show, shortly that this is a false claim).

(Also note here that Marcus Aurelius wrote this statement while he was somewhere in modern Germany, militarily putting down revolts against the Roman Empire, of which he was both Emperor and chief warlord!)

Analysis of those three points

Let me now look at each of those three reservations in turn, before coming to my conclusion.

1. Firstly: Marcus's *foolish* claim that "I can (not) be *harmed* by any of them…"

In a blog post in 2011, I remember writing this: "Of course, we need to note that this is not the 'common sense' understanding of ***harm***. After all, Marcus knew that several previous Roman emperors had been seriously harmed (killed) by their political enemies. And Seneca, a great Stoic philosopher, was himself put to death by Nero during the crushing of a conspiracy to assassinate Nero. So, logically, he must be speaking of 'harm' here in the classical Stoical sense of 'moral decay' or 'moral deviation'."

But the *common meaning* of harm includes physical injury, loss of face, status, dignity, or personal property. And in this definition of harm, the common one, we can be harmed by others who mean to harm us. We can also be emotionally upset by their attitudes and behaviours towards us.

So, my clients would be *poorly served* by me if I told them: "When you go into public places, you will meet all kinds of difficult people, *but* none of them can *harm* you!"

That would *not* be true. They *can* be harmed by others; and they must be clear about that. They also have a responsibility to know how to *protect themselves* in the presence of others who might harm them.

So it would be an example of *extreme Stoic self-delusion* if I taught my clients that *nobody could harm them! That the only harm is to have your ethical stance in life undermined! To be drawn into moral deviation or decay.*

~~~

2. Secondly: Marcus's *untenable* idea that my clients *cannot* be angry with their tormentors.

I cannot teach this to my clients, because I want them to have access to their *reasonably angry responses* when anybody tries to oppress or exploit or otherwise harm them. I want them to be able to *defend themselves, assertively* (not aggressively) – and to do that they need to be able to feel *appropriate anger*.

The Stoics made the mistake of thinking that all emotions are a result of *false* beliefs[44] (and Albert Ellis copied this into his system of rational therapy, and Aaron Beck followed suit!) But this is clearly untrue, as it is *obvious* (when you *think* about it!) that a person *who believes, accurately*, that they are about to be killed by a violent assailant, will feel strong, logical, and rational feelings of fear and dread! Stoics are committed to being *unemotional*. From Cynicism, Epictetus had learned that he should strive to be "as unfeeling as a stone" – see Irvine (2009)[45] – and though Stoicism is supposed to be in the middle ground between Cynicism and moderate emotionality, there is evidence that both Epictetus and Marcus Aurelius tended to drift towards the Cynic position from time to time – and this probably constitutes *the core of their extremism!*
~~~

3. Thirdly: Marcus's *strange* idea that to work against one another is to oppose Nature.

I cannot agree to teach my clients this *naïve view* of human cooperation and competition. In E-CENT theory we teach that the line between good and evil runs right down the centre of the human heart; that we each contain a constructive, pro-social tendency (the 'Good Wolf' state) and a destructive, anti-social tendency (the 'Bad Wolf' state). We need to cooperate with each other for the common good, but we must not lose sight of morality. We must not cooperate with people who are promoting evil. We must, in fact, to the degree that we can, work *against* those people who are promoting evil – and this is not against 'our Nature', because *our Nature is shaped by culture,* and our nature/culture is split between the Good and the Bad.

~~~

Marcus Aurelius was not who we think he was!

And here's the paradox. If you sit down and read through Marcus Aurelius' ***Meditations***, you get the sense that you are reading the journal of a saint; a sage; a monk or hermit. A man who is filled with love for his fellows. But you are not! (He is actually said to have *reviled* mankind! [Irvine, 2009]).

Marcus Aurelius wrote Book II "among the Quadi on the river Gran" in central Europe, where he was crushing a rebellion against the Roman Empire. Marcus was *at war* with the peoples who were subjected by the tyranny of the Roman Empire, throughout most of his forty years of adult life, during which time he was the Emperor and military leader of the most aggressively expansive empire seen up to that time in ancient history.

When he retired to his tent to write the opening lines of Book II, he may have had to wash the blood of battle from his hands before handling his journal. How convenient that he believed that the subjugated peoples, who were oppressed by him and his armies, on behalf of his empire, *were not upset by his oppression of them* – which (Stoicism believes) was a matter of 'indifference' – but rather upset by their *opinions* of the Roman army of occupation!

And how *insincere* that he should write that "to work against one another therefore is to oppose Nature, and to be vexed with another or to turn away from him is to tend to antagonism".
~~~

How can he - a full time warlord! - use that word, "antagonism" in that way, after a hard day's bloodshed in putting down rebellion and revolt by an oppressed people?

A little knowledge is a dangerous thing. I learned that lesson the hard way, when I learned that the philosophy of psychotherapy developed by Dr Albert Ellis was hidebound by his *emotional damage* in childhood; his (self-acknowledged) *amoralism;* his *mild autism;* and his *avoidant attachment style.* I learned in the process that you had better know the provenance of any idea you decide to take into your mind, because ideas carry the birthmarks of their creators, and screwed up individuals can only produce screwed up philosophies of life!

And one of the screwiest philosophies of life is this: *I am a bamboo! I can withstand the hurricanes of a mad neoliberal culture, which demands endless commitment of time and energy to my work, for a reduced salary, and total insecurity of employment!*

~~~

I could write a five volume treatise on the limitations and errors of Stoicism, but that would bore you to death. Here I will simply present three final points on Stoicism. These are:

Two criticisms of Marcus Aurelius' philosophy of life. Both of them come from D.A. Rees, the Oxford scholar who wrote the Introduction to Marcus's *Meditations* (1946/1992).

And a suggestion that perhaps counsellors and therapists should develop a good understanding of modern research on *resilience,* to pass on to their clients, instead of relying upon *a few random quotations* from Stoic philosophers.

Firstly: Stoicism *effectively* denies the *social* nature of humans, while affirming it *in theory;* and then they make the mistake of thinking we can pick and choose how we *respond* to our experiences, as if we were separated from experience by a huge space in which we get to *think, consciously,* about how we will respond to each experienced as it happens; and decide whether or not to 'let it in'! Or, as Rees expresses it:

"The Stoic ideal is radically self-centred (*Meditations* xii, 1); one's concern is solely with one's own thoughts, with one's own moral purpose; and in laying its stress upon the 'assent' of the individual to those ideas which
~~~

obtrude upon his attention, insisting that this is purely under the control of his will, Stoicism seems to open the door to *an unlimited degree of wishful thinking*". (Pager xi)

Secondly: Humans are *social* animals, socialized and educated by family, community, school and mass media. We are subject to all kinds of *social pressures* which shape our trajectory through life. Or, as Rees has it:

"Stoicism was forced to disregard in its doctrine of freedom those *all-pervasive social pressures* which radically condition our beliefs and attitudes, of which Aristotle had shown more awareness, and upon which thinkers of the nineteenth and twentieth centuries have laid so much stress" (Page xi).

Finally: There are (at least) two extensive discourses on 'resilience' in the world today. The first argues *against* the idea that we must all become resilient to cope with *a permanently insecure world*, in which we cannot use politics to change reality[46]. (The ruling class can use Buddhism against us all!) (Evans and Reid, 2013)[47] While the second, in the realm of counselling, psychology and personal development, argues that we need to be able to bounce back when life knocks us down. (Tartakovsky, 2017)[48].

If I advocate the second discourse, there is nothing to stop people from the first discourse using my words to support their contention that 'Everybody should be much more resilient, and therefore we do not need to be so caring, or focused on welfare, or social security, and so on'.

This is a big problem in counselling and therapy. I sincerely believe that the ideas that Carl Rogers and Albert Ellis developed, to help their clients, have seeped into the wider culture and are now used to advantage those who wish to exploit and oppress ordinary people. (Can't you just imagine a Wall Street Banker *accepting himself unconditionally* as he engages in socially destructive practices? And can't you imagine how relieved he would be to be able to blame the victims of the recklessly engineered bank crash of 2008 by asking then: "What are you *telling yourself* to make yourself so upset about *my innate right* to ride roughshod over democracy and the rights of the individual?") Therefore, we have to be careful how we *express* our therapeutic philosophies, so they cannot easily be used to *worsen* social and political realities outside the therapy room!

In this spirit, I want to make the following points: Perhaps we should abandon any references to Stoicism in counselling and therapy, and replace them with advice on how to become more resilient in the face of *unavoidable* life difficulties. Southwick and Charney (2012)[49] – two medical doctors – suggest that a useful curriculum for the development of greater resilience would include:

- Developing optimism (and overcoming learned pessimism);

- Facing up to our fears (or being courageous);

- Developing a moral compass (or learning to always do what is the *right* thing, rather than what is opportunistically advantageous);

- Developing a spiritual, faith, or community connection that is bigger than the self;

- Connecting to others for social support;

- Finding and following resilient role models;

- Practicing regular physical exercise;

- Working on brain-mind fitness, including mindfulness and cognitive training (but they overlooked the impact of food and gut flora on the brain-mind, so that needs to be considered also);

- Developing flexibility in our thinking-feeling-behaviour (including acceptance and reappraisal);

- Focusing on the meaning of your life, the purpose of your life, and on desired areas of personal growth.

Perhaps a consideration of these ideas could take us beyond *the 'wishful thinking' about impossible goals* set by Zeno, Marcus and Epictetus (and Albert Ellis, and some other CBT theorists).

But we should also focus on the political sphere, and recognize that we need to *promote moral politicians,* and to wash the servants of big capital out of government as completely as that is possible!

~~~
~~~

Chapter 10: Some more problems with Buddhism & Stoicism

In E-CENT theory we have taken some *moderate Buddhist* and *moderate Stoic* ideas as *points of departure*, but we have also found serious flaws in both of those philosophies.

For examples:

1. Regarding Buddhist theory: The opening lines of the Dhammapada are as follows:

"What we *are* today comes from our thoughts of yesterday, and our present thoughts build our life of tomorrow: our life is the creation of our mind". (Page 1)[50].

In ***my view***, we need to significant amend that statement to take account of the following three points:

(1) "What we are today comes from *our thoughts (and feelings)...*" *about our experiences*...

So, we are not talking about *disembodied thoughts*, devoid of a stimulus in an *external reality*. And we are not talking about beings that can think *independently of their basic emotional wiring!* People are *emotionally wired up* by nature and their earliest relationships, and they live in *the real world* of good and bad experiences! They have body-brain-minds, and their so-called thoughts - which are actually *thoughts/feelings/perceptions* combined - are *strongly affected* by diet, exercise, relationship support or its lack, external stressors, and so on.

And I would also amend the Buddha's second reference like this:

(2) "...and our present thoughts..." (*Plus our feelings and actions, including eating, sleeping, relaxing, exercising, etc.*) "...build our life of tomorrow..."

So our thoughts (*about* our experiences) *do not act alone*; they are not the *sole determinant* of our lives.

And I also want to challenge his view about 'the mind':

(3) "...our life is the creation of our mind" he claims. (*But he forgot to add: Plus* our relationships; plus our experiences; plus our diet, exercise, stressors

- including economic and political circumstances, family life, and on and on).

So the Buddha can easily *mislead the unwary*; as the unwary were misled by Albert Ellis and Aaron Beck - who *downplayed* the role of the environment in human experience; with Ellis denying the role of early childhood in shaping the later life of the social-individual. Those theorists also overlooked the importance of our eating of unhealthy diets; and our failure to exercise our bodies; or to get enough restorative sleep; all of which impacts our emotional states.

To serve our clients well, counsellors and psychotherapists need to be *critical thinkers*; to be awake; to be well informed (meaning widely read, and subject to multiple influences); and to think for ourselves. We need to become modern polymaths - to the extent that this is possible; to be multi-disciplinary; to cross all boundaries of research and theorizing; so as to avoid simplistic nonsense, like the Buddha's model of the human mind; or the extreme Stoic model of human disturbance, which found its way into rational therapy (REBT) and cognitive therapy (CBT).

Buddhist ideology downplays the impact of the environment upon human organisms, in a way which is corrected by modern social psychology. (Social psychology is an attempt to understand and explain the various ways in which "we, as individuals are influenced by the actual, imagined or implied presence of others". Allport, 1985)[51]. If we are to develop a theory of human emotions, we must not follow the Buddhist dumping of this impact of the social environment on the thinking, feeling and behaviour of our clients, lest we end up *blaming the client* for their disturbance, as was done by Freud, Klein, Ellis and Beck. (Indeed, it was Dr John Bowlby who most strongly emphasized the importance of early childhood *relational experiences*: the impact, for better or worse, of our early social relationships upon our attachment style, and our chances of having a happy marriage in adult life.

Because this went against both Freud's and Klein's perspective - [which blamed the child for their own emotional disturbances] - Dr John Bowlby was ostracized by the British psychoanalytic community for decades - because they insisted upon *blaming the clients' 'phantasies'* for their upset emotions.)[52]

However, the mindfulness aspect of Buddhism, especially Zen Meditation, is very helpful for all of us, counsellors and clients alike, because it stops us ruminating on past problems, or anxiously anticipating future difficulties. Here is an illustration of how to understand 'mindfulness', or awareness of the present moment:

"The greatest support we can have is mindfulness, which means being totally present in each moment. If the mind remains centred, it cannot make up stories about the injustice of the world or one's friends, or about one's desires or sorrows. All these stories could fill many volumes, but when we are mindful such verbalizations stop. Being mindful means being fully absorbed with the momentary happening, whatever it is - standing or sitting or lying down, feeling pleasure or pain - and we maintain a non-judgemental awareness, a 'just knowing'." Ayya Khema[53].

However, here's one serious caveat: It is *not* a good idea to try to use mindfulness to suppress or deny our feelings about our distressing experiences. That will not work. We have to *file* our distressing experiences in the past, or they will *insert* themselves into our future! And the only way I know to file our distressing experiences in the past is to *experience their emotional content fully*; to <u>*digest*</u> those emotional experiences; to <u>*complete*</u> them; and thus to burn them up; and *file* them in inactive files in our long-term memory. In the process we get to *re-frame them*; to see them differently; to drain them of their original meaning and their distressing *emotional charge.*[54]

~~~

2. ***Regarding Stoic theory:*** Here I will present a brief restatement of some of the points made in Chapter 4, with some elaboration and clarification.

The most famous saying of the Stoic philosophers in the world of cognitive counselling systems today is this belief: "People are *not* upset by the things which happen to them, but rather by their *attitude* towards those things". This *extremist* belief is central to Rational Therapy (REBT), Cognitive Therapy (CT) and CBT in general.

That belief is also very similar to the opening statement of the *Dhammapada*, in that it both *blames the client* for their interpretation of their experience, and ascribes to them *the capacity to be indifferent* to their environmental insults, hurts and defeats. (This inference is clear from verses 2 and 3 of the Dhammapada, page 1). But only a lump of wood, or a stone, or some other
~~~

inanimate object, can be truly indifferent to particularly intense environmental stimuli.

A *wise person* may well choose to ignore some environmental insults, hurts and defeats; to downplay them; or to reframe them, so they seem less painful. But not all of our clients can claim to be *wise* upon *first* encountering us. (And many of them will fail to achieve significant levels of wisdom, no matter how long they work with us; and almost none will rise to the level of Stoic functioning, just as ***most Stoics*** fail to rise to the level of the theoretical '*indifference to externals*' which Stoic theory demands of its adherents).

In time, we might teach some of our clients to be *somewhat* wiser - using some *moderate* Stoic principles – but we *should not* attempt to teach them the more *extreme* principles, such as that shown above; partly because we would have to *blame them* for their distress, to begin with; and then we would have to move on to *advocating super-human goals for mere humans.*

But there are some *moderate principles* of stoicism that we should try to practice and preach.

The most helpful principle of Stoicism, which is also found in Buddhism, is this, from Epictetus's *Enchiridion*:

"Freedom and happiness consist of understanding one principle: There are certain things we can control and certain things we cannot control. It is only after learning to distinguish between what we can and cannot control – and acting upon that knowledge – that inner harmony and outer effectiveness become possible".[55]

If some of the things that negatively affect me, in my current social environment, are *within my control*, then it makes sense to try to correct and control them: to change them. And if something proves to be *beyond* my control (or *most likely* beyond my control) then it makes sense not to rail against that fact, but *to learn to accept it* (which will take time and effort, and courage and fortitude, and wisdom).

But that is *not* (ultimately) what is taught by the major Stoic philosophers, when they deploy their more extreme principles. For example, in his ***Meditations***, Marcus Aurelius defines 'harm' as being the ability of some outside agency to damage his 'individual ethical stance'. And he then declares an absolute principle that: *Nobody has the ability to damage my individual ethical stance*. Hence, *logically*, nobody has the ability to *harm* him.

Hence, his final conclusion: *Nobody can disturb me!* (That makes it difficult to understand *why he committed suicide* (by refusing to eat) when he was told he had a terminal illness (Irvine, 2009, page 199). Since the terminal illness 'could not harm him', according to his theory, why not await death with a peaceful heart, which he encouraged others to do? A mystery? Or plain hypocrisy? Or a failure to know himself well enough to know that he was not as stoical as he assumed himself to be!)

(See the ***Introduction*** to the ***Meditations of Marcus Aurelius***, by D.A. Ross)[56].

The problem with the conclusion (that nobody has the ability to harm me) is that only a rare sage could live a life based on the idea - the *fantasy* - that *a hatchet through my skull does not constitute harm, since it leaves my individual ethical stance intact.*

Or, that somebody murdering my baby and raping my wife cannot disturb me, *because it leaves my individual ethical stance intact.*

These are *unreachable* goals, and *inhuman* beliefs, which could never be *universalized* as an approach to life. And therefore, counsellors and psychotherapists should not (morally) imply that these are goals which are achievable by average counselling clients; and that the client is somehow remiss for not acting like a lump of wood!

And neither should we teach our clients to *become like a bamboo;* nor to stay in uncomfortable situations until they become comfortable with them. We have to be much more humane than that; and much wiser than that; and to understand the ways in which all these philosophical aspirations can be used by exploiters to squeeze the life out of their employees and others. Remember Shami's mistake, described in the Foreword, above.

~~~

So, while we can learn some things about *moderating our desires* and *distinguishing* between what is a *realistic* goal (to be pursued) and an *unachievable* goal (to be abandoned) - we must not spread *the lie that our clients are not disturbed by their social experiences! They are!*

I obviously cannot justify making that statement without backing it up. So I need to provide evidence for the general reader of this book to show that people are actually upset by what happens to them?
~~~

At the height of my time as an REBT therapist, I was fond of using the following thought experiment to demonstrate that people are *not* upset by what happens to them:

Thought experiment

Three men who work in a factory are issued with identical brown envelopes on the same day at the same time. The content of the envelope is a virtually identical letter, the only difference being that each letter is addressed to its intended recipient. The letter says: "You are sacked. Your employment with this company is hereby terminated. Please find a cheque for one weeks' wages, attached. Thank you, and goodbye!"

Do they all necessarily react in the same way? No.

One may become *depressed,* by focusing on the fact that he has failed to keep his job, and therefore blames himself. He becomes depressed.

Another may become *angry,* by focusing on the insulting behaviour to which he has been subjected, by an employer who had promised him promotion and secure employment, if he worked double shifts for a month, and this is the rotten ingratitude with which he has been 'rewarded'.

The third man may be *pleased,* because he had become tired of the job anyway, and now has a perfect excuse to spend the next month fishing, before looking for a new job.

I used to think that this *proved* that people are not upset by what happens to them. But it does not. Why not?

Here is a better thought experiment:

Ten women work in an insurance company. They are all laid off (made redundant) on the same day, with the same standard letter, and a single week's pay. The personnel manager speaks to each of them on the way out, and writes this report to her boss: "The ten former employees, have now left the building. I spoke to each of

> them on the way out. Seven of them are very upset, because they feel the chill winds of economic insecurity. Three of them seemed to be okay".

Does this prove that the seven (who *were* disturbed) were not upset by *what happened to them*? No!

The seven who were upset are responding in a *typical* manner to financial problems and material insecurity. The three who seemed to be okay are the *exceptions that* ***prove*** *the rule*. And what is the rule here?

> ***RULE: That most people who are made redundant will feel more or less upset, because working people depend upon their employment to pay for their food and accommodation, etc.***

People who are made redundant are *most often* upset, because *of being made redundant*. Of course, their attitudes towards personal security may differ slightly, one from another, and that will, logically, affect the *intensity* of their upsetness. But they will *mostly* be upset, because of the implications – the *practical, REAL WORLD* implications – of not having an income in the period up ahead.

Being made redundant is an example (I think) of what Dr Hans Selye called 'a stressor'[57]. And the attitudes of the sacked employees is what Selye called 'a conditioning factor'. Although it is often difficult to distinguish between these stressors and conditioning factors, we know that people are conditioned to depend upon employment as the source of their financial security. When particular effects of social conditioning (like being a dutiful wage-earner) meet particular life stressors (like sudden, unexpected redundancy), *predictable emotional disturbances will occur* within the affected individual. From this kind of equation, we can fairly conclude that *people (in general) are disturbed by what happens to them*, given their prior social conditioning, and the ***facts*** of their daily lives.

What I want to teach my clients is a set of strategies which will help them to quickly – but not normally *immediately* (and certainly not *easily*) – reduce those upsets about life's slings and arrows of discontent.

~~~
~~~

Part 3: How to Re-frame Your Problems:

The Nine Windows Model of E-CENT theory

We humans do not look at the world through our eyes, but rather through our 'frames of reference'. A frame is a set of inferences about an object or event. This set of inferences – or hunches, guesses, feelings, and so on – determine what the event or object means to us, or how it 'shows up' for us. Most of our frames of reference, which guide our daily actions in the world, are non-conscious, but they nevertheless control our behaviour, from non-conscious levels of mind.

In this section I want to teach you nine potent ways of framing your problems, so that they will show us as less distressing, which will allow you to be more resilient in the face of those problems.

~~~
~~~

Chapter 11: My Nine Windows Model - Or nine ways to re-frame your problems

The Nine Windows Model of E-CENT Counselling

A powerful way to re-frame and re-think your problems

By Dr Jim Byrne

~~~

The Nine Windows Model of E-CENT[3] counselling is a way of helping individuals to rethink and re-frame their upsetting or distressing problems, without engaging in *confrontation* and/or *conflictual argumentation* with them.

It consists of an experiment, in which the person needing help is asked to *imagine* how their problem would look ***and feel***, when viewed through nine different window frames - each of which provides a slightly different 'context' for the problem.

The context is provided by a philosophical statement (or belief), such as 'life is difficult'; or 'some things are beyond my control'. And the person is asked to look at a ***specific problem*** - which is disturbing or distressing them - through those nine different windows, or contexts; frames; or philosophical lenses - as if they are true beliefs.

Here's how it works:

Think about a current problem that you have, which is serious enough to require urgent treatment. This problem might make you feel angry, anxious, depressed, or some other seriously painful emotion.

---

[3] This model was developed by me, Jim Byrne, around 2014, and originally consisted of just four windows, mostly derived from Buddhist sutras and moderate Stoical principles. I then expanded it to five and then six windows, but had to modify it because one or two extreme ways of reframing had crept into the system, mostly from Buddhism. Then it increased to eight windows, and very recently I added number nine.
~~~

Try to create a visual image or representation of that problem. Then look through each of the following nine 'windows' in turn, (as if looking at that serious problem), and ask yourself the questions suggested:

\~~~

Window No.1: The frame around this window says:

"In life, there are certain things I can control, and certain things that are beyond my control".

Looking at my chosen problem:

*- Am I currently upset because I am **trying** to control something that is **beyond** my control? (For examples: Other people are beyond my control; though some of them may be more or less open to being influenced by me. The economy is beyond my control; as it government policy [today, and for the foreseeable future!] And so on.)*

- If I give up trying to control what is clearly beyond my control, how much happier would I feel? (Normally, a lot!)

\~~~

Window No.2: The frame around this windows says:

"Life is difficult for** all **human beings, at least some of the time, and often much of the time".

Therefore, since I am a human being, life is sometimes going to be difficult for me, as it is when I am confronted by my current problem. If my problem is one in which somebody is acting illegally towards me, I should seek legal help. If they are acting immorally against me, I have to ask myself if I can stop them, and if not, I should consider putting myself beyond their influence or control. Once I have taken care of my legal and moral situation, I should ask myself:

- So why must life not be difficult for me (in this problem situation)? Why must I (alone, among humans) be exempted from suffering?

Since I am human, it follows that I will experience difficulties! (And if I cannot control and eliminate them, then I will have to learn to accept them – without subjecting myself to sadistic, illegal or immoral victimization!)

- Is there any reason why I should be exempt from having problems?

- Is there any good reason to believe that I cannot cope with having this current problem?

∼∼∼

Window No.3: The frame around this window says:

"Life is much less difficult when I avoid picking and choosing what happens, or how it happens; or if I pick and choose more modestly, sensibly or reasonably."

- So, if I am experiencing difficulty right now (in relation to the problem I am viewing through this window), doesn't that mean I must be (unrealistically) picking and choosing?

- And isn't it true that life would be much less difficult if I were to pick and choose more moderately, more modestly, more realistically.

- How can I change my choices and preferences in order to show that I am picking and choosing realistically and reasonably and modestly?

- I must keep my expectations in line with everyday reality.

∼∼∼

Window No.4: The frame around this window says:

"Life is both difficult and non-difficult".

- So if I am very upset, might it not be because I am exclusively focusing on the ***difficulties****, and overlooking those bits of my life which are* ***not difficult*** *(for which I could be grateful)?*

- What happens to how I feel if I add back in the 'missing' non-difficult bits of my life?

- I must make a list of those positive things I have in my life for which I could feel grateful, such as my eyesight or hearing; my ability to walk or talk; and so on.

∼∼∼

Window No.5: The frame around this window says:

"Life could always be* very much more difficult *than it currently is for me".

- So am I making the mistake of thinking it is already (and always) 100% bad?

- Or as bad as could be? (What if a crocodile was eating my rear end off, in addition to my current problems? What percentage badness would that be?)

- Think of those things that I may lose later in life, which I still currently have. (Such as my hair, some of my teeth, my unwrinkled skin. My youthfulness, or whatever). How does that make me feel?

- Write down three things for which I can be grateful right now. ('Count your blessings'!)

\~~~

Window No.6: The frame around this window says:

"Life is a school which obliges us all to learn how to survive and grow. So, I must pay attention, and learn quickly".

*- Which **aspect**(s) of my current problem should I pay attention to?*

- Is this problem a repeating pattern? If so, why do I keep getting to this point? Am I creating or attracting this problem by some unhelpful behaviour or thought/ feeling/perceiving pattern of my own?

*- What **positive lesson** could I learn from my current negative situation(s)? I must write about this, and write down the answer(s).*

- If there was an independent witness present, observing me and how I relate to this problem, what would they conclude? (Write down your answer. It could help to solve your problem).

\~~~

Window No.7: The frame around this window says:

***"I'm okay, exactly the way I am (in terms of appearance, social status, efficiency, and effectiveness, etc.); as long as I am in the habit of acting* morally *and* legally".**

- In what ways am I judging myself negatively? Do I beat myself up for not being able to solve this (present) problem? Do I blame myself for having this problem?

- How justified are those judgements (given that I am a fallible, error-prone human)?

- How could I learn to accept myself more thoroughly, kindly, and charitably? (I must not accept myself completely unconditionally – regardless of my moral and legal actions in the world. But I must learn to accept myself one-conditionally, and that one condition is that I always act as a moral being, following the Golden Rule, of treating other people as well as I would want them to treat me, if our roles were reversed).

\~~~

Window No.8: The frame around this window says:

***"You're okay (you other people), exactly the way you are (in terms of appearance, social status, efficiency, effectiveness, etc.); as long as you are in the habit of acting* morally *and* legally".**

- In what ways am I judging you (another person) negatively?

- How justified are those judgements (given that you [another person] are a fallible, error-prone human)?

- How could I learn to accept you [other person] more thoroughly, kindly, and charitably? (I must not accept you completely unconditionally – regardless of your moral and legal actions in the world. But I must learn to accept you one-conditionally, and that one condition is that you appear to act as a moral being, following the Golden Rule, of treating other people as well as you would want them to treat you, if your roles were reversed).

~~~
~~~

Window No.9: The frame around this window says:

"Winners never quit – but they certainly don't persist in banging their heads on the same section of the wall that obstructs their progress".

- Some people quit too soon, or too easily, and therefore fail to win the prize that they desired.

- Some people keep going, striving and persisting, and they do (often) achieve the prize that they were after.

- And some people keep going, and going, and going, despite the fact that they are clearly flogging a dead horse. This is a form of losing, and failing, and self-disregard or self-abuse! (This is what Shami did, until it ruined his health. He should had paid more attention to the need for balance in his life: meaning 8 hours' work; 8 hours' rest; and 8 hours' play; except sometimes!)

- I must try, try and try again – <u>within reason</u> - to succeed; but not necessarily in the same (unworkable) relationship; or the same (unrewarding or intolerable) business or employment; or on the same path through life.

- Winners are life-long learners, and they have the courage to act on their earned wisdom!

- How can I decide when to persist and when to quit? (I could try using the CoRT tools developed by Dr Edward De Bono[58], applied to my current problem situation).

- Is my current problem a result of bashing my head on the wrong section of wall?

- Is it time to quit on some person, or organization, or some object or thing, or goal, in order to resolve my current problem?

~~~

Reflection: Did this process, of viewing a current problem from nine different 'directions' or perspectives, or through nine different 'lenses', or 'frames', change how it looks and feels to you? (Normally it will!)

~~~

We can summarize the Nine Windows in the following illustrations:

Window No.1: The frame around this window says:	**Window No.2**: The frame around this windows says:	**Window No.3:** The frame around this window says:

"In life, there are certain things I can control, and certain things that are beyond my control".	*"Life is difficult for all human beings, at least some of the time, and often much of the time".*	*"Life is* **much less** *difficult when I avoid picking and choosing what happens, or how it happens; or if I pick and choose more* **sensibly** or **reasonably."**

Window No.4: The frame around this window says:	**Window No.5**: The frame around this window says:	**Window No.6:** The frame around this window says:

"Life is **both** *difficult and non-difficult".*	*"Life could always be* **very much more difficult** *than it currently is for me".*	*"Life is a school which teaches you how to survive and grow. Pay attention. Learn quickly".*

Window No.7: The frame around this window says:	**Window No.8:** The frame around this window says:	**Window No.9:** The frame around this window says:

"I'm okay, exactly the way I am (in terms of appearance, social status, efficiency, and effectiveness, etc.); as long as I am in the habit of acting **morally** *and* **legally***".*	*"You're okay (you other people), exactly the way you are (in terms of appearance, social status, efficiency, effectiveness, etc.); as long as you are in the habit of acting* **morally** *and* **legally***".*	*"Winners never quit – but they certainly don't persist in banging their heads on the same section of the wall that obstructs their progress. And they don't stay in self-destructive situation when they are free to leave".*

~~~

If you review this nine windows model every day, for 30, 60, 90 or 120 days, you should be able to re-wire your brain with a self-supporting philosophy of life, which will help you to be more resilient in the face of any future difficulties. And it will help to clear up your current problems.

But you have to do the homework, diligently, systematically, for significant period of time, to gain the benefits, because it takes time to re-wire your non-conscious brain-mind.

To paraphrase Paul McKenna's expression: "*Repetition* is the mother of self-change".

~~~

Part 4: Developing a Resilient Body-Brain-Mind – The body angle

In Part 4, we will be looking at

- The importance of sleep, and the value of getting enough of it, of the right quality – in Chapter 12;

- The importance of diet and nutrition – in Chapter 13;

- The value of physical exercise, and some of the best forms – in Chapter 14;

- And the importance of Progressive Muscle Relaxation (PMR), and how to do it – in Chapter 15.

Chapter 12: The importance of sleep

Preamble

Insufficient sleep - less than eight hours per night, every night - can and will cause physical health problems, and mental and emotional problems. And you will not be resilient enough to deal with the stress-inducing problems of your daily life if you get an inadequate amount or quality of sleep.

This chapter first appeared as a co-authored chapter, by Renata Taylor-Byrne and Jim Byrne, in our book on lifestyle coaching and counselling, where it was Chapter 5[59]. (For a fuller treatment of sleep science, please see Taylor-Byrne, 2019[60]).

The impact of sleep on mental health and emotional wellbeing

By Renata Taylor-Byrne and Jim Byrne

~~~

Introduction

If you want to be more resilient, and to be able to stay in control of your anger, anxiety and depressive tendencies, under pressure, then you have to give a high priority to your sleep patterns, on a nightly basis.

What do the experts say about the impact of sleep disturbance, sleep loss, deprivation, or sleep insufficiency?

Firstly, according to Dr James Maas (1998)[61], an early expert on sleep science, if you are getting less than eight hours of sleep each night, including at weekends, then you are one of the millions of chronically sleep-deprived individuals, who normally are unaware of how sleepy and ineffective they are, or how much more effective they could be, including emotionally, if they got enough sleep.

Later, Shawn Stevenson (2016)[62] argued that every aspect of your mental, emotional and physical performance is affected by the quality of your sleep.

And in 2017, Matthew Walker[63] wrote that if you sleep less than six or seven hours a night as a regular habit-pattern, then this will destroy your immune
~~~

system and double the likelihood of you developing cancer. Such low levels of sleep would make you more susceptible to the development of Alzheimer's disease, and if you had just one week of such reduced sleep, it would destabilise your blood sugar level to the extent that you could be diagnosed as pre-diabetic.

And of course, most sleep science commentators refer to the negative impact of sleep insufficiency on mood and emotions, including depression, anxiety and anger causation.

Indeed, Walker (2017) considers that sleep is the foundation upon which diet and exercise need to stand, if the whole system is to work well.

If you have an inadequate sleep pattern, this cannot be compensated for by good dietary and exercise practices!

~~~

In this chapter, we will look at the following subjects:

Common sense ideas about sleep;

Distractions from sleep;

Problems caused by sleep insufficiency;

The benefits of sleep; and:

Insomnia and sleep insufficiency; as well as science-based, researched remedies for sleep problems.

The primary importance of sleep

In our earlier book on diet and exercise - Taylor-Byrne and Byrne (2017)[64] - we presented a range of studies which show that human emotional disturbances are caused, or affected, for better or worse, by what we eat, and fail to eat; how we exercise, or fail to exercise; and we also referred in passing to sleep as another major factor in determining our mental health and emotional well-being.

This range of three major sources of good or poor physical and mental health, and high or low levels of emotional well-being, are well documented in the scientific literature. (Lopresti, 2013)[65].
~~~

And many theorists would say that sleep is *the most important* of these; followed by diet; and then exercise. (Of course our attitudes of mind, and our environments, are also important, but they are dealt with elsewhere in this book).

For example, as Walker (2017) points out, although it's not good for us to go without food and/or liquid for one day, we can fairly easily recover from that deprivation.

However, on the other hand, if we were to go without sleep for *one night*, it would have a significantly damaging effect on us, both mentally and physically. So this shows *the relatively greater need* for sleep sufficiency.

Walker goes on to say that: "I was once fond of saying, 'Sleep is the third pillar of good health, alongside diet and exercise'. I have changed my tune. Sleep is more than a pillar. It is the foundation on which the other two health bastions sit." (Walker, 2017. Page 164).

This lines up with the views of Professor Colin Espie[66], who wrote that:

"Alongside eating and breathing, sleep is one of the fundamentals of life, and arguably the most important - you could survive for three times as long without food as you could without sleep, and 17 hours without sleep produces performance impairments equivalent to 2 alcoholic drinks."

If you do not sort out your sleep hygiene, it is unlikely you will be able to greatly improve your sense of emotional wellbeing, and physical and mental health, by diet and exercise alone.

If you fix your sleep, but fail to improve your diet and nutrition, it is unlikely you will be able to make up the deficit via exercise alone.

So we have to take sleep very seriously, followed by diet and exercise, if we want to be happy, healthy and physically and emotionally well.

Common sense views of sleep

William Shakespeare, in his play, *Macbeth*, expressed a profound truth when he declared that, "'Tis sleep that knits the ravelled sleeve of care!'" And we have always taken this to mean that the cares and worries of the day are resolved by a good night's sleep, as a *sleeve* is fixed by *darning* or re-knitting. Some people have contested this simple interpretation, and insisted that the word intended here was 'sleave' of care, and not 'sleeve' of care; where 'sleave' is a bunch of silk filaments as worked by silkworkers. (McGuinness, 2013)[67].

Macbeth's mind is not just unravelled, but knotted and tangled, with a web of difficult emotions, like a tangled knot of silk filaments, and it's a good night's sleep, according to Shakespeare, which will help to unknot those emotions, and sort them out in order to present a viable resolution.

"Sleep brings to order this bundle of emotions as the hand of a silkworker unravels a tangled sheaf of sleave-silk." (McGuinness, 2013).

To be clear, a 'sleave', in silk work, as a noun, is defined like this: "...a filament of silk obtained by separating a thicker thread." Hence, sleep is represented as untangling the strands of our day which have become tangled, and especially those which are emotionally charged, stressful and difficult to process. Thus Shakespeare is saying that sleep helps to sort out our stresses and strains, and makes sense of our days.

Surprisingly, as we will see later, sleep is not just about sorting out thoughts and feelings, but includes a physical and hormonal tidying up of the brain's structure. Indeed, as Matthew Walker (2017) points out, Shakespeare knew that sleep "...is 'the chief nourisher in life's feast'." (Page 108 of Walker, 2017).

Shakespeare was not the only great artist who studied the effects of sleep on the mind.

According to John Steinbeck, the American author of the novel, *The Grapes of Wrath:*

"It is a common experience that a problem difficult at night is resolved in the morning after the committee of sleep has worked on it."

The sleeping brain has an enormous capacity to resolve the stresses and strains of competing demands of a too-busy day. And, as it turns out, it also helps to prepare the brain-mind for the day ahead.

Another famous American author, Ernest Hemingway found that sleep was the best time of his life, and his waking hours were more difficult:

"I love sleep", he wrote. "My life has the tendency to fall apart when I'm awake, you know?"

Of course, we are not advocating 'escape into sleep'. Rather, we advise our clients to make sure they get at least eight or nine hours sleep, of good quality, every night, so that they have the best chance of processing the experiences of the preceding day, and preparing for the stresses and strains of the following day.

And this recommendation is backed up by scientific studies, as well as common sense, as we will see below.

Distractions from sleep

Many people allow themselves to become distracted from the need to sleep. They may be ambitious, and spend too many hours working. To them, we give the advice that they should follow the 8-8-8 rule:

- Do eight hours work;

- have eight hours rest (sleep);

- and divide the remaining eight hours between play and self-care activities, like shopping, cooking, dining, conversing with family and friends, and so on.

(This is the advice I would have given to Shami – see the case study in the Foreword – if he'd consulted me about his tendency to overwork!)

This balance will ensure that their working hours are *optimally productive*, and that their health will be sustained for *long-term productivity*.

Over-working may seem productive in the short-term, but will most often prove to undermine physical health and emotional wellbeing in the longer term; and it is *actually* less productive in the here and now (because the 'saw blade' of our mind becomes dulled; and needs rest and sleep to sharpen it!)

When people of this authors' generation were growing up (in the 1950's and '60's), there were very few distractions from going to bed when it got dark. The public houses closed at an early hour (about 10.30 pm on a week night). The three available TV stations (in the UK) closed down at about 11.00 pm. And there was still a residual awareness that it is important to get eight hours sleep, if you wanted to feel well and fit and happy the next morning. This was also an era of (relatively) full employment, and so most people needed to get up early each morning, to go to work in factories, offices, transport systems, hospitals, and, to a lesser extent, shops.

Today, all of this has changed.

Now we have 24-hour cities, where the bars never (or rarely) close.

TV stations broadcast around the clock.

And, even if there is nothing worth watching on TV, the Internet *narrow-casts* lots of seductive material in the form of videos and blogs, and chat rooms.

And then there's the *ping* of incoming emails. And the *ping* of instant messages to mobile phones.

And the TV screen and the computer screen and the mobile phone screen have all found their way into too many bedrooms; distracting people from sleep.

Indeed, the *blue light* from those devices – which is short-wavelength light – is twice as powerful at suppressing the release of the hormone, melatonin, as ordinary incandescent light bulbs. And when melatonin levels are too low, it is very difficult or near impossible to sleep.

So, at the very least, people who are overexposed to blue light before bedtime, or who have blue light devices in their bedrooms at bedtime, lie awake in their beds for a long time before getting to sleep. This is called 'sleep onset insomnia'.

Melatonin is a hormone which is secreted in response to the failing daylight, and normally switches on around 9.00 pm. But is can be delayed by over-exposure to artificial lighting, especially blue light from LED's.

Simply reading an iPad at night can inhibit the release of melatonin by 50%.

And what are the consequences?

- It takes much longer to fall asleep, (because your body-brain-mind has to wait while the melatonin level is built up again);

- and this sleep disruption affects your level of energy, your mood, and alertness, the following day;

- as well as your longer term biologically-programmed sleep rhythms.

(See below for insights into dietary and exercise effects upon sleep and sleeplessness).

Problems of sleep insuffiency

Why we need sleep

The science of sleep suggests that, while you are asleep, your body is busy:

- detoxifying itself, including getting rid of waste products, resulting from stress and strain during your waking hours;

- repairing tissues;

- and also balancing or rebalancing your hormones.

These various biochemical processes are so complex that it is not difficult to see how things might go badly wrong if the body does not have enough time to do this repair and maintenance work.

Insufficient repair and recovery work could "...impact emotional regulation, memory, mood, and other factors..." (Osmun, 2015).

And, according to Mauss, Troy, and LeBourgeois (2013)[68], who tested hypotheses linking poor quality sleep and poor quality of emotional self-regulation, in a laboratory setting:

"Participants with poorer self-reported sleep quality exhibited lower CRA (or cognitive reappraisal ability [or ability to *re-think* or *emotionally reframe* a problem - Eds.]), even after controlling for fourteen potential key confounds (e.g., age, negative affect, mood disorder symptoms, stress). This finding is consistent with the idea that *poorer sleep quality impairs individuals' ability to engage in the crucial task of* ***regulating negative emotions***."

According to Strine and Chapman (2005)[69], about 26% of (American) adults get insufficient sleep, on at least 14 days out of 30.

This lack of sleep has a negative impact on "...general health, frequent physical distress, frequent mental distress, activity limitations, depressive symptoms, anxiety, and pain": (Strine and Chapman, 2005).

These authors also found that once sleep had been lost in this way, this led on to a higher likelihood of use of tobacco, lack of physical exercise, obesity, and (among men) heavy drinking of alcohol.

And Osmun (2015), having reviewed a significant slice of the scientific research on sleep, concluded that: "...the research makes a strong case for getting a good night's sleep on a regular basis, but particularly before reacting to emotional events or making difficult decisions."

How much we need, and the effects of not getting it

So, people often get insufficient sleep because of:

- all the *distractions* (which encourage them to stay up too late);

- *pressures* to over-work, which come from the poor state of the Anglo-American economic system, and over-ambition; and

- *disruptions* like caffeine, alcohol, and computers, phones, TVs and so on, in the bedroom.

Furthermore, as James Maas (1998) pointed out, people tend to overestimate the amount of sleep they are getting, and many who think they are getting seven hours - (which is one or two full hours less than their [normal] minimum need for healthy living) – are actually getting closer to six hours, which is woefully inadequate.

Most adults need between 7.5 and 9 hours of sleep per night to be happy, healthy, emotionally well and successful, according to Dr Maas (1998).

Matthew Walker (2017) whose scientific research is more up to date, would put that figure higher, at 8 to 9 hours. And people in the 16-24 age range need nine or more hours of sleep each night to ensure reasonable cognitive functioning during the following day.

Daytime exhaustion, cognitive fog, physical illness, irritability, anxiety and depression can be expected to follow from repeated episodes of sleep deprivation. (Sources: Walker, 2017; Maas, 1998; and Stevenson, 2016).

Seven major negative results of sleep insufficiency

What are some of the effects of not getting enough sleep? According to Strine and Chapman (2005):

"Sleep-related problems, which affect 50-70 million Americans, involve all areas of life, including cognitive performance, emotional well-being, work and leisure-time activities, and general physical and mental well-being".

And the range of research studies that we have reviewed suggest that you can expect some or all of the following:

1. Your emotional intelligence will be reduced. Here are three studies that support this conclusion:

Firstly, Walker (2017) conducted an experiment in his sleep lab, to show how the lack of sleep affects people's emotional intelligence.

He took two groups of people and placed them under two different experimental conditions:

- One group had a full night's sleep, and

- the other group had insufficient sleep.

Both groups were then (separately) shown a range of pictures of individual human faces, which displayed a wide range of emotions, varying from friendliness through to intense dislike and anger. The participants had to individually assess this range of facial expressions, to decide if they were displaying threatening or friendly messages. While they were engaged in this activity, their brains were being scanned in a Magnetic Resonance Imaging (MRI) machine.[70]

The results of Walker's experiments were as follows:

- If participants had had a good night's sleep beforehand, then they had no difficulty in distinguishing facial expressions ranging from hostility through to benevolence. Their assessments (spoken, and neurological, confirmed by the MRI scans) – unlike those of the sleep deprived condition - were accurate, showing that the quality of their sleep had helped them in their reading of facial expressions.

- But in the sleep deprived condition, participants found it much harder to differentiate between the facial expressions displayed on the faces in the range of pictures shown to them. This clearly has huge implications for emotionally intelligent functioning in our personal and professional lives.

Secondly, Gordon (2013)[71] states that

"...people who are more sleep deprived report feeling ***less friendly, elated, empathic***, and report a ***generally lower positive mood***".

This report shows that one bad night of sleep can have a negative effect upon moods and emotions. Again, this will affect that aspect of emotional intelligence which allows you to read and manage your own emotions. And when we fail to manage our emotions well, there is often damage done to our relationships at home and in work or business.

And, ***third***, (and finally), inadequate sleep, in terms of quality and/or quantity, was found to reduce research participants' ability (in laboratory experiments) to regulate their negative emotions (Osmun, 2015; and Mauss, Troy, and LeBourgeois, 2013).

This occurs because lack of sleep reduces our ability to brush off intrusive negative thoughts, which then become worry and preoccupation, which interfere with our ability to manage our emotional encounters with others.

~~~

2. Your concentration will be negatively affected. In an online blog, Dr Simon Kyle summarizes several research studies that show a definite link between inadequate sleep and problems concentrating on essential tasks. He summarises the results like this: "...increased sleepiness and fatigue are associated with the inability to concentrate or 'think clearly'. Indeed, along with impaired energy/fatigue and mood, concentration is one of the most common daytime issues reported by patients with insomnia disorder - this is what was found in *the recent Great British Sleep Survey*. This inability to concentrate might reflect (or suggest) an issue (or problems) with sustained attention or shifting attention. In studies where sleep-deprived subjects have been tested after sleep loss, it is commonly the case that they will take longer to respond to a stimulus that appears on the screen (and experience more attentional lapses; failing to respond within a certain time interval). A study in insomnia patients found that a complex attention task - where subjects had to respond on a computer screen to the letter 'p' but not the letter 'd' - revealed impairments in reaction time to making this judgment." (Kyle, 2018).
~~~

~~~

3. Lack of sleep can lead to depression, sometimes as the main cause, but often combined with other causes, such as lack of physical activity, and/or poor diet. (Strine and Chapman, 2005; Kyle, 2018).

According to Asp (2015)[72]:

"Not getting enough restful sleep can affect your emotional health. In other words, a chronic lack of sleep can cause depression. Although it is unlikely that lack of sleep alone can be the sole cause of depression, it combined with other factors can trigger depression in some people. Links between depression and lack of sleep have been commonly found in studies".

Other studies have linked lack of sleep to depression and anxiety, via the mechanism of intrusive, repetitive thoughts, and a lack of ability to disengage from negative stimuli. (Nota and Coles, 2018)[73].

Dr Simon Kyle draws attention to the Great British Sleep Survey's conclusion that lack of sleep leads to low mood: "Emotionally, we may find ourselves more irritable and lower in mood, as a result of poor or insufficient sleep. Research has consistently found that sleep deprived people show less stable patterns of behaviour and are more likely to be emotionally labile. Indeed, the Great British Sleep Survey revealed those suffering from insufficient sleep *were **twice** as likely to suffer from low mood* as those who sleep well."

Of course, the other side of the equation is this: When you become depressed, this can further disrupt your sleep. You may find you have difficulty getting to sleep; staying asleep; or that you wake up in the early morning feeling tired.

~~~

4. Sleep loss can lead to anxiety: According to researchers at the University of California, at Berkley, sleep loss increases feelings of anxiety, especially among individuals who are prone to worry. (Nauert, 2018)[74]. The Berkley research report begins like this:

"UC Berkeley researchers have found that a lack of sleep, which is common in anxiety disorders, may play a key role in ramping up the brain regions that contribute to excessive worrying."

"Neuroscientists have found that sleep deprivation amplifies anticipatory anxiety by firing up the brain's amygdala and insular cortex, regions associated with emotional processing. The resulting pattern mimics the abnormal neural activity seen in anxiety disorders." (Anwar, 2013)[75].

The researchers also suggest that if you can fix your sleep problems, you can also reduce your anxiety conditions.

~~~

5. Anger problems can also be linked to inadequate sleep. According to Gordon (2013)[76]:

"Both correlational and experimental ... evidence suggest that when people are sleep deprived, they feel more ***irritable, angry*** and ***hostile***".

Like other emotional problems, the causation of anger tends to be multi-factorial; it comes from many supplementary sources; like diet, exercise, sleep deprivation; and poor stress management in general. A blog post by 'My-Sahana' cites nine sources of anger-including problems, of which lack of sleep is one:

"Not sleeping enough can result in feeling edgy and easily irritable. Chronic insomnia, sleep apnoea or other sleep disorders can be linked to recurrent bouts of anger". My-Sahana (2012)[77].

~~~

6. Inadequate sleep is linked to physical illnesses, including heart disease, cancer and other physical illnesses.

According to the NHS Choices (UK) website, lack of sleep affects physical health as much as emotional wellbeing:

"Many effects of a lack of sleep, such as feeling grumpy and not working at your best, are well known. But did you know that sleep deprivation can also have profound consequences on your physical health?"

The bottom line of their statement was this:

"Regular poor sleep puts you at risk of serious medical conditions, including obesity, heart disease and diabetes – and it shortens your life expectancy." (See NHS Choices, 2015)[78].

~~~
~~~

7. Insufficient sleep can also cause early death, as suggested above by NHS Choices (2015). This finding is corroborated by one meta-analysis, in the UK and Italy, which analysed 16 studies involving a total of 1.3 million people, before reaching this conclusion:

"People who sleep fewer than six hours a night are more likely to die early". (Cited in an article by Rebecca Smith, medical editor of *The Telegraph*. See Smith, 2009)[79].

Famous cases of sleep-deprived individuals, and the negative consequences

We spent a little time exploring famous cases of sleep-deprived individuals who, as a consequence, did not manage their emotional lives very well; or who damaged their brains in the process.

The first possibility that came to mind was Sylvia Plath. She famously wrote this:

"I wonder why I don't go to bed and go to sleep. But then it would be tomorrow, so I decide that no matter how tired, no matter how incoherent I am, I can skip one hour more of sleep and live." (The Unabridged Journals of Sylvia Plath).

Perhaps the fact that she did not live beyond the age of ***thirty years*** was, to some degree, linked to her skipping of 'one more hour of sleep'!?!

Rihanna - the famous pop singer – made public statements about her difficulty resting after touring in 2011, mentioning getting less than 3 hours a night for several weeks. And then again, she has great difficulty controlling her body weight, which swings up and down dramatically. She may be *comfort eating* to compensate for her lack of sleep.

A famous American baseball player - David Ortiz – who plays for the *Boston Red Sox* - reported difficulty turning his mind off and getting to sleep. Later, this lack of sleep was blamed for a massive slide in his sporting performance.

Jay Leno – the host of the American TV hit, 'The Late Show' - broadcast the news in 2007 that he sleeps about five hours per night. And he got away with it for years. But then, in 2009, he suddenly missed two shows. He admitted suffering from *exhaustion*. (Surprise, surprise!) And now (in 2018) Leno is 67 years old, and just as committed to *overworking* as always. But the scientific research shows that he will have shortened his life expectancy, reduced his happiness and emotional intelligence, reduced his capacity to concentrate, risked physical disease, and lowered his quality of life by skimping on sleep in order to overwork.

Then there are the cases of Margaret Thatcher and Ronald Reagan, both of whom skimped on their sleep, and both of whom ended up *losing their brain-minds to Alzheimer's disease!*

And now, Donald Trump announces that his long-term success is based on the fact that he only sleeps for five hours per night! Enough said! But is it actually true that his sleeplessness made him successful? This is a highly questionable assertion, given (1) that he inherited billions of dollars from his father; and (2) the number of ***business failures*** he has experienced. One of the most famous was Trump Airlines. According to Jacob Koffler, on the ***Time*** blog:

"**Trump Airlines:** In 1988, Trump bought Eastern Air Shuttle, an airline service that ran hourly flights between Boston, NYC and DC for 27 years prior, for $365 million. He turned the airline, once a no frills operation, into a luxury experience, adding maple-wood veneer to the floor and gold-coloured bathroom fixtures. The company never turned a profit and the high debt forced him to default on his loans. Ownership of the company was turned over to creditors. It ceased to exist in 1992". (Koffler, 2015)[80].

Looking through the blog post by Koffler (2015), it looks to us as though the following businesses were Trump failures:

- Trump Airlines; Trump Vodka; Trump Casinos (which apparently filed for bankruptcy four times!);

- Trump: The Game (a board game, which lasted one year);

- Trump Steaks (Lasted a few years. According to Koffler: "The company has since been discontinued – maybe it had something to do with the Trump Steakhouse in Las Vegas being closed down in 2012 for 51 health code violations, including serving five-month old duck.").

- Trump Magazine (lasted just 18 months);

- GoTrump.com, a travel search engine (lasted one year);

- Trump University (ended badly);

- Trump Mortgage (lasted one and a half years).

That makes 9 major failures.

And what about the successes:

+ The Grand Hyatt Hotel;

+ Trump Tower;

+ Wollman Rink;

+ No. 40 Wall Street;

+ Trump Place;

+ The Apprentice (TV show);

+ Trump International Tower Chicago.

That makes seven impressive successes.

So **nine** major failures, and **seven** impressive successes.

Not a great balance to achieve by somebody who goes for just 5 hours sleep per night!

A bit more sleep might have helped his business decisions. And his lack of sleep will have caused him a loss of longevity, poor mood control, and reduced emotional intelligence! (Who would have guessed it?!)

The benefits of sleep

Scientific research and traditional wisdom confirm the following benefits of a good night's sleep:

Benefit # 1. Increased capacity to cope with stress and strain.

One report concluded:

"...consistent sleep may serve as an effective strain intervention, thereby preventing negative acute and chronic health effects." (Barber and colleagues, 2009)[81].

And Osmun (2015) reports on scientific research which shows that subjects responded to emotional experiences less reactively after a good night's sleep (Van der Helm, et al. 2011)[82].

Osmun (2015)[83] also argues that "sleep plays a protective role in emotional processing", based on research by Van der Helm and Walker (2009)[84]; in which they "...survey an array of diverse findings across basic and clinical research domains, resulting in *a convergent view of sleep-dependent emotional brain processing*."

And it is not without significance that Van der Helm and Walker (2009) titled their article: *Overnight Therapy? The Role of Sleep in Emotional Brain Processing*. For it seems sleep had significant therapeutic effects upon the emotional centres of the brain.

~~~

Benefit #2. Deep sleep improves emotional intelligence, making it easier for us to read other people and to manage our own emotions. One significant study, in which Matthew Walker was the lead researcher, found that "...quality sleep matters. The deeper the sleep, particularly REM sleep, the better you'll be able to assess the emotions of those around you." (Source: The Brain Flux blog, 2008).

~~~

Benefit #3. Willpower and self-control are also affected by quality of sleep, though the research in this area is not as well developed as we would like. One significant study - by Pilcher, Morris, Donnelly and Feigl (2015) - at Clemson University, Department of Psychology, came up with this conclusion:

"Good sleep habits and effective self-control are important components of successful functioning. Unfortunately chronic sleep loss and impaired self-control are common occurrences for many individuals which can lead to difficulty with daily self-control issues such as resisting impulses and maintaining attentive behaviour. Understanding how self-control is depleted and how good sleep habits may help replenish and maintain the capacity for self-control is an important issue. A sleep-deprived individual who has expended the necessary resources for self-control is at an increased risk for succumbing to impulsive desires, poor attentional capacity, and compromised decision making." (Pilcher and colleagues, 2015)[85].

~~~

Benefit #4. Better mood control, through the capacity to read social situations, and to manage repetitive thoughts, and to change significant appraisals of distracting concerns.

~~~

Benefit #5. Reduced tendencies towards anxiety and depression.

- **Firstly**, let's look at anxiety. According to Calm-Clinic online:

"It's said so often it has become cliché, but the truth is that the mind and body are genuinely connected. The way your body feels affects the way your mind feels, and vice versa. ... That's why ***one of the most important tools for fighting anxiety is sleep***, and that's also why not getting enough sleep for multiple days in a row also known as 'sleep debt' can be a serious problem for those living with anxiety and anxiety disorders". (Calm-Clinic, 2018)[86].

- **Secondly**, on the link between sleep-debt (or cumulative sleep loss or insufficiency), and depression; according to the National Sleep Foundation (USA):

"The relationship between sleep and depressive illness is complex - depression may cause sleep problems and sleep problems may cause or contribute to depressive disorders. For some people, symptoms of depression occur before the onset of sleep problems. For others, sleep problems appear first. Sleep problems and depression may also share risk factors and biological features and the two conditions may respond to some of the same treatment strategies. Sleep problems are also associated with more severe depressive illness." (NSF, 2018)[87]

~~~

Benefit #6. Better physical health. As argued by NHS choices (2015), better health is linked to good quality and quantity of sleep; and inadequate sleep leads to major physical diseases.

~~~

Benefit #7. More enjoyment of life. In her blog, titled ***Happier***, Nataly Kogan writes about, 'The magic of a good night's sleep: Because an exhausted person is never a happy person'.

Here are two brief extracts:

"Even though most of us don't get nearly enough sleep these days, everyone knows that sleep is important: human beings need sleep to live and function. But what a lot of people don't know or misunderstand about sleep is how important it is to our overall sense of happiness and wellbeing.

...

"Even when people describe their own levels of happiness, being well-rested comes out on top. Researchers Daniel Kahneman and Alan B. Krueger found in their research on life satisfaction a direct correlation between sleep quality and overall happiness. In fact, they found sleep quality was the single most influential factor in rating daily mood, too. A recent Gallup poll got the same results: people who get adequate sleep are more likely to rate their lives as happier." (Kogan, 2018)[88].

Insomnia: the curse of sleeplessness, and how to treat it

Some people, who know that sleep is a wonderful part of life, still have difficulty achieving it. For example, in David Benioff's novel, *City of Thieves,* we read this:

"I've always envied people who sleep easily. Their brains must be cleaner, the floorboards of the skull well swept, all the little monsters closed up in a steamer trunk at the foot of the bed."

And traditional Irish wisdom teaches us that "A good laugh and a long sleep are the two best cures for any problem."

Insomnia is a growing problem in the Anglo-American world, due to the pressures of neoliberal economic policy, and growing inequality, and intensified exploitation of workers at every level. Insomnia is defined as the inability to fall asleep, in the first ten or twenty minutes of being in bed. It can also include the tendency to wake up again, a couple of hours after going to bed.

Sleeplessness is a horrible place to be. Not only will it rob you of the peace and happiness of a gentle tomorrow; but it's torture to endure.

As Emil Cioran writes: "Insomnia is a vertiginous lucidity that can convert paradise itself into a place of torture."

Or, as Jessamyn West expresses it: "Sleeplessness is a desert without vegetation or inhabitants."

As early as 1998, Dr James Maas, an American sleep expert, wrote that, "About 70% of the (American) people are not sleeping well for at least one or two nights each week".

Similar statements have been made about the British population, and sleep problems have most likely worsened on both sides of the Atlantic since that time.

Why is this a problem? As we saw above, at the very least, lack of adequate sleep will reduce your emotional intelligence, reduce your effectiveness in the world, and render you less dynamic than you could be. And you will be less happy, and prone to depression and other emotional disorders. It is widely recognized that, unless you get enough rest and sleep, you will tend to be irritable and anxious. (Wagner, 1996)[89].

In working with insomnia, and general sleep hygiene, with our counselling clients, we tend to offer the following advice:

1. Make sure you get plenty of physical exercise, and breathe in good quality air during each day. And make sure you get out in direct sunlight for at least one full hour each day during the summer time, and two or more hours in the winter. (See Endnote[90] on the effects of physical exercise on insomnia).

2. Eat a healthy diet, which omits most caffeine, all gluten, and keep your sugar and processed carb consumption very low. Eat complex carbs, as in vegetables and gluten-free grains, with a small amount of protein.

3. Avoid stimulants, like caffeine, nicotine, chocolate, or sugary foods, from 12.00 noon onwards. These stimulants are likely to keep you awake. Also, do not eat large meals before bedtime. You should breakfast like a king (or queen); lunch like a prince (or princess); and have a modest evening meal. Some experts recommend mixing protein and carbs at breakfast time (such as eggs on toast); lunch based on protein and salad (or cooked) vegetables; and an evening meal based on carbohydrate with salad (or cooked) vegetables. The carbohydrate will tend to make you feel relaxed and tired enough to sleep.

4. Manage your bedroom sleeping space, so it is calm, cool (but not cold), private, and as dark as possible.

5. Pick a time for bed which is at least nine hours before you have to get up for work; and strive to always go to bed at that time, even at the weekends (with a few, rare exceptions!)

6. Invest in a good quality mattress, which should be firm enough to support you, but not so hard as to be uncomfortable.

7. Wind down in preparation for bed. Do not do any vigorous activity in the hour before your bedtime. But do make sure you do vigorous exercise most days of the week, well before bedtime: such as first thing in the morning; or walk home after work; or go swimming in your lunch break.

8. If your insomnia is particularly bad, take a hot bath before bedtime. And/or meditate about an hour before bedtime. And/or have an audio relaxation CD on an audio machine by your bed, and listen to it while you fall asleep. We recommend some of the relaxation CDs by Paul McKenna and/or Glenn Harrold.

9. Get in the habit of writing out your problems in a diary, journal or notebook, about one hour before bedtime: (as described by Hubbard 2018[91], commenting on the research report by Scullin and Krueger et al, 2018[92]). Our advice, based on this research, and earlier research, is this: Make a written plan to fix your problems, and then let them go. Before bedtime tonight, write down whatever is on your mind; and then wrote the main activities you need to engage in tomorrow; and then your mind will be cleared of those things you could have ended up mulling over in bed.

10. If you can't get to sleep, after 30 minutes in bed, get up and read something relaxing, until you feel tired enough to sleep. Or do a boring household chore.

11. Do not get up early just because you wake up early. Aim to get at least eight or nine hours of restful sleep every night. Stay in bed until you've got your healthy allocation of sleep.

~~~

Additionally, Wagner (1996) recommends that you pay attention to your consumption of vitamins B complex and vitamin C. Vitamin B6 is particularly important, it seems, because it is implicated in converting tryptophan to serotonin, the neurotransmitter that *many theorists believe* promotes normal sleep. We teach our clients that they need to take regular
~~~

supplements of particular vitamins to control their stress level. These include:

- Vitamin B complex.

- Vitamin E, natural source - 400 iu strength.

- Vitamin C powder - 2,000 to 3,000 mgs per day, minimum.

(You can always check these recommendations with a nutritional therapist, or your preferred medical practitioner).

You may also benefit from an extra strong magnesium supplement, of 400 to 500 mg, three times per day. (Wagner, 1996).

You could also drink camomile tea from lunchtime onwards; and have an infusion of valerian and hops before bedtime; or *kava kava*.

Do not take sleeping pills, as they will destroy the quality of whatever sleep you do get, by disrupting your REM sleep. And in any case, drinking tart cherry juice, from the Montmorency cherry, is much more effective at boosting your melatonin levels, which are necessary for sleep to occur. (See Howatson *et al*, 2012)[93].

Finally, develop a good, positive, flexible philosophy of life, which includes the idea that there are only certain things you can control; and you have to give up trying to control the uncontrollable. (See the ***Nine Windows Model*** in Chapter 11, above).

~~~
~~~

Chapter 13: The importance of diet and nutrition

The nutritional quality of the food that you eat is hugely important for your physical and mental health, and your emotional wellbeing[94]. There are some foods that you definitely need to avoid, and some foods that you definitely need to consume. However, there is no *universal agreement* about the latter point: which foods to eat. National governments around the world normally issue guidelines for what a 'balanced diet' looks like, which reflects some mainstream perspectives, plus the interests and beliefs of various *food producers*. There is a great deal of divergence between nutritionists, nutritional therapists, food scientists, and others as to what people should and should not eat.

In this chapter, I will present some extracts from my book on lifestyle counselling and coaching for the whole person, which contains a lot of information which was researched by Renata Taylor-Byrne (and published in Taylor-Byrne and Byrne, 2017). In particular, I will present guidelines on the main foods to avoid, and some ideas of what might constitute a healthy diet, which will support your sense of physical and mental strength, flexibility and resilience.

Diet and nutritional advice and guidance

Here is an extract from Chapter 4 of my lifestyle counselling book (Byrne, 2018):

The importance of food for the body-brain-mind

Firstly, we can't function properly without food, because food provides the energy for physical and mental activity, and the material to rebuild our cells. Inadequate nutrition impacts our ability to live, work, communicate, heal, and fight off all the viruses and germs which are present in the atmosphere. We need to have a diet which has all the essential amino acids, vitamins and minerals, complex carbohydrate, fats, and fibre. These should come from healthy sources of *unprocessed* food, plus some nutritional supplements. The Mediterranean diet is highly rated, plus the Nordic diet, as potential models to follow; or rather to build upon and to personalize.

Some others were also commended, for short-term use; such as (aspects of) the Paleo, Atkins, and Ketogenic diets - which might, unfortunately, be too high in meat content, which causes inflammation; and inflammation is linked to mood disorders. For example, the 25-year ***China Study*** – Campbell and Campbell (2006)[95] -found that the people who ate the most vegetables were the healthiest, while the people who at the most meat suffered the most ill health.

Some of the evidence in favour of high-fat, low carb diets – like the Paleo and Atkins diets - may be misinterpreting the findings (e.g. Elliott, 2014)[96]. Although Elliott goes along with the idea that it is the high-protein, high-fat content of the Atkins/Paleo-type diets that reduces depression; Mozes (2015)[97], looking at the effect of carbohydrates on the incidence of depression, shows a better understanding.

Alan Mozes reports that:

"The study (under consideration) involved 70,000 women aged 50 to 79. The findings, the investigators said, only show an association between 'refined' carbs and elevated depression risk, rather than a direct cause-and-effect relationship".

But could it not be the case that the Atkins/Paleo diets work, not because of the high fat, high protein end of the equation, but because of the 'low carb' end of the equation; which must (most often) also be 'low *refined* carbs', as opposed to 'low *wholegrains* and *vegetables*'? (Although wholegrain bread is often higher in sugar content than other breads!)

Certainly the research cited by Mozes (2015) seems to suggest this view as a valid interpretation, where he writes that *"...the women who consumed diets higher in vegetables, fruits and whole grains had a lower incidence of depression".* (However, this does not prove that *everybody* can tolerate grains!)

Complex carbs, in the form of vegetables, and whole (gluten free and gliadin free) grains, seem to be okay (for many people, much of the time), and are not at all in need of being replaced by proteins and fats!

By eliminating *refined carbs,* in the form of junk foods and highly processed foods, the Atkins/ Paleo diets make it impossible to evaluate the impact of protein and fats *per se!*

Some new research is clearly needed to separate out these competing interpretations.

(And some people may need to avoid all grains, and/or all dairy products, at least some of the time; and some will have to permanently exclude them. But they should do this by *experimentation*, under the guidance of a *qualified* nutritional therapist – in order to avoid problems of malnutrition!)

Balanced diet and toxic foods...

What is a balanced diet?

Firstly, at the moment, there is *no universal agreement* about the definition or content of an ideal, balanced diet; and national guidelines vary considerably between, say, Britain and the USA; and both of those guidelines differ significantly from the Mediterranean and Nordic diets. However, we know (some of) what is bad for us, and we have some clues as to what may often be good for people, but we also have to allow for individualized diet and nutrition plans, because every human body is unique, based on a personal history of eating, which has *interacted with* a particular genetic heritage.

The official British guide to nutrition suggests that we should eat about 30% grains; 30% vegetables and fruit. And about 40% split equally between (a) dairy products, (b) meat and fish, and (c) nuts and seeds.

We recommend that you experiment with that kind of guideline; perhaps moving the proportion of vegetables up to 40% or higher; but also consider the elements of the Mediterranean diet and the Nordic diet, both of which have high levels of oily fish and vegetables. Oily fish (which is high in omega-3 fatty acids) is important for brain and heart health, and also for preventing depression, anger and anxiety. So it is probably a good idea to have oily fish (like salmon and/or sardines) once or twice each week. Also, if you have problems with grains, increase your vegetable consumption; reduce your grains; and keep your meat consumption low (especially grain-fed meats, because they tend to boost your omega-6 levels, which promote inflammation; and inflammation is linked to both depression and most physical diseases). For a more detailed set of dietary guideline, please see Part 1 (sections 3[a] and [b]) of Taylor-Byrne and Byrne [2017]). And bear in mind that you can always consult a nutritional therapist for confirmation of your own conclusions about your dietary needs.

~~~
~~~

However, in practice, most people do not follow official nutritional guidelines. For example, on average, the British population is currently eating more than half of its food from *ultra-processed sources*. To state that more precisely:

"Half of all the food bought by families in Britain is now 'ultra-processed', made in a factory with industrial ingredients and additives invented by food technologists and bearing little resemblance to the fruit, vegetables, meat and fish used to cook a fresh meal at home". (Boseley, 2018)[98].

What this could mean is that poorer people are eating a lot more than 50, or 60, or perhaps more than 70% junk food, while richer people eat less than 50%, or 40, or 30% junk food. And there are very serious health implications - including mental health implications - of eating more than a very small amount of junk food. (Brogan, 2016[99]; Perlmutter, 2015[100]; Holford, 2010[101]).

And over the years of counselling individuals, we have found that people who eat sugary, yeasty foods, like breads, cakes, biscuits, sweets and puddings - which is to say, high sugar, high grains and high dairy diets - are prone to develop a form of *gut dysbiosis* called *systemic Candidiasis* – or generalized *overgrowth* of Candida Albicans in the large intestine – which shows up as *unaccountable* anxiety or depression, combined with low levels of energy or chronic fatigue. (See Taylor-Byrne and Byrne, 2017).

~~~

Personalized diet

The safest way to follow healthy diets seems to us to be this: Get a couple of good recipe books which emphasize the kinds of foods found in elements of the Mediterranean, Nordic, and Vegetarian diets; and Chapter 11 of the China Study, which emphasizes eight principles of food and health. And, if you can afford it, consult a good nutritional therapist.

According to Leslie Korn:

"No single diet is right for everyone. Each person has a different cultural-genetic heritage and therefore a different metabolism. Some people, like the Inuit, require mostly meat and fish, whereas people from India do well on a predominance of legumes, vegetables, fruits, and grains. Most people require a mix. However, that mix of food can vary greatly. Know your ancestral and genetic heritage and try to eat for your individual metabolic type". (Page 14, Korn, 2016)[102].
~~~

But there is one thing we can safely predict, based upon scientific studies which are cited in this book: No race of people will *ever* exist, who can, *for long,* remain physically and mentally healthy on a junk food diet; or an inadequate diet in terms of nutrients![103], [104].

Invest time and effort in shopping for *raw ingredients,* and spend *time* in the kitchen engaging in food preparation. This can become a highly enjoyable way to spend your time, and it's a great way to express *love* for our nearest and dearest! Food made with love, and raw, natural ingredients, is a source of great joy.

Make more than fifty percent of your meals raw salads, combined with nuts and seeds. (And some theorists think we should always eat fruits at a time separate from our main meals, unless our main meal is just fruit!).

Eat lots of plant based proteins: such as, vegetables (avocado, broccoli, spinach, kale, peas, and sweet potato); legumes (such as lentils and beans); nuts and seeds (including sesame, sunflower, almonds, walnuts, and hazelnuts); non-dairy milk (such as almond, coconut, and/or oat milk); gluten-free grains (quinoa, amaranth, and buckwheat [if you can tolerate them] and brown rice). And take Spirulina and Chlorella supplements for their nutrient and protein content.

Supplement with: Vitamins B, C and E (at the very least!); plus omega-3 fatty acids (as in fish oils, like cod liver oil), Co-enzyme-Q10 (Footnote[105]), and live acidophilus and other live bacteria[106].

Eat some fermented foods, like Miso, Kimchi and sauerkraut (if you can tolerate them. People with overgrowth of Candida Albicans should avoid these foods, however!). Chew your food well, with 50 chews per mouthful as a common recommendation (Enders, 2015[107]). And use a squat-toilet (if at all possible) to optimize elimination (Enders, 2015). (And if you don't have a squat toilet, use a foot stool – sit on the toilet with your feet on the stool [of about six inches in height] - to simulate the traditional squatting position).

Drink eight glasses of filter water per day.

Do some reading about diet and nutrition, and find out for yourself.

Monitor the effects of dietary changes on your moods, emotions, energy levels, and sense of wellbeing; and adjust accordingly. The best way to do that is to keep a food diary for a few weeks, and record everything you eat and drink. And also record your exercise and sleep patterns.

And check each day to see how you feel: *Is your energy up or down since yesterday? Is your mood up or down since yesterday? Do you feel physically better or worse than yesterday? Any sign of skin allergies? Or bloating? Or headaches? Or other pains?*

And if any of those indicators is negative, that should be linked back to what you ate 24 to 30 hours earlier (approximately). Plus what has been happening during those 24 to 30 hours: like sleep disturbance; lack of physical exercise; increased stress from any source; the emergence of a problem that you feel you cannot handle; and so on. (If you can't track it back on your own, see a professional helper – such as a nutritionist, a health coach, or an alternative health practitioner - to support you).

As a general rule, consult a suitable nutritionist, medical expert or health coach, when and if necessary. (And also read Part 1 of Taylor-Byrne and Byrne, 2017).

~~~

Beware toxic foods

Secondly, beyond sensitivity to grains and dairy products, there are foods whose ***toxicity*** is very *high*, and it is only in the last twenty years or so that people have been able to gain access to research studies and investigations which have looked at those 'foods' which, though always on sale in the supermarket and shops, are really bad for our bodies and brains.

Let us briefly review the top six toxic foods:

1. The **first** culprit is ***trans-fats*** (also called hydrogenated fat, and nicknamed "Frankenfats"). They begin life as harmless vegetable oils, which are then industrially processed by superheating processes which add hydrogen atoms to the oils.

Why are these vegetable oils put through this damaging process?

Because it makes the fat much easier to use in the manufacturing of bread, cakes, biscuits; snack bars; ready meals; and it is preferred by fast food shops and restaurants. It is much cheaper than real butter or natural vegetable oils. These trans-fats last longer than healthier fats, which means processed foods can last longer on supermarket shelves – but the effects on the body are grim!
~~~

Because the trans-fat is created by being boiled at very high temperatures, this affects its chemical structure. This type of fat is thus unnatural and (wo)man-made, and causes chaos in our body and brain on a cellular level. For examples: it affects the enzymes that our body needs to fight cancer; and it has been implicated in a major study which showed a connection between rage and the consumption of trans-fats. Trans-fats also interfere with the insulin receptors on the body's cell membranes, which promotes obesity. And they cause major blocking of the arteries! Recent studies have linked trans-fats to both depression and anger management problems. (See Taylor-Byrne and Byrne, 2017).

2. The **second** enemy of our body-brain-mind is ***sugar***. It's described as the enemy of the immune system, because it takes four hours for our immune response to recover from the effects of consuming sugar. Sugar reduces the ability of the immune system to protect us properly; increases inflammation in the body (which is linked to the causation or triggering of depression, and all physical illnesses); interferes with the proper functioning of our brain cells; and makes our blood sugar levels fluctuate wildly (which causes stress symptoms, including anxiety). Sugar creates fat around our internal organs; causes obesity and diabetes; attacks the collagen in our skin; stiffens our skin and causes wrinkles; and increases blood pressure! It is also implicated in heightening the stress response, when we face any difficulty in life.

3. The **third** enemy? It's ***alcohol***, described by Patrick Holford as 'the brain's worst enemy'. Its effects include: unhelpfully dissolving essential fatty acids[108] in the brain; negatively impacting the way our memory works; draining certain B vitamins, vitamin D and calcium from our body; and damaging our ability to get a good night's sleep. It leaches water from the cells of our body, creating dehydration and producing large amount of 'free radicals', which increase the risk of hormonal cancers, particularly breast cancer. It is also implicated in depression and suicide ideation, suicide completion, and self-harm.

4. **Caffeine** is next in line in terms of its harmful effects: it overstimulates the heart, stomach, pancreas and intestines. And it reduces calcium, potassium, zinc, vitamin C and the B vitamins. It also alters the acid/alkaline balance in the body in a negative direction; plays a part in premature ageing; and affects our sleep. Its main negative effect on our emotions is to simulate anxiety, and to trigger panic attacks.

5. **Processed food** is the next problem (and much processed food is also 'junk food'). When people are short of time, they are very tempted to get processed food for meals, because of the convenience. Processed foods are normally faster to prepare, but if they have been altered in any way, apart from being washed and packaged, then they normally become suspected of being 'junk foods'. Junk food (which is most processed food) is food which has been altered from its raw, natural state by chemical or physical means. It is sold in jars, tin cans, bottles, and/or boxes. And it has very dodgy add-ons, like excessive amounts of salt, sugar and transfats, and artificial flavours and colours. They also often have constituents that are low in nutrition. Because there can be so much fat, sugar and salt in processed food, this increases the risk of high blood pressure; and the increase in sodium increases the risk of stroke. Furthermore, processed foods create constipation due to lack of fibre. And they can increase the risk of depression, according to a research study by Akbaraly et al (2009)[109], which compared the level of depressive symptoms of middle-aged people on diets which were *either:* (1) high in processed food; or (2) high in wholefoods. Those on a diet high in processed foods had a 58% increased risk for depression over a five year period, according to the research findings. (Wholefoods are normally bought in the state in which they came out of the ground or off the trees and bushes [fruits and vegetables]; or they have remained minimally changed post-harvesting, and essentially left in their natural state [like wholegrains, legumes, etc.]).

6. What about ***gluten***? This is an enemy for our bodies because of the way gluten behaves when it's in our intestines. Gluten is actually the name of the mixture which is formed (or expanded) when cereal flours (like wheat, rye or barley [or contaminated oats]) are mixed with water. When these two substances are mixed together they expand the chains of proteins called gliadins and glutenins. These substances tend to create inflammation, and to pull the cells of the gut walls apart, producing a condition called 'leaky gut'. This allows whole molecules of food to escape into the blood stream, and travel to the brain. And, according to Dr Giulia Enders' (2015) book on the guts, this also tends to break down the blood-brain barrier, and allow food particles to affect the brain, causing inflammation. (Inflammation is now recognized as the main cause of all the major diseases, including the emotional problem of depression, and possibly other emotional problems, like anxiety).

Many people are *gluten intolerant*. This is called **Celiac disease**, and people with this condition have to avoid all forms of gluten, otherwise they will further damage their guts. Some other people (perhaps 26% or more of us) have non-Celiac gluten sensitivity (NCGS), which damages our brains, but not our guts. And people with neurological damage of unknown origin should therefore always be tested for NCGS. There may be other people who have a form of non-Celiac gluten sensitivity which causes abdominal discomfort, pain, and gas. And there may be people who think they have gluten sensitivity, but who actually have gut problems resulting from the Fructans in fruits and vegetables, or other food stuffs. (These people can be helped by the Low FodMaps diet. See Taylor-Byrne and Byrne, 2017).

Because of this situation, many people are now opting to avoid gluten. The official advice to those people is to get themselves tested, for both Celiac disease and Non-Celiac Gluten Sensitivity (NCGS), to make sure they are treating the right condition! But some of us, such as this author, have chosen to avoid almost all gluten, without being tested for NCGS.

Technically, the gliadin within gluten draws apart the 'tight junctions' between the cells that form the walls of our intestines. This leads to an increase in the space between the cells, allowing toxins and larger molecules of food, (which would normally pass down through the intestines, and be eliminated), to be released into the blood-transporting system of our bodies, causing havoc in the form of bowel problems, celiac disease, headaches, brain inflammation, anxiety and depression, and more. Apparently many people are unknowingly suffering from the side-effects of gluten, according to Julia Ross (2002); and researchers have found that symptoms of depression tend to disappear when wheat and other grains have been taken out of the diet. (But we can always use gluten-free whole grains, if we find, by experimentation, that we can tolerate them in our diet. On the other hand, many people find they have little or no tolerance for any form of grains. [Brown rice may be the most benign grain]).

The importance of nutritional supplements for mental health

Having looked at toxic foods, we then went on to look at nutritional supplements, like vitamins, minerals, Co-Q-10, gut bacteria, and so on (in Taylor-Byrne and Byrne, 2017).

The question as to whether nutritional supplements actually help us improve our physical and emotional well-being was addressed.

The findings show a range of opinions on their effectiveness, which we have reviewed and resolved.

The NHS Direct UK, considers that nutritional supplements are *unnecessary* unless there are specific *reasons* why someone may need extra nutrients, such as pregnant women; and women who may be breastfeeding; and young children who may have a lack of variety in their diets.

Also, doctors may prescribe specific nutrients e.g. the recommendation to take iron supplements when a patient has iron deficiency anaemia.

We reject this view, of the *limited* need for nutritional supplements, as being ill-informed. This NHS viewpoint is based on the flawed assumption that everybody either does, or could, eat a balanced diet, which would give them all the nutrients they need. This is a false premise, because most people do *not* eat a balanced diet; would not know what a balanced diet *looked* like; and would also find it hard to get *all the nutrients they* ***need*** from modern, processed, *denatured* foods!

There are also contrasting views on this subject, held by the following experts: a professor at the Yale School of Public Health's Division of Chronic Disease Epidemiology; and Patrick Holford; and Dr David Perlmutter.

Professor Susan Taylor-Maine considers nutritional supplements to be inappropriate because: 'They deliver vitamins out of context' (Ballantyne, 2007)[110];

And Patrick Holford, a British nutritional expert, considers them to be *essential* as we need good nutrition for the creation of optimum mental health.

(See Part 1, section 5, of Taylor-Byrne and Byrne, 2017)

~~~

For us, the most powerful arguments are these:

(1) Much of our food is now denatured, and low in nutritional value.

(2) Most people would not know how to put together a balanced diet for a day, not to say a week, so they tend to miss out on many nutrients.
~~~

(3) Therefore, nutritional deficiencies are highly likely to be widespread and serious.

(4) Furthermore, nutritional deficiencies are definitely implicated in the causation of not just physical diseases, but also emotional problems and mental illnesses. Therefore it makes sense to take multivitamins and minerals, plus vitamin C and vitamin B complex, and a strong, natural source vitamin E (400 iu), even if it could be shown that *some proportion* of those supplements are then urinated out of the body. Depressed individuals have been found to be deficient in Magnesium, so it makes sense to supplement with Magnesium citrate. (Deans, 2018)[111].

This approach - of using nutritional supplements, *in combination with* the best *wholefood* diet you can devise for yourself - is a safer option than relying on an *inadequate diet* for our full range of nutritional needs.

Furthermore, Dr David Perlmutter considers that we need to use probiotics (or live, friendly bacteria, like Acidophilus Bifidus), as supplements, if we want to have a healthy gut and brain. He was inspired by the views of Nobel Laureate Elie Mechnikov, who considered that a proper balance of good and bad bacteria in the gut was an essential factor in making sure human beings live a long and healthy life.

Since Mechnikov has put this theory forward his views have been confirmed by many scientific studies. Perlmutter states the view that the research results confirm that '*Up to 90% of all known human illness can be traced back to an unhealthy gut.*'

~~~

And here is a quick summary of Dr Jim's Stress and Anxiety Diet. The full diet can be found in Taylor-Byrne and Byrne (2017):

Dr Jim's Stress and Anxiety Diet

In Part 3 of Taylor-Byrne and Byrne (2017), Dr Jim Byrne introduced his stress and anxiety diet. This came out of his years of struggling with the side-effects of *Candida Albicans* overgrowth, which include low energy and low mood, plus anxiety. He described how he used supplements and a particular diet to overcome those side effects, and to boost his mood and
~~~

stabilize his emotions. The anti-Candida diet eliminates almost all sugar, yeast and fermented foods: (see Chaitow, 2003[112]; Jacobs, 1994[113]; and Trowbridge and Walker, 1989[114]). But you still have to find a way to balance your consumption of protein, carbohydrates and fats.

From this experience of managing his own gut-brain-mind interactions, he was sensitized to any new research he came across, on any aspect of the body-brain-mind and emotions, and he passed this learning on to any of his counselling clients who showed an interest, or a need to know about it.

He then describes certain pieces of advice, from the Stress Management Society, and other authors; and from the Paleo, Nordic and Mediterranean diets; which can normally be expected to have a positive effect upon mood and emotions; but watch out for the down side of the Paleo diet, which may be too high in animal fats. (The China Study showed that the people who ate the most meat had the most disease!)

Some of his key recommendations included:

Don't skip breakfast; eat a balanced diet (which has to be established by trial and error); avoid sugar, caffeine, alcohol, gluten, and dairy products. (One cup of real coffee per day is probably okay; and one glass of wine every other day; but sugar and gluten should be avoided completely! Some theorists think we can get away with one or two junk food meals per week, but no more than that!)

Close to 70% percent of your diet should be in the form of low-sugar vegetables (and [gluten free] grains, and legumes, if you can tolerate them), with fibre intact; plus 10% in fats; 10% nuts and seeds; plus the remainder (of approximately 10%) in the form of meat, fish and eggs. It's probably best to avoid milk and cheese, but then you have to get your calcium from vegetable sources and/or supplementation.

Try to eliminate all *processed* grains (e.g. white bread, white pasta, etc.), but keep whole grains (if you can healthily tolerate them!) at about 20% of your diet (and make sure they are gluten free). He also talks about the importance of adequate water consumption, meaning six to eight glasses per day of filtered tap water, or glass-bottled mineral water. Eating snacks (like nuts and seeds and apples, etc.) mid-morning and mid-afternoon is also an important form of blood-sugar management.

Raw food is very important, because cooking kills so many nutrients, including all vitamins. And organic vegetable are best, and should be emphasized ahead of fruit, because fruit sugars, taken in excess, can cause physical and emotional health problems. For some people, who are particularly sensitive to sugar, even vegetables have to be selected for low-sugar content (as described in the ***Low FodMaps*** diet). (Some people are fructose ***intolerant***, and have to avoid fruit completely. While some are fructose ***sensitive***, and have to ***reduce*** *fruit consumption*).

Jim recommends various supplements, especially vitamin B, C and E, for stress management; plus a good strong multivitamin supplement, with the full range of minerals.

The body needs every single nutrient known to science (according to Dr Leslie Korn, 2016).

One of the best ways to proceed is probably to take a good, complex multivitamin and mineral supplement every morning; plus magnesium, (400 iu's); plus a yeast-free B-complex tablet; and two or three grams of vitamin C powder in water per day.

Plus a natural source vitamin E capsule (400 iu's); plus omega-3 fatty acids (in the form of foods and supplements). Plus a *friendly bacteria* supplement, like ***Acidophilus***, or preferably a multi-strain variety, in capsule form.

~~~
~~~

Chapter 14: The importance of physical exercise

"If regular exercise could be bottled, it would be a miracle drug. Basically, everything in your life gets better if you find time to exercise regularly".

Ben Silberman[115].

~~~

Physical exercise not only strengthens your body, by strengthening your muscles, but it also releases feel-good hormones, which lift your mood; and it also washes stress hormones out of your body.

It seems that eastern exercise systems - like yoga and Tai Chi/Chi Kung have some advantages over western approaches, because the eastern approach switches off your fight-or-flight response, and switches on the relaxation response, immediately you start exercising.

If you go to a western gym, on the other hand, and do weight training or circuit training, initially your stress level will go up, and will take quite some time to come down again. When it does come down, it will fall to a lower level than it was at when you entered the gym.

But yoga and Chi Kung will immediately bring your stress level down, which is better for your body. On the other hand, we could all benefit from some 'bone loading' exercises, like press ups, and weight or resistance training.

The strength of your core muscles - abdominals and back muscles - will have a big effect upon how resilient you feel in your everyday life; and your core strength will also support your mental strength (all other things - such as diet and nutrition, sleep, and relaxation - being equal).

The main body of this chapter is extracted from Taylor-Byrne and Byrne (2017):
~~~

Extract 1:

Introduction

> *"Exercise strengthens the entire human machine – the heart, the brain, the blood vessels, the bones, the muscles. The most important thing you can do for your long-term health is lead an active life."*
>
> Dr Timothy Church (2013)[116].
>
> ~~~

Exercise is good for your body-brain-mind, boosting health and strength and emotional buoyancy. According to Dr Mark Atkinson (2007): *"Thirty minutes of moderate-intensity exercise, five times a week, is associated with numerous health benefits. These range from improving mood and self-esteem to reducing the risk of cancer and heart disease"*[117].

In the western tradition of physical exercise, three forms of exercise are recommended:

1. **Aerobic training**, which includes brisk walking, jogging, cycling, swimming, etc. (We [Renata and Jim] enjoy brisk walking, and dancing vigorously to pop music). Thirty minutes of brisk walking per day is sufficient to lift depression and reduce anxiety. And : *"Swimming for just half an hour three times a week can lower stress levels, raise mood, lower incidences of depression and anxiety and improve sleep patterns"*. (Source: Just Swim)[118]. Furthermore, running for just thirty minutes per time, three times per week can also lift mood and reduce depression by 16% (according to a recent study by the University of London)[119].

2. **Weight training**, which includes press-ups, sit-backs, climbing stairs, cycling, dumbbells, barbells, kettlebells, etc. (We [the authors] use press-ups and sit-backs; the 'Plank' position from Pilates; carrying some weight from the shops on a regular basis; and the 'PowerSpin' rotator). Weight training, or resistance training, is also good for improving mental health and emotional wellbeing.

According to a meta-analysis of several studies, *"...resistance training (or weight training) is a meaningful intervention for people suffering from anxiety"* (O'Connor and colleagues, 2010).

And: *"Four studies have investigated the effect of resistance training with clinically diagnosed depressed adults. The results are unanimous; large reductions in depression from resistance training participation"*. (O'Connor and colleagues, 2010)[120].

3. **Flexibility and stretching exercises**, which includes yoga and Chi Kung (Qigong, from Tai Chi), both of which are introduced and described, and extensively explored, below.

~~~

There is lots of evidence that physical exercise reduces all forms of stress. This includes:

(1) *Transitory stress,* which crops up when we run into a threatening or dangerous situation, or we experience a momentary loss. And:

(2) *Continuous stress,* arising out of nagging overloads of work and difficult life challenges.

The main forms of emotional expression in which stress manifests are: anger and anxiety.

Depression is not normally conceptualized as being a feature of the stress model, but rather of grief.

Healthy stress (or Eustress) is a response to a pressure bearing down on an individual, with which the individual can cope. Unhealthy stress (or Distress) occurs when this pressure is greater than their coping resources.

When the pressure is too great for their coping resources, the individual may respond with either explosive or implosive anger - as in either rage outbursts or silent sulking - or with acute or chronic anxiety - as in generalized anxiety disorder, social anxiety, or panic.

Depression is related to *the grief response,* and is normally about loss or failure, whether real or symbolic. A person may become depressed after losing a job, a loved one, or losing face, social status, etc.

However, physical exercise helps to reduce all of these emotional states:

- anger,

- anxiety

- and depression.
~~~

...

~~~

Extract 2

Indian and Chinese exercises for health

Yoga

There is lots of evidence that *yoga* can help with the symptoms of depression and anxiety, with childhood autism, and even with schizophrenia and psychosis.[121] Some of this evidence is weak, and additional studies are needed.

There is also evidence that yoga can calm down angry, reactive people:

'...with a growing body of research backing yoga's effectiveness as an anger "de-fuser," physiologist Ralph LaForge regularly advises physicians to recommend yoga to their hostility-prone cardiac patients. LaForge is managing director of the Lipid Disorder Training Program at Duke University Medical Centre's Endocrine Division in Durham, North Carolina, where ground-breaking research has taken place on "*hot reactive" personality types – that is, people who react to anger more explosively than most... Yoga, particularly therapeutic forms like restorative yoga*[122]*,*" says LaForge, "*has proven to be a valuable method of cooling hot-reactives down.*" (Alan Reder, 2007)[123].

Alan Reder continues like this: 'Stephen Cope suggests that asanas (or hatha yoga postures - of which there are between 32 and 84 - Eds) may be in fact the best yogic antidote for anger "*because asanas allow you to move the energy.*" He cautions against meditation (or sitting still - Eds) for folks in an explosive state because meditative awareness just feeds the flames once the temperature has reached a certain point.'

Reder makes a very important point when he says that not everyone should use the same anger management strategy. Specifically, he writes that: *'Cope's observations underscore the fact that anger manifests differently in each person, and must be treated differently as well.*

'Some of us get so revved up by our catecholamines (or stress chemicals) that we can't think straight. In those cases, experts have found that methods such as deep
~~~

breathing, moderate exercise, or walking away from a provocative situation are the best way to lower the arousal level.

But for those who are milder by nature, awareness can accelerate anger's rush through, and out of, the body. "Yoga helps people stay with the wave of anger all the way to the other end," explains Cope.'

So focus your awareness on your anger to dissipate it, ***if you are mild mannered by nature;***

But move your body in some form of moderate exercise, and do some deep breathing, ***if you tend to be more hot-tempered.***

Reder (2007) continues: '*Besides asanas (or yoga poses), Cope touts a yoga-based technique taught at the Kripalu Centre for Yoga & Health in Lenox, Massachusetts, for integrating emotional experiences. The technique, called "riding the wave," employs five sequential steps: Breathe, Relax, Feel, Watch, Allow.*'

Clearly, based on what has been said above, this process should only be used by people of mild manner, and not hot tempered individuals.

This is the process:

1. **Breathe** 'into' your belly (by lowering your diaphragm and expanding your belly). Do not allow your upper chest to rise; or gradually reduce the extent of the rise of your upper chest.

2. **Relax** your entire body. (It helps if you have previously done conscious relaxation exercises to appreciate how this feels, and how to do it. You could buy a relaxation audio program, for this purpose. Or check out *Progressive Muscle Relaxation* in Chapter 15, below).

3. **Feel** whatever sensations are coursing through your body. (Do not try to suppress any angry feelings. But also do not indulge them. Just *feel* them).

4. **Watch** your mind. (Whatever arises in your mind should be allowed to arise, so long as you have been training yourself to feel compassion for those people who frustrate and thwart you!)

5. **Allow** things in your body and mind to be the way they are – and the anger will gradually burn itself out through awareness.

And repeat steps 1-5 again, and again, until the anger has fully passed.

~~~
~~~

More generally: According to Johnna Medina, in an article titled, '*How yoga is similar to existing mental health therapies*':

'The ancient Eastern practice of yoga combines mindfulness training with exercise (hence the term, "mind-body"). For years, practitioners all over the world have reported receiving mental and physical health benefits from yoga.'[124]

You could attend a class in which you practice yoga, and then continue to do the exercises at home when the class has ended; or, if you are good at learning from books and/or videos, you could study those kinds of resources.

~~~

Chinese exercise systems

Does the Chinese system of Qigong (or Chi Kung) – which is related to Tai Chi - have a similar effect on anxiety, depression and anger?

Marcus James Santer reflects on his own experience of using Qigong/Chi Kung to cure his own depression - and get off anti-depressants. His reflective study begins like this:

"In this post I'd like to look at what it is that makes Qigong/Chi Kung such a powerful tool for overcoming depression, anxiety, worry, fear and for raising self-esteem and resistance to stress.

"I know from my own personal experience of using Qigong to get off anti-depressants ...

"You can think of Qigong as a tool for increasing your emotional immune system."

...

He ends with this conclusion:

"Qigong *is a powerful tool for overcoming mild to moderate depression, for overcoming anxiety, worry and fear. It is a potent way to raise self-esteem and increase your resistance to the stresses and strains of modern living.*

"These 'illnesses' are known as empty illnesses because we don't know the cause of the symptoms and/or the location of the illness is not known. Western medicine does not have a brilliant track record at treating such empty illnesses, often resorting to the prescription of drugs to treat the symptoms whilst the root cause is untreated.
~~~

"I must point out that in cases of severe and long standing emotional problems, Qigong alone may not be enough and you may need the help and support of a skilled counsellor or psychotherapist." [125]

~~~

Michael Tse (pronounced Shay) is a Qigong master who has a large international following, and who practices in Harley Street, London and St. John's Street, Manchester, in the UK; and also overseas. He has made the study of Qigong his life's work, and in his book *'Qigong for Health and Vitality'* (1995)[126], he outlines what the benefits are of practicing this exercise method.

In terms of stress prevention, he considers that if you have a healthy body you will have a healthy mind, due to the inseparable connection between the body and the mind. As people do these slow, gentle, traditional Chinese exercises, their energy level increases, as does their skill at assessing their own body's state and whether or not they are over-working themselves. He states:

"When you lose the ability to judge your body's condition, you can easily become ill or suffer from chronic conditions like ME, heart disease and even cancer". (Page 37)

Tse considers *daily practice* of Qigong to be essential in order to reap the benefits, and he explains that, as a result of daily practice, our brains perform better, improving our memory and attention to detail. Also, in terms of handling anger or other aspects of living, he states that Qigong will enable people to become calmer; more accepting of the flow of life; and physically relaxed.

To reduce depression, he recommends specific exercises (Page 39) and states:

"Qigong brings us back to nature, enabling us to stay away from what is artificial and letting the natural senses return".

~~~

A preliminary study by Linder and colleagues shows that Qigong may be beneficial for relieving stress, although more study is warranted in this area[127]. A much later comprehensive review by Jahnke and colleagues (2012) produces compelling evidence that Tai Chi and Chi Kung can help with depression, anxiety and self-efficacy. This is what they concluded:

"Conclusion: A compelling body of research emerges when Tai Chi studies and the growing body of Qigong studies are combined. The evidence suggests that a wide range of health benefits accrue in response to these meditative movement forms, some consistently so, and some with limitations in the findings thus far. This review has identified numerous outcomes with varying levels of evidence for the efficacy for Qigong and Tai Chi, including bone health, cardiopulmonary fitness and related biomarkers, physical function, falls prevention and balance, general quality of life and patient reported outcomes, immunity, and psychological factors such as anxiety, depression and self-efficacy. A substantial number of RCTs (Randomized Control Trials) have demonstrated consistent, positive results especially when the studies are designed with limited activity for controls. When both Tai Chi and Qigong are investigated together, as two approaches to a single category of practice, meditative movement, the magnitude of the body of research is quite impressive."[128]

In Jahnke *et al* (2010) you will find this statement:

"A substantial body of published research has examined the health benefits of Tai Chi (also called Taiji) a traditional Chinese wellness practice. In addition, a strong body of research is also emerging for Qigong, an even more ancient traditional Chinese wellness practice that has similar characteristics to Tai Chi. Qigong and Tai Chi have been proposed, along with Yoga and Pranayama from India, to constitute a unique category or type of exercise referred to currently as meditative movement.[129] *These two forms of meditative movement, Qigong and Tai Chi, are close relatives having shared theoretical roots, common operational components, and similar links to the wellness and health promoting aspects of traditional Chinese medicine. They are nearly identical in practical application in the health enhancement context, and share much overlap in what traditional Chinese medicine describes as the 'three regulations': body focus (posture and movement), breath focus, and mind focus (meditative components)".*[130]

~~~

It may be that Qigong can help with anger, in particular with a belly-breathing exercise which is assumed to heal the liver. But since we can teach belly breathing as a way of calming down the body, we will stick to that approach in this book. Any deep breathing techniques that you study within Tai Chi or Qigong are likely to be helpful in controlling your anger. But remember, with hot-headed individuals, *movement* is probably most important.

~~~

Exercise and the brain-mind

Here's a short extract from a paper which we (Renata and Jim) wrote in 2011, which was essentially a book review of Ratey and Hagerman's (2009) book – *Spark* - on the subject of how exercise improves the brain.[131]

This is how we commented towards the end of our paper:

"If you value your brain, and want to keep it in good shape, then exercise is going to appeal more and more to you. Why? Because: 'The better your fitness level, the better your brain works', say Ratey and Hagerman (2010, page 247). They mention that research from epidemiologists to kinesiologists confirms this connection (between fitness and brain functioning) repeatedly. They also mention that: 'Population studies including tens of thousands of people of every age show that fitness levels relate directly to positive mood and lower levels of anxiety and stress'.

"Jeannine Stamatakis writes: 'To see how much exercise is required to relieve stress, researchers at the National Institutes of Mental Health observed how prior exercise changed the interaction between aggressive and reserved mice'. If the reserved mice had a chance to do some exercise before encountering the aggressive mice, then they were a lot less stressed by that conflict experience. 'Although this study was done in mice, the results likely have implications for humans as well. Exercising regularly, even taking a walk for 20 minutes several times a week, may help you cope with stress. So dig out those running shoes from the back of your closet and get moving'. (Scientific American Mind, Vol. 23. No.3, July/August 2012; page 72).

~~~

Professor Sapolsky on exercise for stress

Finally, in this section, the views of Robert Sapolsky on the benefits of exercise will be summarised. He has been researching and writing about the effects of stress on human beings for many years. He is a professor of biology, neuroscience and neurosurgery at Stanford University, and a research associate with the Institute of Primal Research, National Museum of Kenya. He is the author of a book titled, *'Why Zebras Don't Get Ulcers', (2010)*[132], which is a guide to stress and stress-related diseases, and how we cope with them.

When Sapolsky describes the techniques he uses to control his own stress, he starts with exercise, and states that he uses this technique most
~~~

frequently. And in his book he describes the many benefits of physical exercise. In relation to blood pressure and resting heart rate, for example, he states that regular exercise will lower them both, and increase lung capacity at the same time.

Exercise also reduces the risk of a range of cardiovascular and metabolic diseases, and so lessens the chance of stress making them worse.

Exercise makes us *feel* better, and uplifts our *mood*, and this is because of the release of beta-endorphins. These are neurotransmitters, which are chemicals that pass along signals from one neuron to the next. Neurotransmitters play a crucial role in the function of the central nervous system, and in mood change; and beta-endorphins are more powerful than morphine. (See Bryant, 2010)[133].

New imaging methods have allowed researchers to study the pattern of behaviour of neurotransmitters in the body, and the flow of endorphins as they interact with human brain cells, confirming that they play a part in the 'feel-good effect that we get from exercising'. So they are natural pain-killers and mood-lifters - (according to Charles Bryant, 2010).

In addition, Sapolsky (2010) states that you reduce physical tension in your body by doing challenging physical exercises. And there is also evidence that if you are well-exercised, then your reaction to psychological stressors is reduced considerably.

Significantly, because you are keeping to your self-chosen exercise regime, you get a sense of achievement and self-efficacy, which is very rewarding.

However, Sapolsky points out that there are several provisos, in his opinion:

(1) You will get a more cheerful mood and a reduced stress response if you exercise – but this will only last for a period of time that can vary from between two hours up to a day after the exercise session. So the benefits wear off if the exercise is not repeated regularly; thus suggesting the need for *daily* exercise!

(2) He also makes the point that you will *only* reduce your stress levels through exercise if you *want* to do it. Sapolsky states:

"Let rats voluntarily run on a running wheel and their health improves in all sorts of ways. Force them, even when playing great dance music, and their health worsens". (Page 491)

The research studies, according to Sapolsky, show very clearly that moderate aerobic exercise, (which you can do whilst talking, without getting too much out of breath), is better than anaerobic exercise - (which is short-lasting, high-intensity activity, where your body's demand for oxygen exceeds the oxygen supply available, and you use energy that is stored in your muscles).

Sapolsky recommends that exercise be done in a consistent, regular pattern and for a prolonged period of time: *"It's pretty clear that you need to exercise a minimum of twenty or thirty minutes at a time, a few times a week, to really get the health benefits."* (Page 402).

And finally he recommends that you don't overdo it.

However, if you were to *never* exercise, then there would (obviously) be no health benefit for you. On the one hand, Sapolsky is saying that a big amount of exercise improves your health a great deal. On the other hand, he cautions against doing *excessive* amounts of exercise as this could damage various physiological systems in the body.

~~~

The search for the ideal exercise routine

Choosing the right exercise system for yourself is a very personal process. This can take time as there is now a dazzling array of sports and exercises to choose from. Experimenting with them, and finding the ones that suit you best, can be very rewarding, whether it's a team game like football, volleyball, or basketball; or more sedate group exercises like Tai Chi or Qigong. And many people have gained a great deal from yoga and Pilates, or simple walking.

(We [Jim and Renata] like to do Qigong [pronounced Chi Kung] every morning after meditation. Plus some calisthenics, like press ups and sit backs; the plank; and I [Renata] also like to do some Yoga stretching exercises. Jim sometimes runs on the spot; and walks around the house for a few minutes every thirty minutes of the working day. He also does some warm-up exercises, and another Chinese system called Zham Zhong, which is pronounced 'Jam Jong'. [From time to time, we both 'lose' these habits, and have to start all over again to re-establish them!]).

One thing is clear: We need, and greatly benefit from, exercise.
~~~

We benefit both mentally and physically.

Physical exercise enriches our lives, helps us to resist diseases, enables our brains to develop, and reduces the impact of the many stresses and strains we are all subject to in the modern world. And as shown above, physical exercise contributes to emotional control - which means reducing our tendencies towards anger, anxiety and/or depression. For these reasons, we recommend that our clients do an average of thirty minutes of physical exercise per day, for at least five days per week. Simple walking, at your own page, for thirty minutes each day is as good a place as any to start.

If you want to be resilient you have to attend to your physical exercise needs!

Happy exercising!

~~~
~~~

Chapter 15: The importance of progressive muscle relaxation

By Renata Taylor-Byrne, March 2020

Introduction

> *"Why use sedatives and tranquilising drugs with their many side effects, when nature has provided a built-in device free from all such defects (a built-in tranquiliser)?"*
>
> Oscar G. Mayer, (In Jacobson, 1976).[134]

Progressive muscle relaxation is a technique that will greatly improve the quality of your life, including your resilience in the face of life's difficulties! It will reduce your anxiety, boost your energy, make you sleep better at night and improve your sports abilities. Furthermore, it will make you less susceptible to heart attacks, and high blood pressure; and it will boost your immune system; to name just a few of the benefits you can gain from practicing this system of relaxation on a regular basis.

The creator of this technique was Dr Edmund Jacobson (1888 –1983). He was a physiologist, and physician in psychiatry and internal medicine. He spent seventy years researching and developing the key insights of scientific relaxation, based on observing tension within the human body. Starting in 1908 at Harvard University, followed by Cornell University, and after that Chicago University, he then set up his own institution in Chicago called the Laboratory for Clinical Physiology.

What Dr Jacobson developed was a simple technique which, if practised daily, reduces physical tension throughout the body-brain-mind.

'Why is this a valuable process?' you might ask.

And my answer: Because the reliable, measurable reduction in levels of physical tension has *beneficial effects throughout* the body-mind. People have more energy, less illness, anxiety and depression; and this slowly transforms people's self-confidence. They are able to sleep better and to banish insomnia; and their memory reliably improves.

Most people don't realise that they become *increasingly physically tense* as they try to solve the daily problems of their lives. This tension uses up lots of their physical energy.

Because of this phenomenon, of accumulation, or building up of physical tensions, day in and day out, people develop anxiety, depression, and a range of physical illnesses: such as high blood pressure, heart attacks, peptic ulcers, spastic colon and nervous indigestion.

The process of progressive tension works like this: As we handle the daily tasks and challenges of life: like work, commuting, and managing the home; physical tension slowly builds up in our bodies as the day progresses. And this accumulating tension is added to by a steady bombardment of bad news via mobile phones, the TV and newspapers.

This accumulated tension interferes with our ability to get to sleep reasonably quickly, to recharge our batteries. And if we have poor quality sleep, we begin the next day feeling tense before our work challenges begin!

In an effort to escape from the demands of our lives; and to relax and enjoy ourselves; we go on holidays. But this strategy can easily backfire as we experience the challenges of air, road and rail travel, and/or hotel and accommodation hassles. People increasing turn to drugs of one sort or another - (including alcohol and/or street drugs, or pharmaceutical drugs from their doctor) - to escape their tense and stressed life situations.

What Dr Jacobson has demonstrated over the decades is this: You can switch off the tension of daily stress and strain by learning how to relax your muscles, which automatically relaxes your central nervous system, including your brain-mind. Progressive muscle relaxation (PMR) is like taking a natural, internally available tranquilizer!

In addition to taking care of the tension of the daily grind; progressive muscle relaxation can also be used (doubled up) at times of particularly high stress and strain; for examples:

- job interviews, making presentations, dealing with difficult people;

- before examinations, or auditions, or taking a driving test;

- or taking part in sports events and other areas of skill performance.

~~~
~~~

Progressive Muscle Relaxation (PMR) defined

> *"Nature does not excuse us when we display ignorance of the laws of health".*
>
> Jacobson (1963).[135]

~~~

In this chapter I will define Progressive Muscle Relaxation and describe its development as an efficient and very effective relaxation technique which has been thoroughly tested for its therapeutic power.

Examples of case studies showing its ability to heal very serious health problems will be described; and some recent research studies will show that it is highly relevant for our present, high-stress culture.

Then the topic of insomnia, and how daily progressive muscle relaxation can greatly help, will be explained. The final part of the chapter will be a description of the technique which you can try out for yourself, and further information about the benefits including my own feedback on having experimented with the technique for the past three months.

~~~

(1) The definition of Progressive muscle relaxation

> *"We must learn tension control just as we learn French, the pianoforte or golf. Nature favours us with instincts which our parents readily turn to account to teach us to walk in infancy. However (nature) does not teach us to control ourselves, else we might have fewer addicts to sedatives, tranquilisers, alcohol and such (drugs)".*
>
> (Jacobson, 1963, page 29).[136]

~~~

Progressive muscle relaxation (PMR) is a technique whereby a person (a client) sees a relaxation therapist, and slowly learns, through the tensing and releasing of body muscles, to *not do anything at all* to their muscles. Relaxation is the *total* absence of any muscle movement in the body.
~~~

Jacobson elaborates on this point like this: "According to my experience, those who preach 'relaxation exercises' have not quite understood that to relax is simply **not to do**; it is the total absence of any muscular exercise". (Jacobson, 1976, page 34)[137].

He considered relaxation to be the complete physiological *opposite* of being excited or upset.

Matthew Edlund, M.D.[138] has described Jacobson's technique as being 'paradoxical' because you start to become relaxed *without* making any effort to become relaxed. Paradoxically, you focus on muscle tension at first, and then switch off the tension to leave yourself in a state of relaxation.

Jacobson's clients included engineers, journalists, lawyers, doctors, bankers, dentists and people from all the current businesses and professions which were operating in America from the 1920's up to the 1980's. When his first book - which was entitled "Progressive relaxation" - was published in 1929, he was told by the workers and printers at the Chicago University Press who produced his book, that they *in particular* experienced a great deal of tension. And later in his career he came across union members in the garment and other industries, and assembly line workers, who displayed evidence of extreme tension.

His theory was that clients experienced tension because they had hyperactive bodies and minds, and the build-up of tension in the body resulted in the following symptoms:

- anxiety, and high blood pressure,

- cardiovascular disorders, and nervous indigestion,

- peptic ulcers and spastic colon.

People were trying to cope with a very fast and constantly changing society – even in those much slower than today, days - and the problem was that their efforts to cope were using up lots of energy.

This energy, which is called *adenosine triphosphate*, comes from the food we eat. And Jacobson compared it to the petrol supply in a car. Just like the petrol in a car's tank, we have a limited amount of "personal petrol" (or fuel) which we need for our brain, nerves and muscles, and it comes directly from the food we eat.

This energy supply is used up by the activities we do to achieve our goals. When we have a job to do, we use some of our 1,030 skeletal muscles, which we contract and relax as necessary, in order to get things done.

But what Jacobson learned from experience of seeing clients was this: None of the doctors who had dealt with his clients, before they came to him, had told them about the need to *control their energy usage* as they lived their lives.

Those clients were well versed in the reality of running a business or profession. Thus they knew that, if they spent too much money, they would risk damaging their business, and, potentially, bankruptcy.

But they had *no idea* that they needed to manage their own *personal* supply of *physical energy*. Here is what Jacobson found:

"I have had experience with the top management of some of the (American) nation's most successful corporations. The officials conducted business duties with outstanding efficiency and success, yet spent their personal energies quite extravagantly.

"I was shocked to find that 40% of the top executives of one leading corporation had blood vessels that were beyond cure. They were paying with their lives for (unregulated) energy expenditure." (Jacobson, 1976, Page 12).

~~~

(2) How our muscles become tense and cause problems for us

When we perform any activity, we use our muscles, by contracting (or tensing) them. This reduces the length of the muscle fibres temporarily.

Within the muscles there are two sets of nerves:

- One set of nerves transmits information *to* the muscles, and:

- The other set of nerves takes information *from the muscles to the brain and the spinal cord.*

The information transmitted from the muscles via the nerves is electrical in nature, but it moves more slowly than the electricity we use in our daily lives.

When we tense our muscles, in order to carry out some act, we spend personal energy and this is in the form of increased nerve impulses. As stated earlier, this personal energy, which we burn up in our brains, muscles and nerves, is called *adenosine triphosphate*. Jacobson (1976) states: *"At every*
~~~

moment you depend on your personal energy expenditures – namely you burn adenosine triphosphate in your muscle fibres, in your nerve cells and fibres and in your brain cells and fibres. In this burning of fuel you resemble a car or an aeroplane, which likewise burns fuel in order to move". (Page 11)

Furthermore, the energy that people use up as they go about their daily lives (which has to be acquired through the food they have eaten) can be measured with electrical machines.

Jacobson created a machine called an 'integrating neurovoltmeter' which simply means a way of measuring *muscle and nerve tension* of different intensities. It was able to measure mental exertion down to one ten-millionth of a volt. As people become more tense, there can be an increase from 1 to 70 electrical discharges per second, from nerves and muscles.

He described human beings as having a brain-nervous-muscular system which is a very complex "electrochemical-mechanical integrated system" which serves people as they go about their working lives. But nature, although *providing* ways in which people can control and manage the energy they use up in the course of daily life, *doesn't* show human beings how to do that.

People have to find out for themselves about energy conservation, and that was what Jacobson wanted to help them with. They needed to understand that tensions would build up in their bodies and cause serious health problems if they didn't learn to manage this process. He made the study of tension in the human body, and the reduction of it, his life's work.

Jacobson gives an example in his (1976) book, titled 'You must relax', of how three different people - a soldier in a battle, a student working in an examination room, or a runner taking part in a marathon, would all have high levels of physical tension. And if these people were wired up so the electrical impulses could be recorded, then this high level of physical tension would be confirmed by the results, showing a high frequency of electrical impulses.

And if these three people were to go to a more peaceful environment, and have a rest, lying down, there would *in most cases* be a reduction in the electrical impulses recorded on the equipment. But this *doesn't always follow* because there are people who have highly active, high pressure lives and when they try to switch off, they are unable to do so, because the nervous stimulation messages that they receive from their muscles and nerves has become normal for them.

A closer look at how tension and stress builds up in our bodies

If we don't give ourselves time to *relax and recover* after we have exerted ourselves - (for example by doing a hard day's hard day's work; tackling a sudden problem; dealing with an accident; or any one of the many challenges that humans of all ages meet regularly) - then we can cause problems for ourselves.

Here's why we have to relax: Our bodies have developed through centuries of evolution, so that we are able to handle stressors, and then *recover* from them quickly, by calming down and resting. We've got a very efficient, in-built system for handling pressure. It's called the 'fight or flight' response, and our bodies react with the release of stress hormones which help us cope with the problems that arise.

But once the problem has passed, we have an automatic recovery system which kicks in, and this is called the 'rest and digest' system. Meyer, quoted at the start of this chapter, described it as our 'inbuilt tranquiliser." These two different, but inseparable, types of responses are part of our autonomic (meaning 'automatic') nervous system, which protects our body-mind through appropriate activations and deactivations of our energy release system.

The autonomic nervous system makes sure that, after we have dealt with a sudden crisis or stressful event, our digestion *slowly* returns to normal; our breathing slows down, as does our heart rate; and we get back to full energy conservation mode.

But if we *don't* give ourselves time to recover in-between these stressful events, we stop the natural recovery process from taking place. Our bodies experience more and more stress without this safety valve, or recovery stage, to dissipate it. Then there is a gradual accumulation of *excessive tension* in our muscles, and stress hormones in our blood and body tissues.

That is where Jacobson's Progressive muscle relaxation can help us.

"Tension disorders are more common than the common cold" stated Jacobson in his 1976 book. He concluded, from his professional experiences, that many disorders of the body are a ***direct*** result of physical tension. For examples: states of fear and anxiety; high blood pressure; nervous indigestion; heart problems; and peptic ulcers.

His goal was to show people how to *manage* their bodily energy carefully, so that they could reduce their physical tension levels. He set up an organisation in Chicago called the Foundation for Scientific Relaxation. It was a non-profit organisation and it provided training for doctors and other professionals involved in health education.

Dr Martin Turner and Dr Jamie Barker - authors of 'What business can learn from Sport psychology', (2014)[139] - are convinced that *daily practice* of Progressive Muscle Relaxation (PMR) is needed before you can experience the benefits in reduced stress levels. (In other words, it's not enough to do it *occasionally*!) They recommend *checking your heart rate* before and after the practice of the technique, which will provide you with reassuring information that the technique is actually working. And they also conclude that PMR will improve your performance in different areas of your life and your work.

One of their findings is this: *"After a week's practice you will notice an increase in your ability to self-regulate"...* (Defined as "managing your actions, thoughts and feelings so you achieve your valued goals' - RTB.)... *and begin to see the value in integrating muscle relaxation into part of your preparation for important performance situations, or alternatively as an integral part of your daily routines".* (Turner and Barker, 2014: page 173).

Case studies: Several examples of how progressive muscle relaxation can help

(1) The first example:

Jacobson gives a description of the use of his 'scientific relaxation' technique (which he described in his 1976 book) and explains how, during the Second World War in America, USA Navy cadets, aged 19-22 (straight from schools and college), were involved in flying aircraft during warfare against enemy planes.

As a direct result of the continuous flying missions that the cadets had to complete, (which they couldn't withdraw from - [remember *Catch 22*]), as well as other challenges, the cadets started having nervous breakdowns and other indications of the strain - meaning accumulated physical and mental tensions - that they were under.

As an experimental solution, the US navy decided to send five of its officers (nicknamed the 'Navy Five') to Jacobson's Education Department, based in his Laboratory for Clinical Psychology in Chicago. There they got instructor training in how to teach Progressive Muscle Relaxation (PMR), for 6 weeks; so that they could then go back to their bases and train the new intakes of cadets in progressive muscle relaxation (PMR), and the principles of scientific relaxation.

The message that Jacobson wanted to get across was this:

"Scientific relaxation is not just lying down or sitting in a quiet manner with good intentions. It's as technical an undertaking as running a plane, which many of the cadets were striving to learn". (Page 33)

But how could Jacobson and his colleagues make sure that the 'Navy 5' instructors were *really* learning to relax? They would have to measure their starting tension levels, and the ending relaxation levels.

Fortunately, this had already been catered for, in an earlier period of Jacobson's work. In order to measure the level of physical tensions in the bodies of his clients, Jacobson and his colleagues, with the collaboration of the Bell Telephone Company Laboratory, had created *a tension measuring device* called an 'integrating neurovoltmeter'. This measuring equipment was so sensitive that, even if a muscle looked relaxed, any slight tension could be recorded, down to *one millionth of a volt of electricity.*

The evidence from the results produced by the electrical equipment showed clearly that the Navy instructors were learning to relax their muscles.

The instructors *also* needed to learn that *physical exercise,* on the one hand, and *muscle relaxation,* on the other, were ***two separate processes***. For example, Jacobson had established that, if you worked all day in an office, stuck behind a desk, even though you were not moving around and exercising, you were still using your body muscles; even though the movements were not as apparent as those of a manual worker or sportsperson. Therefore, he was able to conclude that, someone who *looks* physically inactive can have *unseen* levels of tensions in their muscles.

After their training period in Chicago, the Navy instructors returned to their **Pre-flight training bases** in different parts of the US. They then, in turn, taught 95 officers the skills of relaxation training, so they could become instructors also; and in the next seven months, 15,700 cadets were instructed in relaxation skills.

The ***American Journal of Psychiatry*** published the results of the training, which were summarised as follows:

- *The nervousness and fatigue amongst the cadets was reduced, and they reported much better sleep.*

- In addition, when the accident rates of the untrained cadets were compared with those of the trained cadets, *the accident rates were lower with those cadets who had received the training.*

- There was also *a high level of appreciation for the relaxation training* from the cadets, their instructors and from people who had simply seen the beneficial effects of the training on the young cadets.

~~~

(2) An individual example:

In 1976, Jacobson wrote about Mrs Hardy, a client that he treated with PMR. She had been suffering from cyclothymic depression. (This is a type of mood pattern which is characterised by alternating, short episodes of depression and hypomania; in a milder form than that of bipolar disorder). Her depression had lasted for several years. She was worried about her age and how long she would live, and she was convinced that she would never be able to stop worrying about it. As a result, she had very high levels of physical tension. (This suggests her depression was preceded by *anxiety* and *tension*!)

Jacobson taught her to notice when she was tensing the muscles in her body, and how to stop tensing them. And gradually, as a result of daily practice, she began to spot the signs of tension in her body and when she was tensing her muscles unnecessarily. This allowed her to desist from tensing, which left her body in a state of relaxation.
~~~

She learned this new **relaxation habit** lying down; and also in her daily life with her family, as she cooked, cleaned and ran the home. And as she did this awareness exercise, she realised that no-one was forcing her to tense up part of her body. She had been doing it herself all the time.

Jacobson stated: *"She was doing something with her muscles just as definitely as if she were sweeping a room or washing the dishes. Anxiety was **an act** which (at least in part) she was performing and need not perform."* (Page 40. ***Emphasis added***).

What she was doing with her muscles became apparent to her when she had a very low level of tension in her muscles and she discovered the following: *"… To her surprise, perhaps for the first time in years, she found herself free for the moment from the severe anxiety which previously had oppressed her constantly."* (Jacobson, 1976).

As she continued with her treatment, she was advised to keep practising the muscle relaxation exercises. And the outcome was that she stopped worrying about the difficulties of getting older.

When her level of tension was measured electronically, it confirmed her progress - she was able to go back to the job that she had been doing, handle money problems easily, and she was able to join her husband in his business.

The final comment on how she had changed as a result of the relaxation exercises was expressed by Jacobson as follows: *"She became free of the fears that had held her as a slave. She became confident, self-assured and cheerful."*

~~~

(3) The third example:

Jacobson also describes a client who came to his clinic: *"Towards the end of World War 1, a patient who came from the United States Army, described how his parachute failed to open when he pulled the cord. He fell to earth and the parachute fell on top of him and broke his back."*

The surgeons in the US army were able to treat his injuries successfully but he was left with persistent pain which didn't reduce in its intensity. So the man travelled to Jacobson's Chicago clinic for treatment. He was given several months of Progressive Muscle Relaxation (PMR), and daily practice was *essential* to help his pain management. The result was that he slowly experienced a reduction in the pain from his injuries, and one day, feeling
~~~

better, he visited a golf course (which he had never done before) to see what the sport was like.

He started trying out the game, on the golf course. And as he did so, his behaviour was observed by several golf professionals. They watched his movements and they became convinced that he possessed a natural flair for the game and encouraged him to learn to play golf. He took their advice on board and started learning to play properly. The result: "*...he became one of the outstanding golf professionals of the country*". (Jacobson, 1978, page 143).

Recent research studies

Because so much of Jacobson's own research was conducted up to the 1970's, I want to present two recent research studies which confirm the power of Positive Muscle Relaxation (PMR):

(1) PMR and Anxiety: Research in Greece in 2019

The most recent research study, that I could find, was conducted in Greece, in January 2019, with 50 long-term unemployed people.[140] They had been suffering from anxiety disorders, and the participants were split up into 2 groups. One group of thirty individuals were put on an 8 week progressive muscle relaxation training programme, and the control group did not receive any training.

At the start of the research study, the participants' level of stress, anxiety, depression, integrity; their health-related quality of life; and their sense of safety and security; were all measured. And at the end of the research, the result was that the intervention group (which had the training in PMR) had improved results in all those aspects of their functioning which had been measured by the researchers.

So, even though the intervention group had statistically higher levels of depression, anxiety and stress *before* the intervention, they gained a significant reduction in those levels because of the PMR; whereas in the control group, no significant difference was observed.

Between the two groups, the differences were statistically significant. To summarise the findings, the intervention group showed a *decrease* in the evidence of depression, anxiety and stress; the quality of their life and general mental health had improved; and they felt more of a sense of coherence about their lives.

~~~

(2) PMR and pain: Research in Egypt in 2018

A research study which took place in 2018 is another example of the power of PMR: After having a caesarean section, a lot of women suffer pain, disturbed sleep, and difficulty moving and walking. A research study was undertaken at the Damanhur National Medical Institute in Egypt with a group of women - 80 in number - to see if Progressive Muscle Relaxation (PMR) could help improve their recover from their operations.[141] The research study took the form of a randomised, controlled clinical trial, and 40 women were assigned to a study group and 40 women were assigned to the control group. The women in the study group were shown how to do PMR, and then did it themselves. The results appeared to be quite conclusive:

- When the quality of the sleep experienced in the two groups were compared, 62.5% of the PMR group had nourishing sleep, compared to 5% of the control group.

- The level of pain they experienced by the control group was described by them as being at a level of 70%. On the other hand, in the PMR group, pain was 'significantly absent' from the whole of this group.

Therefore the conclusion made by the research team was that PMR significantly reduced pain and made women's physical activities less painful and restrictive, and there was a definite improvement in sleep quality. The researchers concluded in their report that their findings were similar to others in the same area of research: That the pain that mothers who had experienced caesareans was reduced by PMR through the operation of several body systems.

They observed that it reduces the stress hormones of epinephrine (adrenaline), catecholamines and cortisol. Also, the deep breathing technique used, increases the oxygen levels in the body, and reduces the oxidative factors, and as a result of this, less pain is experienced. PMR can
~~~

also restrict the reaction of the sympathetic nervous system (the 'Fight or flight' response) and stimulate the parasympathetic response (the 'Rest and digest' part of the autonomic nervous system) by restricting the feedback pathway from the brain-mind to the muscles; and as a result, *block* the biological response to pain. As a consequence, it may lower the heart rate, the level of blood pressure and the metabolic rate.

The outcome of the research study, the researchers concluded, was that post-caesarean women who practiced the PMR technique have lower post caesarean pain, a better quality of sleep and a reduced level of restriction on their physical activities than those who received just the routine nursing care.

How progressive muscle relaxation helps with insomnia

> *"The reason you can't sleep is because some of your muscles are tense when they shouldn't be. Who is responsible for this tensing? Your grandmother? Your boss? No – you are responsible – you are doing it".*
>
> (Jacobson, 1978, page 93)

Jacobson described several factors that made it difficult for people to get a decent night's sleep. These included:

- having cares and worries,

- over arousal from modern life,

- discomfort about decisions which they had taken, which activated their conscience, and:

- dietary stimulants like tea, alcohol, or lack of food.

Another factor is the job occupations that people have. Many people's jobs keep their minds constantly and fully engaged in their daily work; and being mentally very busy during the day, without breaks, creates tension in the body, and this tension doesn't suddenly evaporate from people's bodies at bedtime.

Jacobson goes on to say: *"You may want to state that when you are tense, you just can't help it. That is what is called a 'good alibi'. If you want to continue to be tense, and need an excuse to do so, all I can say is that your excuses are excellent".* (Jacobson 1978, page 93).

This however is a little harsh, because human beings are largely non-conscious creatures of habit. Jacobson shares with Albert Ellis this tendency towards blaming the (largely non-conscious) client for choosing to stress themselves. This is untrue and unscientific thinking.

Unless and until you are shown that you can tense your muscles; that you are tensing yourself (unwittingly); and how to *stop* tensing yourself; nobody has the right to blame you for your tension.

Jacobson knew from all the years of research that he had undertaken, that when a person relaxes completely, they fall asleep automatically. And clients who suffered from insomnia were over concerned with not sleeping, moving around in bed repeatedly, reorganising their bedding, and generally keeping up tension levels in their bodies. He states: *"What prevents slumber and keeps us awake is quick changes."*(Jacobson 1978, page 106).

He further stated that he had observed a lot of sleepless people and seen that they altered their body positions *repeatedly*, and this was counterproductive because constant movements simply kept the insomnia going. (But he failed to notice that this was not voluntary action, but habitual patterns of movement).

His research findings suggested that individual would fall asleep more quickly and easily at night if they stuck to the daily pattern of practising the PMR relaxation strategies. A tense body with tense muscles will predictably prevent sleep for a long time during the night.

But if you learn to become aware of and to deliberately *let go of* tension in your muscles, slowly you will become more and more relaxed, and you will get the full benefits of a good night's sleep in time. (Aim for at least 8 hours of sleep every night). The more relaxed you are, the quicker you will be able to get to sleep and achieve the mental nourishment that only sleep can give the body.

If you have had insomnia for several years then Jacobson's realistic advice is that you will recover from it less quickly than someone who has had it for a relatively brief period of time: *"If you've got severe, chronic insomnia what you most require is a long course in nervous re-education"*, he stated (Jacobson 1963, page 111).

At this point, Jacobson is being more realistic. Human beings are creatures of habit, and the longer we practice a habit for, the longer it is likely to take us to change that habit.

~~~

How to do practice the PMR technique

Here are some brief guidelines for doing the PMR practice:

Choose a place where you can be alone for 15 – 20 minutes, for daily practice. Make sure that the room is quiet, and warm enough; and there are no loud sounds to distract you.

Now follow this sequence of activities:

1. Lie on a beach mat or bath towel on the floor; or on a long couch or settee.

2. What you are going to do is *tense up* and then *relax* each of the main muscles of your body, for a count of 5 seconds; and then release the muscles, and focus on the pleasant feeling of relaxation for a count of 10 seconds[4].

Do not tense any muscle to the point of causing pain or a muscle strain. (If you feel a muscle is cramping, stop tensing for a few seconds and try again. If you get cramp in any let muscle, get up and walk around until it goes.)

This process, of tensing and relaxing, helps to educate your body and mind about the distinction between the *feeling* of tension and the *feeling* of relaxation.

Here is the sequence to follow:

(a) Focus your attention on your toes, and curl them. Feel the tension in your toes; hold it for a count of 5 seconds; and relax. Feel the sensation of relaxation for a count of 10 seconds.

(b) Now focus your attention on your feet, and press them both forward, as far as the toes will go. Count to 5 seconds, and then relax completely for 10 seconds.

---

[4] If you are not used to counting seconds, try this method: "One thousand and one; One thousand and two; One thousand and three; One thousand..." etc.
~~~

(c) Next, pull your toes back as far as they will go, to tense your lower legs. Count to 5 seconds, and then relax for 10 seconds. Savour the feeling of relaxation.

(d) Tense your thigh muscles, by lifting your heels a few millimetres off the floor while keeping your legs straight and tense; hold it for 5 seconds, and relax to the count of 10 seconds.

(e) Now breathe out completely, and contract your abdominal muscles. Hold it for 5 seconds; and relax. Savour the relaxation response for 10 seconds.

(f) Tense your chest: Breathe in until your lungs are full. Tense the muscles of your upper chest and upper back. Count to 5 seconds, and then relax for 10 seconds.

(g) Now raise your shoulders as if trying to get them to reach your ears. Hold it for 5 seconds; release suddenly; and enjoy the feeling of relaxation for 10 seconds.

(h) Next, make fists with your two hands, to tense your hands and forearms. Count to 5 seconds while tensing; and then relax them for 10 seconds.

(i) Tense the front of your upper arms (biceps). Make fists, and fold your arms so as to try to touch your shoulders with your fists. Hold it in tension for the count of 5 seconds; and then release suddenly, and savour the sense of relaxation for the count of 10 seconds.

(j) Tense the back of your upper arms (triceps). Make fists. Face the back of both fists towards the floor, and straighten both arms as hard as you can. Feel the tension in your triceps for the count of 5 seconds; and then relax to the count of ten seconds.

(k) Tense your neck by pushing your head backwards against the surface you are resting on. Count to 5 seconds, and then relax for 10 seconds.

(l) Now tense your jaw: Bring your teeth together very firmly by biting hard, and pull back the corners of your mouth (but avoid straining or paining your jaw muscles). Count to 5 seconds, and then relax for 10 seconds.

(m) Then, press your lips together tightly, while trying to smile. This will tense your lips and face muscles. Hold it for the count to 5 seconds, and then relax to the count of 10 seconds.

(n) Now press your tongue against the roof of your mouth, to tense your tongue and throat. Hold it for the count of 5 seconds; and then relax for 10 seconds.

(o) Squeeze your eyes tightly shut, to tense the muscle around them; and hold the tension for 5 seconds. Then relax for 10 seconds.

(p) Now tense up your forehead by raising your eyebrows. Hold the tension for 5 seconds, and then relax for 10 seconds.

~~~

This whole process will most likely take you seven or eight minutes to complete. Now you have done it, treat yourself to a further ten or fifteen minutes of rest, while you savour the feeling of relaxation throughout your body. I suggest that 15 minutes would be the minimum amount of time for the whole process. When you have finished tensing and relaxing the different parts of your body, then just lie still.

You may find you fall asleep quite naturally and this is a good way to combine learning about your body tension and releasing it, and having a daily siesta. You will feel refreshed, and with renewed energy, after the PMR process is complete.

This is crucial point: For this technique to work, and provide maximum benefit, you need to do this *every day*. Try to make sure you do not miss a session. You will get an energy boost from this relaxation technique; plus big benefits for your heart and blood pressure; and for your stress and anxiety levels.

The 'abbreviated' progressive muscle relaxation technique

Jacobson's progressive relaxation technique (PMR) has been acknowledged by health care professionals throughout the world as being very effective in many different healthcare contexts. It is a technique that anyone can learn and use for themselves, and this increases their sense of self-efficacy and control over their bodies. It's also a lot cheaper than drugs and doesn't have the negative side effects that drugs have!

Progressive relaxation technique (PMR) teaches the client to raise their awareness of the muscles in their body; then as they *notice* the tension,
~~~

slowly letting go of it, in each of the main muscles of the body. If this is done regularly (daily is best), the client become more and more able to spot the tension in their muscles as it arises. And the more they practise, the more they can automatically spot and release unnecessary tension.

A modification was made to Jacobson's PMR technique by Joseph Wolpe (pronounced 'Welpay'); a South African psychiatrist. This was because Jacobson's original training of his clients in the relaxation process took a long time and was very detailed about the exact procedure for relaxing the muscles. The original version of progressive muscle relaxation stipulated daily exercise times of one hour a day and over 50 training sessions (about three muscle groups per session) were considered necessary.

After mastering the basic relaxation exercises, then 'differentiated relaxation' could be added. This means that to get more benefit for your body and mind, you could experiment with the use of progressive muscle relaxation in everyday life (e.g. when reading and writing at work or when driving a car). It was recommended that you used the necessary movements to carry out a daily task, and any muscle groups that were *not needed* to do the activity, were to remain as relaxed as possible.

Practising the full progressive muscle relaxation technique every day, in the way Jacobson recommended, would mean that it could take 3-6 months before a client had learned the relaxation technique, so Joseph Wolpe altered the process by reducing its length.

Wolpe, practiced psychiatry in the US; specialised in behaviour therapy; and created a treatment to help desensitize patients with phobias by *exposing them to their fears gradually*, one step at a time).

Wolpe[142] built upon the research findings of Jacobson, and made it clear that relaxation was an *essential* part of systematic desensitisation, which was the name of the treatment he created.

Systematic desensitization has helped many people recover from fear and panic attacks. He used progressive muscle relaxation (PMR) but considered that a shorter version would be more practical for his clients.

So progressive muscle relaxation was re-named as 'abbreviated progressive muscle relaxation training' (APMRT) and this quicker form is still used today, as it is more practical and easy to accomplish, once a person has learned the technique; and it is still very beneficial for the body. And the version described above is closer to Wolpe than it is to Jacobson.

Conclusion

In this chapter, I have defined PMR (Progressive Muscle Relaxation), and described how and why our muscles become tense and cause us all kinds of health problems. I then cited three case studies which show how effective PMR is when measured scientifically. Then I presented two case studies from 2018 and 2019, which also confirm PMR's effectiveness for the treatment of a range of social/emotional/pain problems. I then looked at the way PMR helps with insomnia.

Subsequently, I described the process of doing PMR so you can do it yourself. And I referred to the fact that Joseph Wolpe has argued for the use of a quicker, easier approach to PMR/desensitization. However, the guidelines that I have offered in this chapter are a quick version of PMR, taking as little as 15 to 20 minutes per day.

Here is a list of some more of the most powerful benefits of PMR that I mentioned in the first part of this chapter; this time from Maria O'Toole (2005). In her encyclopaedia, she states that, when individuals use PMR on a regular basis, they find that:

- there is a reduction in anxiety levels;

- the ability to concentrate is enhanced;

- panic attacks take place less often, if at all;

- creativity and spontaneity are elevated;

- there is an increased feeling of being able to manage emotional mood states;

- people are able to become more adept at facing up to sequenced fearful situations; and finally:

- they have higher levels of self-esteem!

~~~
~~~

During the four months in which I (Renata Taylor-Byrne) have been experimenting with doing daily PMR, I have found that:

- the quality of my sleep has improved,

- my sense of well-being and autonomy has increased,

- my anxiety level has plummeted,

- I have more energy,

- and my sleep-efficiency has improved: (which means the amount of time that I'm asleep, each night, is higher now, as a proportion of the total amount of time that I'm in bed).

- I also fall asleep more quickly than I used to, because I can quickly scan my body for signs of tension and relax any tense muscles, using the knowledge gained from daily practice of Jacobson's/Wolpe's PMR technique.

~~~

At the start of this chapter I quoted the words of Oscar Meyer, a lifelong friend of Jacobson's. I truly agree with his view that, (with daily progressive muscle relaxation), we can bring about the use of our 'inner tranquiliser'; which makes us more resilient. I strongly recommend that you give it a try and enjoy the very real benefits!

~~~

Chapter 16: Developing self-management skills

Introduction

If you want to be resilient in the face of life's challenges and difficulties - to be fit and well enough to overcome the many hurdles that will block your path – you must know how to *manage yourself* for optimum performance, physically and mentally.

In this chapter I will present the E-CENT approach to developing self-management skills that I originally published in my book – *Holistic Counselling in Practice* – which first appeared in 2016, but which was re-issued in modified form in 2019[143]. Here it is:

Defining self-management

Although each individual is actually a social animal - shaped and conditioned by their family of origin, their schools, the mass media, and so on - *we nevertheless can decide to take responsibility for managing ourselves and our lives.* That is to say, if somebody, or something, *wakes us up* to the reality of a crossroads junction we are facing in our lives, we can take conscious responsibility for *choosing* the road we will follow. (If nobody or nothing wakes us up, we will continue to follow our non-conscious patterns and habits. And it may also be that when we 'choose', we do so because we 'have no choice' but to 'choose' what we 'choose', because, it seems/feels to us that we have to make that 'choice'!)

This process of waking up and taking responsibility means giving up operating 'on automatic' – giving up being a wholly non-conscious automaton. It is not perfectly effortless, this process of taking conscious control. Remember how difficult it was *to change anything* as a result of a New Year's Resolution. The changing of habit patterns is not perfectly achievable. Remember how often your New Year's Resolutions failed!

I have been working on my own self-management for almost forty years, but I have not reached 'the end of the line' yet! Neither am I in line for a medal or trophy for my achievements so far! (Though I have created a healthier body-brain-mind for myself than I previously had; and I've learned to manage my social environment more effectively. And I've achieved a level of 'spiritual connection' to the universe that I could not have imagined 35 years ago! Furthermore, I am very much better at finding the middle way between being way too flexible [in a particular context] or way too inflexible [in another]).

I have changed some old, bad habits over the years; formed some new, good habits; but I have to watch my behaviour daily, "as though I were a bandit lying in wait", as Epictetus put it. (Epictetus, 1991).

'Self-management' means that I set goals for myself; I seek wisdom for myself; I try to guide my life by the best knowledge, and emotional intelligence, that I can find and/or generate. This is not an easy task, and in fact it is a lifelong journey of discovery, trial and error, progress and slipping back, and so on.

E-CENT counselling theory advocates the use of some of the most helpful aspects of some of the most useful philosophies of life available to us: like *moderate* Stoicism, *moderate* Zen Buddhism, and some aspects of moral philosophy. (But we avoid extreme Stoicism and extreme Buddhism, because they teach that we can be indifferent to adversity, like a block of wood, a stone, or a bamboo tree in a tropical storm!)

The moderate philosophies, which we advocate, should ideally be combined with the best aspects of modern psychology; and the best of the self-improvement literature available in bookshops and on Amazon and other online book stores.

Identifying self-management aims and goals

Most people have their self-management aims and goals back to front. Many people seem to go after *wealth* before *health*; and *status* before *happiness*; and *career 'successes'* before *the sense of making a contribution*, or of *finding their life's work*.

E-CENT theory advocates the hierarchy of 'unifying principles'[144] - or principled aims - presented in the next section, below - which have been developed and followed by Jim Byrne and Renata Taylor-Byrne over a period of almost forty years.

This is a full 'curriculum for life', and it could take a whole lifetime to implement it. So do not overload yourself; and do not give up just because it is difficult to change old habits!

It has taken some *persistence* on our parts to keep going with this curriculum, when we were tired and discouraged; or we felt lazy; or we could not see the point in the immediate moment.

Winston Churchill famously advocated that we should "Never, ever, ever, ever, ever give up!"

However, this advice is *too extreme*. In E-CENT theory, Window No.9 takes a more flexible approach. This is the middle way, if you like, between giving up *too easily*, and *never* giving up at all (even when you suspect that *you are like a frog being boiled alive in some corporate soup tureen!)*

Let me remind you of Window No.9, from Chapter 11 above:

Window No.9: The frame around this window says:

"Winners never quit - but they certainly don't persist in banging their heads on the same section of the wall that obstructs their progress".

- Some people quit too soon, or too easily, and therefore fail to win the prize that they desired.

- Some people keep going, striving and persisting, and they do (often) achieve the prize that they were after.

- And some people keep going, and going, and going, despite the fact that they are clearly flogging a dead horse. This is a form of losing, and failing, and self-disregard or self-abuse! (This is what Shami did, until it ruined his health. He should had paid more attention to the need for balance in his life: meaning 8 hours' work; 8 hours' rest; and 8 hours' play; except sometimes!)

- I operate on the principle that I must try, try and try again – <u>within reason</u> - to succeed; but not necessarily in the same (unworkable) relationship; or the same

(unrewarding or intolerable) business or employment; or on the same path through life.

- Winners are life-long learners, and they have the courage to act on their earned wisdom!

Ask yourself:

- How can I decide when to persist and when to quit? (I could try using the CoRT tools developed by Dr Edward De Bono[145]*, applied to my current problem situation).*

- Is my current problem a result of bashing my head on the wrong section of wall?

- Is it time to quit on some person, or organization, or some object or thing, or goal, in order to resolve my current problem?

~~~

Let us now look at our list of aims, or unifying principles:

Unifying principles from the curriculum for life

1. To be healthy;
2. To be happy;
3. To be a person of integrity, who lives from their 'Good Wolf' side (which means from their *virtues*); and who monitors and shrinks their 'Bad Wolf' side (which means their *vices*)[146].
4. To have at least one ***really powerful*** relationship;
5. To have a few ***successful relationships***, with family, friends, associates, colleagues, neighbours, and/or others.
6. To engage in enjoyable, meaningful work, which is socially valuable or useful;
7. To take care of your physical and psychological wellbeing;
8. To take care of your material wellbeing, and the resources required to do so;
9. To explore the question of what 'spiritual' means for you[147]. Do you have a 'spiritual dimension' to your life? Are you taking care of it? Or are you more community-connected? Or connected to nature?
~~~

Primary areas for goal setting:

To optimize the chances of achieving those unifying principles (or aims) in practice (within which you may also have more specific, short term and medium term goals), E-CENT theory advocates paying attention to the following aspects of your life:

1. Diet (balanced and healthy); Read at least one good book on diet and nutrition. (See Chapter 13).
2. Daily meditation; Begin with ten minutes of sitting meditation per day, and build up to 30 minutes eventually. (See Appendix B, below).
3. Daily physical exercise; Begin with at least 30 minutes of brisk walking each day; and add on additional exercises, such as yoga or Pilates, or Chi Kung; or weight or circuit training at a gymnasium. (See Chapter 14).
4. Regular relaxation exercises; Use audio CDs, such as one of those produced by Glenn Harrold or Paul McKenna. Or learn and practice Progressive Muscle Relaxation (PMR), described in Chapter 15 above.
5. Daily nutritional supplementation of your diet (with professional guidance where necessary). See Chapter 13.
6. Regular writing therapy (Daily Pages)[148], at least three or four times per week (Julia Cameron, 1992)[149].
7. Developing and using good quality problem solving and decision making skills. (See section 7.6 of my book on Holistic Counselling in Practice)[150].
8. Routinely maintaining reasonable, moral and self-helpful self-talk (or inner dialogue). For example, by learning and applying the Nine Windows Model (in Chapter 11 above); living by the Golden Rule; applying the WDEP model[151]; and writing your Daily Pages every morning to prevent the build-up of stress-inducing, undigested experiences.
9. Daily reading of books that will promote personal development (for at least 30 minutes per day - and if that's too much, then do this three or four times per week).

10. Developing the skills that you need to get, and keep, the kind of job that suits your natural talents and abilities. (Barbara Sher, 1995)[152].
11. Attending to your coaching, counselling and therapy needs, promptly. If necessary, see a competent professional about:

    (a) Giving up playing 'psychological games' (from Victim, Persecutor or Rescuer roles [Stewart and Joines, 1987]);

    (b) Adopting the 'I'm OK – You're OK' life position (Stewart and Joines, 1987);

    (c) Giving up unrealistic or unreasonable beliefs and attitudes, as well as disempowering frames and stories;

    (d) Dealing with your childhood history of (insecure) attachments to parents and others (Wallin, 2007)[153];

    (e) Developing a sound philosophy of life, including some kind of spiritual or connectionist system of thought; and

    (f) Practicing critical thinking skills (Bowell and Kemp, 2005)[154]; etc.
12. Getting a good **balance** (which is called '**pono'** in Hawaiian) of ***work, rest*** and ***play*** (approximately eight hours of each [8-8-8] per day);
13. Avoiding a sedentary lifestyle, which damages health. Get up and move around every fifteen to twenty minutes, for a minute or two each time. Or use a standing desk; stand for 45 minutes; and then lie on the floor and put your feet up a wall, above head height. Some theorists now argue that you should not sit for more than three hours per day!
14. Working for 45 or 50 minutes and resting for 10 to 15 minutes every hour, for a good balance of health and productivity.
15. Developing good ***time management*** skills;
16. Developing a concentration of power on the top priorities of your job, and working to optimum levels of skill and ability.
17. Managing your stress level at home and at work.
18. Developing your self-confidence.

~~~
~~~

Self-management: Summary

Self-management may be summarized as ***striving to be the best you can be,*** when you have fully developed your innate talents; ***to do the best you can do,*** as a social animal, connected to a community; and to ***have the rewards*** that accrue to your efforts in life.

If you try to run that sequence - in the previous paragraph - in the opposite direction, you will most likely be endlessly unhappy. That is to say, if you try to **have** some positive outcome, ***before*** you **do** the work, you will **fail**.

The major challenge is to ***take control of your mind***; to ***protect*** and ***support*** and ***develop*** your body-mind; and to ***discipline*** your daily activities.

A starting point

To get started on this long and detailed journey, do not overload yourself. Do not believe you have to do everything all at once.

Make sure you have a good diary system, and choose between one and three aims from above. Choose the ones that seem ***most important to you,*** right now!

Then choose between one and three goals from the second list.

Write your principles and goals in the front of your diary, and review them every day. This is required to get them into long-term, or relatively permanent, memory.

Make a commitment to work on those principles/goals until you have them working *pretty well automatically* in your life. (This could take days, weeks or months; so do not despair if it takes some considerable time!) It normally takes at least thirty days to get any new, *good habit* reasonably well established. Try writing out the advantages of these changes, to you, and the disadvantages of not making them. Then review those advantages and disadvantages every morning, to get really clear about them, and to memorize them.

Have a reward that you give yourself, such as *your* ***favourite*** *breakfast,* when you've reviewed your 'change agenda' in the front of your diary. And if you fail to review those principles and goals, you don't get your favourite breakfast, but rather your *least favourite* breakfast.

Also have a *penalty* in mind: If night-time arrives and you still have not reviewed your new principles and goals, then you take £2 (British pounds) or $5 (US dollars, or equivalent) and drop this money down the nearest drain! Or burn it, in the case of a $5 dollar bill!

(Make sure this is a real threat; as it will help to strengthen your resolve to make the habit changes you want to achieve! I've done my daily meditation and exercise almost every morning for years – [except when occasionally unwell, or I excused myself because of a tight deadline for some family event] - rather than throw four pounds [£2 for skipped meditation, and £2 for skipped exercise] down the drain. I have probably done my daily exercise about five or six days per week, for ninety-five percent of the past twenty-five years! [I have, of course, occasionally slipped back for a while; and then recommitted to this important activity]).

Those rewards and penalties should help to reinforce the new behaviour of reviewing your new principles and goals each morning; and doing something about implementing the principles and goals in your life.

However, remember, you may often slip back. Accept that that is normal. It is harder to establish a good habit than a bad habit. And it is easier to break a good habit than a bad habit. (The 'devil' has all the best tunes!)

When you slip back, do not beat yourself up. Pay the penalty; refrain from the reward; and **recommit** to the same principles and goals, and start again ***today!***

~~~

Thirty or sixty days into this process, you will almost certainly find that you have begun to be more self-disciplined about reviewing your principles and goals; and putting them into your daily life.

Once you have those first principles/aims/goals securely in your life, as routine habits, go back to the lists of principles and goals above, and choose another one, two or three of each to begin to work on. Add them to the front of your diary.

Review them every morning, with the same rewards and penalties in mind.
~~~

Keep going until you can no longer take any kind of action in the world to improve your life. Hopefully that will be a very long time in the future! If indeed that point can ever be reached by anybody!

~~~
~~~

Part 5: Conclusion

In Part 5 we will review the problem of the Bamboo Paradox, and relate it to western scientific research on the stress response. (See Chapter 17, below).

And then we will summarize the ground we have covered in the whole of this book - (in Chapter 18).

~~~
~~~

Chapter 17: Unravelling the Human-Bamboo Paradox

The problem with the *'bamboo bullshit'* which is broadcast by Extreme Stoics and Extreme Buddhists - and by *apologists* for the neoliberal exploiters who control the world economy and political system today - is that it ignores what we know *from science* about the limits of human endurance in the face of stress and strain.

Western scientific research on stress has shown us that there are three phases in the human stress response:

1. **Too little stress**: This means we are not being *challenged sufficiently* to arouse our body-brain-mind to *optimal activation*. Think of a fit and healthy person who can afford to retire from work, and who does not have any useful work to do from that day onwards. Or somebody who is forced into unemployment by local economic circumstances. Those two individuals will experience roughly the same amount of *mental distress* from being under-occupied, and underused by life.

2. **Optimal stress**, which is called *eustress*: As the level of stress rises, from too little, it moves through a phase called eustress, where our performance is enhanced, and we feel pressured, but not overly so. This is the phase when we experience 'flow', or 'being in the zone', or enjoying the challenge.

3. **'Stress'/Distress**: (What we normally call 'stress' really is 'too much stress', or *distress.*) *Stress,* in this sense, means we are being subjected to *too much pressure relative to our* ***coping capabilities*** *or capacities.*

The tipping point

Some stress is necessary to get us into action each day, and to keep us pursuing our goals. This kind and level of stress, mentioned above, is called "eustress", or benign stress. However, when stress rises above the level at which it motivates us, it starts to have a negative, over-loading effect. This type and level of stress, technically called "distress", causes us to malfunction and to become emotional strained, and inefficient or ineffective in our work. In normal, everyday language when we talk about stress we really mean "distress", or excessive stress. (This is illustrated in Figure 17.1, below).

Figure 17.1 is an illustration of *the Yerkes-Dodson law.* The Yerkes-Dodson law was created in 1908 by two psychologists: Robert Yerkes and John

Dodson[155]. The law states that *increasing physiological and/or mental arousal will improve performance (such as work performance) up to, but not beyond the point at which it becomes* ***excessive*** *for the person experiencing it.*

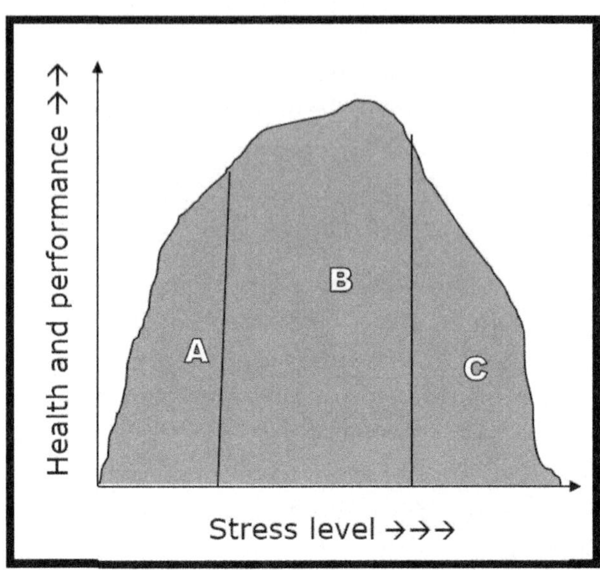

Figure 17.1: Showing the difference between Eustress (B) and distress (C)

Figure 17.1 maps stress along the bottom (X) axis; and health and performance along the vertical (Y) axis. This graph clearly shows that, initially (in section 'A' of the graph) increasing stress levels are associated with increases in health and performance. Then (in section B of the graph) we enter the area called eustress, in which optimum levels of stress ensure optimum levels of health and performance in the world, at home and at work. Then, as we pass beyond eustress (section B) into ***distress*** (section C) both health and performance levels decline rapidly, ending in anxiety, panic, burnout or collapse (sometimes called 'a nervous breakdown').

Exercise 1: *Can you now (or normally) identify the point at which your eustress tips over into distress?*

Can you reduce any pressures in your life so they do not promote distress?

How can you avoid this tipping point?

~~~
~~~

The problem is dis-stress

Once the level of stress in a person's life passes the critical (for them!) level, their work and relationship performances collapse pretty quickly, and they may even experience a 'breakdown'; or feel too ill to work. (This is corroborated by the Yerkes-Dodson Law: *Medium levels of arousal produce best performance levels on complicated tasks*). Anywhere beyond the mid-point in the scale (in Figure 17.1), a person may experience acute anxiety, panic attacks, angry or tearful outbursts, and uncomfortable physical sensations and phobias, such as agoraphobia or claustrophobia. And long-term exposure to acute stress leads to physical organ breakdown, and chronic diseases.

A case study of burnout

As I sat down to write this chapter this morning, I picked up a copy of the ***Sunday Times Magazine*** for November 17th 2019. Renata had told me there was an interesting article in this issue, about men at work.

I turned to page 47, to the 'Man Trouble' column, by Matt Rudd. And I read this piece which tells the story of Peter (not his real name) who was under excessive pressure in his new (recently promoted) job role.

His sleep was largely destroyed; he was working longer hours each day, and working his weekends - just like Shami, my client (mentioned in the Preface, above). Peter was having panic attacks about the impossibility of staying on top of his impossible job, and he'd become isolated from his family, because he worked such long hours.

Eventually, he had to see his medical doctor (GP [MD]), who signed him off work for a week. Peter initially thought this time off work would wreck his career. But he did take the time off, which might have saved his life - as he had considered suicide.

So, how did he resolve his problems?

1. It took eight months to do it, including four months off work, on sick leave.

2. He left his high-pressure job, and (eventually) got a job he loves, which makes him happy.

3. He had four months of counselling, on a weekly-visit basis, which gradually rebuilt his self-confidence.

4. He acknowledged that he was not 'superman', and not 'perfect'. "I do not have limitless energy", he concluded. "And there are problems that no amount of time spent in the office can solve". (That is to say, He is NOT a bamboo; and cannot ever hope to win in life by pretending to be a bamboo; or a lump of wood; or a stone. When we go down that route, we end up like a boiled frog!)

5. He now plays sports every week; spends quality time with his family and friends; does some manual labour regularly; and he has proper relaxation time at the weekend.

As Matt Rudd concluded: "The world does not end if you admit you are struggling. Don't wait until you hit rock bottom". (If only Shami had had this kind of advice!)

~~~

What does Peter's story tell us about the Bamboo Paradox? Initially, he was behaving as if he had an almost infinite capacity to adapt to pressure, like somebody who believes he is a bamboo – that he can withstand tropical storms that bring down lesser trees! However, his body broke down, and caused him to be rescued from this mess; and his counselling experience obviously taught him that he is not a bamboo; that he has very definite limits to his ability to endure punishing levels of work pressure. He gave up his unrealistic expectations of his own capacity to endure excessive stress, and he got a better life as a result. Once he realized that *he is not a* ***bamboo***, he could find an environment in which 'trees like him' could survive and thrive!

More on stress

The distinguishing characteristic of stress (meaning distress) is *heightened physiological arousal*, comprising:

- increased heartbeat,
~~~

- racing pulse,

- deep breathing,

- flushed face,

- butterflies in the stomach,

- accompanied by acute anger or fear, or a combination of the two.

The main direction of causation is shown in Figure 17.2, flowing from bottom to top of the process: beginning with an external stimulus.

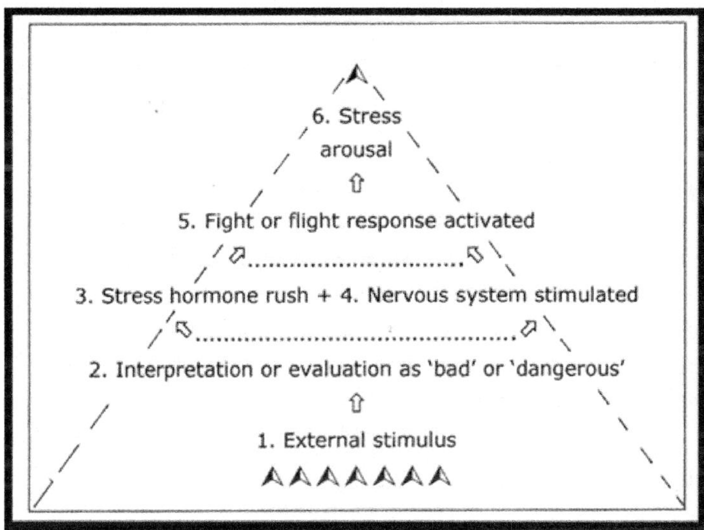

Figure 17.2: Stress Arousal

What Figure 17.2 shows is that, when you - (as a habit-based, body-brain-mind) - interpret or evaluate a particular noxious event as 'bad' or 'dangerous', or threatening in some way, that causes the release of stress hormones, and at the same time your nervous system is stimulated. This causes your innate 'fight or flight response' to kick in, and that is the point at which stress arousal generalizes.

Your digestive system closes down, and blood is sent to the large muscles of your body to support your response of fighting or fleeing. But since fighting or fleeing makes little sense in most 'stressful situations' in the modern world, you get stuck with a permanently (or semi-permanently) ***switched on*** stress response, which serves little or no useful function; and which is continuously wearing down your immune system.

Stress consists of the effects on you of your body going into "a fight or flight response", but then it either *cannot or does not fight or flee.* This is increasingly common in the modern world, because so many of the stressors we face are threats to our egos, or work and lifestyle pressures, and not physical threats, but the non-conscious part of our mind cannot tell the difference. (And you can't hit a bad phone call, or run away from a traffic jam, to quote Paul McKenna - and you often have to stay in very difficult conditions - like exploitative, impossible jobs - before you can find a way out).

Exercise 2: *Does this explanation help you to understand what is happening to you?*

If so, how?(Make a note in your journal or notebook for future reference).

Relating stress to the Bamboo Paradox

The bamboo paradox is this: While a human can be prone to avoid all pressure, and thus to be under-aroused; they can also be persuaded that they are like a bamboo, and then they begin to believe that they can withstand tropical storm-like pressures, and this does them in. Why? Because a human who thinks they can act like a bamboo, and survive any and all external pressures, will break when they get beyond the Eustress zone, described above.

Some simplistic gurus teach this guideline: "Be like a bamboo in order not to break".

But this is a *paradoxical instruction,* because, if you *were* like a bamboo you would not *need* to receive this instruction. But since you may well be naïve enough to *follow* this instruction, you may well end up *breaking your body-mind* by *trying to endure* a situation which is powerful enough to *crush* you!

So, what would be a good and helpful use of the Bamboo metaphor for being flexible?

Let us try a common sense approach. How about this as a guiding principle:

- "Bend under unavoidable pressure, to avoid braking. And then bounce back when conditions improve".

That might seem like a viable principle to guide your action, but it does not stand the test of being applied to the lives of Shami and Peter (in the case studies above)!

Shami bent under unavoidable pressure, but that pressure broke him. So now he seems incapable of bouncing back (alas, poor man!)

Peter tried to bend under unavoidable pressure, but his body-mind crumpled in time to get him out, before he could do irreversible damage to himself. He was able to bounce back (outside of the 'tropical storm') - with psychological and counselling help. And then he wisely chose to look for, and was fortunate to find, work that suits him, in which he can thrive.

Another common sense principle of guidance could be this:

- "Do not give in to pressures you could control. And do not waste energy fighting unnecessary battles".

This might not be good advice, because:

- Shami did not ***recognize*** that he was subjected to ***unreasonable pressure***; and neither did Peter (initially). Neither of them could see either *the necessity to control their work pressures*; or the *possibility* of controlling them. They both behaved like the famous frog in the pan of water, described by Charles Handy. But Peter jumped before he was cooked; and Shami failed to get out of the boiling water, until it was too late.

~~~

Stress is a complex problem. It does not have a single cause, as indicated above. It is multifaceted; that is to say, it has many aspects and is linked to many sources and influences. It is related to your *resources for coping* with major life changes, and your *perceptions* of environmental pressures. It's about what happens to you; how you respond to it; how you then feel and behave; and how you handle those feelings and behaviours.

Environmental factors that *trigger* perceptions that result in stress include: Financial problems; loss or disappointment; threat or danger; excessive competition or conflict; time pressure; noise and pollution; frustration; and many others.

You may also be affected by many life-change stressors, e.g. Moving house; death of your spouse or other loved one; divorce; marriage; redundancy; bullying at work; promotion; demotion; change of lifestyle; etc.
~~~

Your stress level also depends upon such factors as your diet, exercise, sleep, relaxation, and what you *tell yourself* about your life pressures, and so on. (What you tell yourself about those pressures in your life is called your "self-talk", or "philosophy of life"). And a lot depends upon your sense of *control*, which depends upon how you 'frame' your experiences, and the coping strategies you have in place.

Can you control your workload, your work environment, and/or your social life?

Are you confident and assertive enough to at least *try* to control your workload, your work environment, and/or your social life?

Are you *wise enough* to learn how to stoically accept those things which you clearly cannot control?

The more control you have, the less stress you feel, according to the Whitehall Studies, conducted by Michael Marmot, beginning in 1984.[156]

Exercise: *What factors in your life are contributing to your stress level?*

Can you change or control any of those factors? Yes/No?

If yes, which ones:

And what do you intend to do about it?

~~~

Control is an important factor

In the Whitehall Studies, it turned out that the more senior a civil servant was, the *less stress* they experienced, relative to the more junior civil servants in the studies! But *perception* also can play a part here, in that trying to control the uncontrollable is a greater source of stress than learning to accept
~~~

that some things are beyond your control. This idea was first developed by Epictetus, the first century CE[157] philosopher, who argued that

- *Freedom and happiness result from understanding one principle: there are "certain things you can control and certain things you can't". And it's only after you learn "...to distinguish between what you can and cannot control, and to only try to control what seems likely to be controllable, that inner harmony and outer effectiveness become possible".*[158]

~~~

Let's do a little 'thought experiment', to see how we can get beyond the 'common sense' view of people acting like a bamboo. Firstly, let me present a little graph of two people with different levels of endurance or resilience – Person 'A' and Person 'B':

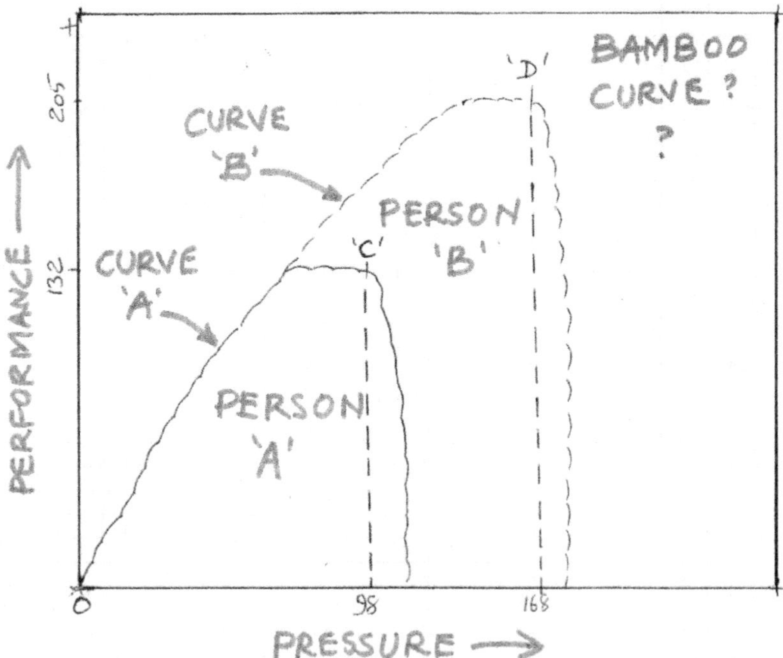

Person 'A' is represented by the small 'bell curve' (or inverted-U) on the left of this illustration; while Person 'B' is represented by the bigger bell curve which extends higher and to the right.
~~~

The horizontal axis of this graph measures 'pressure' - (For example, work over time) – and it extends from '0' to about 270 'units' of (arbitrarily defined) pressure. The further to the right the arrow moves, the more the pressure increases.

The vertical axis measures 'performance' – (e.g. work output) – and it extends from '0' to 240 'units' of (arbitrarily defined) performance.

What can we learn from this graph about Persons 'A' and 'B'?

Firstly: Person A achieved a performance output of 132 units; while Person 'B' achieved a much higher performance output of 205 units.

Secondly: Person 'A' burned out, and their performance collapsed when the pressure of work reached 98 units (measured along the horizontal axis), or point 'C' on their performance curve; while Person 'B' was able to continue working, and increasing their performance, until they reached point 'D' on their performance curve (at an output of 205 units), at which point the pressure rate of 168 broke them down, and they collapsed back to zero!

Thirdly: We can infer that Person 'B' has a higher level of tolerance of pressure than Person 'A'; but that ***they both have their breaking points***, under pressure.

Fourth: If we wanted to apply the common sense theory of 'living like a bamboo' to this graph, where would the bamboo bell curve be drawn? *Nowhere!* It cannot be incorporated into this graph. ***Why?***

(a) Because the only kind of pressure that applies to bamboo (in the common sense theory of resilience) is ***high wind*** and ***stormy conditions***. But in this graph we have been looking at the kind of ***common work pressures*** that apply to most humans to varying degrees. The burnout point occurs at a point where the individual has ***too much work to do***, and ***not enough time*** to do it, and their ***physical and mental (energy) resources*** are stretched to breaking point. ***But pressures of this type do not, ever, apply to a bamboo tree!***

(b) If this graph was changed to look at two individuals who are under economic pressure – too many debts and too little money to pay them – then this would be a common human stress situation; but again, this kind of pressure ***never applies to a bamboo tree***. And people do have their breaking points when it comes to too much economic pressure for too long a time – all other things being equal.

(c) We could look at the vertical axis of this graph, above, as measuring and illustrating work performance (e.g. work output per unit of time); or as resilience in the face of economic pressures; or as resilience in the face of social pressures, such as coping with an unfaithful partner; coping with marital conflict; coping with shaming experiences; and so on. But again, ***these kinds of performance criteria never, ever apply to a bamboo tree!*** But they often apply to a human being; and they often cause a breakdown in human beings.

Conclusion: Humans and bamboos cannot be mapped onto the same kind of graph. Humans and bamboos ***should never be equated or compared***. Humans and bamboos have very different qualities, and very different lives. Human resilience is ***bio-psycho-social***; while bamboo resilience is ***bio-mechanical*** or ***bio-dynamic***.

What does it mean, when I say that human resilience is biopsychosocial?

I mean that it depends upon the known or inferable *ability* of a human body (the 'bio' component) to *withstand stress and strain*. (And this depends upon the absolute strength and flexibility of the human body, as such. And also on what the person does in terms of diet, exercise, sleep, relaxation, and so on).

Human resilience also depends upon the strength of the mind (the 'psycho' component). (And this depends upon mental stresses and strains in the past and in the present; and on the emotional intelligence of the individual; and on their commitment and determination; and a few other factors; including, again, diet, exercise, sleep, relaxation, and supportive relationships, etc.)

And human resilience also depends upon *social messages* (the first part of the 'social component') about what to try to endure, and how to try to endure it. (And this aspect is flexible, and can be distorted by dark forces that want to extract *more profit* from workers, and *pay them less*, and *treat them worse*, etc.) And the second social component is how well connected the individual is to supportive others.

~~~
~~~

Some sources of 'Bamboo bullshit'

Extreme Stoicism and REBT

In this book, I have indicated that Extreme Stoicism is a source of unrealistic expectations of human durability - and that is what I am now calling 'bamboo bullshit'; the crazy idea that a person can decide to withstand any pressure whatsoever that comes their way!

And extreme Stoicism found its way into Rational Emotive Behaviour Therapy (REBT), because Dr Albert Ellis - who created REBT - had learned as a child that nobody cared about him, and so he did not care about himself. He treated himself like a lump of wood, which could endure any kind of suffering, and he tried to teach that ideology to the world. Of course, this played right into the hands of the Chicago School of Economics, which was promulgating a philosophy of unleashing *unrestrained market forces*, in a new economic system (neoliberalism) in which dog would eat dog, and the devil would take the hindmost!

REBT tries to teach the world *infinite flexibility* in the face of adversity. The main manifestations of this ideology in REBT is the concept of High Frustration Tolerance; which is often expressed like this: "I certainly ***can stand*** this adversity". And it is assumed we can withstand anything up to, but not including, our own death.

But that's what Shami must have thought/felt/concluded. He had certainly been introduced to REBT before he met me; and when he met me, I was still teaching the importance of High Frustration Tolerance. To my shame, I had allowed myself to be influenced by Dr Tom Miller, who had elaborated Dr Albert Ellis's system of REBT into a seminar format, in which he taught this principle:

"You can stand anything, up to, but not including, your own death".

What this principle does not consider is this:

Should you - being sensible and self-interested - try to withstand ***anything; absolutely anything***; that life throws at you?

Peter's answer was probably, initially: "Yes, I have to!" But his body, and his non-conscious mind, had other plans; and they quit on him. Collapsed under the pressure. And that saved him from suffering worse problems later one, including the possibility of suicide, or chronic disease.

Shami probably also thought he should persist in working twelve hour days, and getting just a few hours' sleep each night. But his body eventually quit on him, and has not recovered to this day, more than eight years later.

~~~

Neoliberal ideology and the 24/7 world

There is a huge trend among modern employers to treat their employees like ***flexible, bamboo slaves***; who have no need for security of employment; no need for rest and recuperation (after a long day's work); no need for sick pay; holiday pay; an *endless capacity* to endure over-work; and so on. (The same employers pay themselves extremely well; don't work particularly hard; and feather-bed themselves against the chill winds of adversity! And if they lose their money on the stock market, they run to the government for a handout!) So it is important that every employee and their trade union representatives take whatever action they can to ***stop this dehumanizing rot***, which is adding to the public health crisis engulfing the Western world today. People need work, rest and play, in about equal measure. (And, in order to thrive, we all need to live in a more equal society than the US or UK. Equality is better for everybody)[159].

There was a time when governments held employers to account for a 'duty of care' for their employees' welfare. That no longer applies in practice, and work conditions in the western world are now appalling. As an illustration, take the example of the British government's decision to ask former employees of the National Health Service (NHS) to come out of retirement to help out with the current (March 2020) coronavirus crisis. The Guardian newspaper reported, on 5th March that "Retired NHS staff (are) reluctant to return". In that article, Matthew Weaver, reporting on a survey of former NHS staff, wrote: "Many said they did not want to return to a working environment where they suffered stress, bullying, burnout and breakdowns"[160].

And similar stories could equally be collected from across the British economy (including the education sector).

The materialist madness of the neoliberal world – which was unleashed on all of us by Margaret Thatcher and Ronald Reagan, (who followed the
~~~

ideologues of the Chicago School of Economics[5]) - combined with the endless appetite of Hedonic Adaptation - leads individuals to treat themselves as *flexible bamboo machines,* in search of more and more material possessions – or just to make ends meet in a low pay economy. And this is exacerbated by the high tech revolution which has given us the madness of the 24 hour city; the 24/7 internet; and all night TV; combined with 24 hour email services, which contain work emails that demand to be answered at all times of day and night!

A YouGov study from 2018 shows that only 6% of people in the UK work a traditional five-day, nine-to-five week. And more than five million workers regularly work unpaid overtime. (Williams, 2020)[161].

By contrast with this materialist 24/7 madness, it is time to recognize the spiritual beauty of time spent just being. Just sitting quietly doing nothing. Or simply walking in nature. Enjoying the gift of the present moment. And just being a human being, and not a mad, greedy, or *monumentally insecure human-bamboo-nut!*

Practical solutions to the problem of stress/distress

The effects of stress

Stress has negative effects on you in three respects:

(a) It affects your emotional state and your thinking; especially by depressing your mood, and disorganising your thinking.

(b) It affects your behaviour and your bodily sensations; and:

[5] The Chicago School is described as 'a neoclassical economic school of thought' which emerged in the twentieth century, based on the theory of supply and demand. It originated at the University of Chicago in the 1930s. The principal arguments of the Chicago School are that free markets are the best means to allocate resources in an economy; and that there should be little to no government intervention. These theorists believed that this is best for economic prosperity; even though they presided over the collapse of Wall Street in 1929, followed by ten years of stagnation. They also ignore the negative effects of the free market and growing inequality upon the quality of life for everybody. Life is worse for almost everybody under the Thatcher-Reagan reforms, based on Chicago School dogma.

(c) It affects your physical health adversely, especially your heart and your arteries. (Cortisol increases; sex hormones are reduced; and plaque is released into the arteries, causing damage called sclerosis).

~~~

Exercise 3: *In which of these three ways are you affected by your stress problem, (a), (b) and/or (c)?*

~~~

Exercise 4: *More work on identifying the stressors in your life:*

It is important to understand how stress affects you personally. Here is a strategy that you can use, which will take several hours, preferably over a period of days:

(a) Picture in detail what happens to you when you are under major stress. (What happens to your breathing, and your heart rate? Does your mouth become dry, and do your hands shake? Consider your mood and thinking, as well as your behaviour and bodily sensations). Write down your answers in the form of a list, in a journal or stress diary.

(b) Divide your life into major areas, such as (i) Work; (ii) Home; (iii) Family; (iv) Leisure; (v) Holidays, etc.

(c) Identify events or experiences which cause you to have feelings of stress on a typical day in each of these areas: work, home, family, leisure, holidays, etc.

(d) Produce a blank stress map for each of the major areas of your life (listed in (b) above).

Record the top six or eight events or activators, which are currently problems for you, in each area of your life.

(Figure 17.3 below is an example of one such stress map for a specific area of your life. Write the area of your life under consideration in the centre of the stress map).

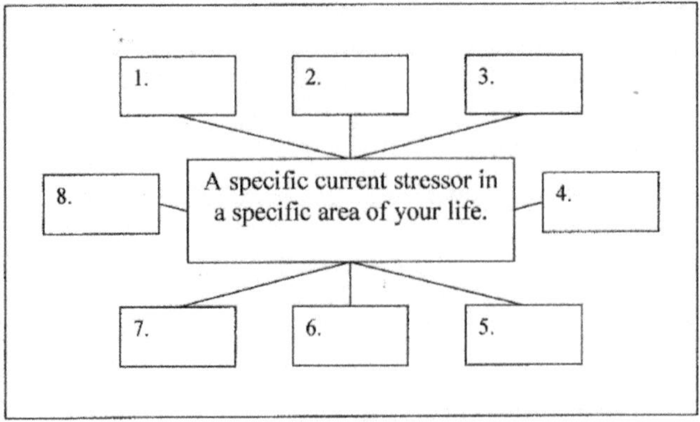

Figure 17.3: Sample stress map...

(e) Reproduce Figure 17.3 on an A4 (or Letter size) sheet of paper, and fill in boxes 1 to 8 with some contributory stressors to this one area of your life. Then take a second stress map, and fill in the contributory factors for the next area of your life. And continue until you have covered all the key areas of your life. The 'areas' of your life might include: Work; Home life; Finances; Career plans; and so on.

When you have listed six or eight contributory factors for each stress activator, in each of the key areas of your life, give each contributory factor a score between 1 and 10,

where 10 = a major stressor;

5 = moderate stress;

and 1 = hardly any problem at all.

(f) Finally, using Figure 17.4 below, list each contributory factor to your stress level in the centre of a stress map matrix, and try to identify three or four actions you can take to cope better with that stressor.

(See matrix below):

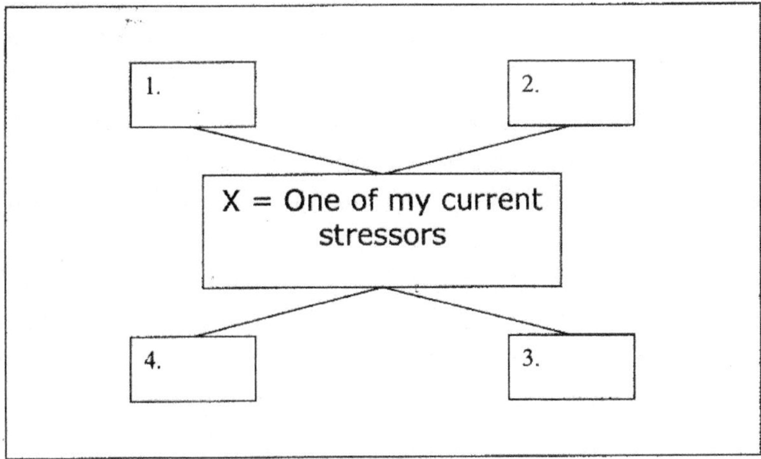

Figure 17.4: Actions I can take to cope with my stressors (one at a time)

Ask yourself these questions: *What can I do about 'X' (in the centre of the illustration, above)? What actions can I take?*

List three or four potential solutions to each of your current stressors.

Once you have a reasonable map of your stressors, you will be in a position to discuss your stress problems with a counsellor, a therapist, your GP (MD), or an alternative therapist; or a good friend. You will also have more control over your stressors once you know what they are. (You could also try writing about one of your stressful situations or events for ten or fifteen minutes every day. This will improve your immune response, and help you to cope with your stressors better).

~~~

How to build resilience

In the Preface to my book critiquing REBT, I wrote about resilience in the following terms:

1. Some people are not sufficiently resilient in the face of life's difficulties. This works against them, because they are crushed by particularly difficult experiences, instead of soldiering on through their difficulties, and coming out the other side.
~~~

Because of this problem of low resilience, it is important that counsellors and therapists teach themselves *how to promote resilient mental attitudes* in their un-resilient clients.

2. The main antidote to low frustration tolerance (LFT), or poor resilience, that was taught by Albert Ellis is the idea that, "I certainly *can stand* (difficult situations)", and he would have cited examples from the lives of the Stoics, including the willingness of Socrates to die for his principles; or Zeno emerging from his shipwreck and soldiering on; or Albert Ellis' own general position – when confronted by fearful situations – of affirming, "If I die, I die!"

But most people are not likely to be easily persuaded to adopt such an extreme Stoic or Buddhist principle. (Interestingly enough, the statement, '*If I die, I die*', is an almost verbatim copy of a statement from the ***Book of Ruth***, which Ellis would have encountered in his Orthodox Jewish Saturday School in New York, when he was a youngish child.)

3. What Ellis would never have taught to his therapy clients, which we in E-CENT teach, is this: *Physical exercise increases resilience*: (Ratey and Hagerman, 2009)[162]. Or this: "Sleep is such a powerful source of resilience...": (Huffington, 2017)[163]. (And I should have added that diet/ nutrition, relaxation, meditation, and walking in nature also increase the resilience of the individual).

In my critique of REBT, I suggested that "...perhaps counsellors and therapists should develop a good understanding of modern research on *resilience,* to pass on to their clients, instead of relying upon a few random quotations from Stoic philosophers". And, I could have added, Buddhist philosophers, and Jewish philosophers.

The concept of Low Frustration Tolerance – from REBT - is too *simplistic,* and *extreme,* to be of interest to most counsellors or their clients. The concept of ***resilience*** is a much more rounded concept, which is developed through a broad range of strategies, and not just telling myself, in the face of any difficulty: "I ***can*** stand this!" (Or "I must act like a bamboo tree, and bend in this force nine gale!")

For example: Southwick and Charney (2012)[164] – two medical doctors – suggest that a useful curriculum for the development of greater resilience would include:

- Developing optimism (and overcoming learned pessimism);

- Facing up to our fears (or being courageous);

- Developing a moral compass (or learning to always do what is the *right* thing, rather than what is opportunistically advantageous);

- Developing a spiritual, faith, or community connection that is bigger than the self;

- Connecting to others for social support;

- Finding and following resilient role models (but not Extreme Stoics!);

- Practicing regular physical exercise;

- Working on brain-mind fitness, including mindfulness and cognitive training (but they overlooked the impact of food and gut flora on the brain-mind, so that needs to be considered also);

- Developing flexibility in our thinking-feeling-behaviour (including acceptance and reappraisal);

- Focusing on the meaning of your life, the purpose of your life, and on desired areas of personal growth.

~~~

A more balanced way of thinking about taking care of yourself in a challenging world would involve both:

- developing supportive 'coping resources' (including adequate sleep, exercise, relaxation and nutrition);

- and reducing the pressures under which you operate (including over-working, under-sleeping, and eating the wrong foods.

Table 17.1 below list a range of things you could focus upon to bring more balance to your life.

Perhaps a consideration of those ideas could take us beyond *the 'wishful thinking' about impossible goals* set by Zeno, Marcus Aurelius and Epictetus - (and Albert Ellis, and some other CBT theorists).

It should also take us beyond the silly concept of "acting like a bamboo!"

But it is going to take a lot of hard work to roll back the mad, 24/7 culture of deregulated markets;
~~~

round the clock mobile technology;

no weekends,

and endless working days – with work emails stressing people well into the night;

plus the need to correct the "market based mentality of the self" (or the self as a marketized-corporate-commodity! [See Williams, 2020]).

In the meantime, we will have to keep ourselves realistically strong (and wise), using the strategies described throughout this book.

Reduce the pressures you can control	**Increase areas of self-support and resilience building**
• Make sure your job is right for you • Don't take work home with you • Switch off work emails at 5.00pm (or the end of your shift); and avoid the Internet during the evening • Reduce work commitments and unnecessary tasks • Say 'No' to unhelpful pressures and new tasks • Keep your affairs well organized; including using a good time management system • Prioritize tasks, and do the *vital few*,' and not the *trivial many* • Keep your expectations in line with reality • Abandon perfectionistic tendencies • Delegate and/or defer anything that is not vital for you to do • Ask for help and support as appropriate • Always pad your travelling time, to avoid the sense of time pressure	• Read a good book on stress management* • Learn how to be an assertive communicator** • Monitor your stress reactions • Practice PMR to relax • Manage your relationships at home to ensure love and support • Manage your health by *preventing illnesses* instead of aiming to cure them • Work on your self-confidence, and your personality adaptations*** • Manage your diet, exercise and sleep well; and keep your life in balance (8-8-8) • Low to no alcohol and caffeine • Avoid smoking and recreational drugs. (Also pharmaceutical drugs!) • Watch comedy films, and avoid the news and current affairs • Develop your sense of humour • Avoid dwelling on negative thoughts about your life

Table 17.1: Managing your stress levels

* Byrne, J. (2012) *Chill Out: How to control your stress level, and have a happier life*. Hebden Bridge: The Institute for E-CENT Publications.

** See Appendices B1, B2, C and D of this book: Byrne, J. (2020) *How to Resolve Conflict and Unhappiness*. Hebden Bridge: The Institute for E-CENT Publications.

*** See: Byrne, J. (in press) *The Confidence to be Yourself: Realistic self-acceptance*. Hebden Bridge: The Institute for E-CENT Publications.

Reflections on Chapter 17

Have you completed Exercises 1 to 4 above? Yes/No?

(If not, when, if at all, do you intend to do so?)

These exercises are designed to help you to apply the theory of stress arousal to your own stress problems.

What have you learned from this chapter?

Do you plan to write this up in your journal or stress diary? Yes/No?

If 'yes', then when will you do that?

How can you increase your resilience without becoming a 'bamboo nut'? (Which aspects of your lifestyle, for example, should you work at changing?)

~~~
~~~

Chapter 18: Conclusion

I began this book by looking at a number of instances of individuals advocating the idea that we should try to behave like a bamboo plant in the face of the stresses and strains of everyday life in the cruel world of neoliberal capitalist exploitation. But bamboo is only 'resilient' in relation to *one* element - high wind. Human beings have to be resilient in relation to a whole host of bio-psycho-social stresses and strains, derived from the political-economic-social systems in which they live.

So, just because *flexibility* is the key for bamboo survival, that does not mean that *flexibility* (and *nothing but* flexibility) is the way for humans to be resilient in the face of social, economic, personal and political pressures. (Sometimes our survival is best served by ***fighting back*** against an unfair political or economic system; or ***leaving*** the scene which is stressing us!)

I then went on to explore some of the helpful aspects of Moderate Stoic philosophy, in Part 1 of this book.

In Part 2, I explored the problem of Extreme Stoicism, which is a misleading philosophy of life, which cannot help us to know our rights; and the limits of our endurance. It also encourages us to accept the madness of the 24/7 culture, with no proper weekend rest; and no proper sleep period at night; and no security of employment.

Then, in Part 3, I outlined my system of re-framing current problems, so that they will show up as less stressful, and help us to cope (provided we are also taking good care of our bodies). This system of re-framing includes elements of moderate Buddhism and moderate Stoicism, plus one Native American insight.

Part 4 reviews the key elements of an effective approach to managing your body-brain-mind - in its physical aspect. This includes considerations of our needs for nutritious foods; adequate sleep; physical exercise; and effective muscle relaxation (as a source of rest and energy recovery). Plus a range of self-management skills and strategies.

In Part 5, Chapter 17, I returned to a consideration of the Bamboo Paradox, and contrasted 'bamboo bullshit' against some practical stress-management strategies; or how to really build resilience.

If you are a human, then *you are **not** a bamboo.*

If you try to behave like a bamboo, then you are making a big mistake.

Bamboo has nothing to teach us about dealing with bent politicians; a cruel economic system; gross inequality; or unfairness or injustice.

Bamboo has nothing to teach us about the science of stress management, as outlined in Chapter 17.

And bamboo has nothing to say about the nature of a healthy diet; adequate sleep; relaxation; or how to exercise for health and happiness. Bamboo is in that sense pretty dumb.

The only things dumber than bamboo are those people who tell you,

"You have to act like you're a bamboo!"

(And those people who listen to them!)

This book has outlined a whole range of ways in which a human can develop their optimum strength and resilience for coping with the kind of world in which we humans live - which is very different from the world of vegetables, like bamboo.

- Keep yourself strong, physically and mentally!

- Treat yourself well, using the concept of *pono*, or *balance*; eight hours work; eight hours reset; and eight hours play each day.

- Make sure you manage your diet, exercise, relaxation and sleep for optimum health and vitality.

And do what you can, with what you have, where you are, to change the political and economic world into a better place for happy humans to live!

~~~
~~~

References

Akbaraly T.N., Brunner, E.J., Ferrie, J.E., et al. (2009) 'Dietary pattern and depressive symptoms in middle age'. *The British Journal of Psychiatry, 2009 Nov;195(5):* 408-413. doi: 10.1192/bjp.bp.108.058925.

Anwar, Y. (2013) 'Tired and edgy? Sleep deprivation boosts anticipatory anxiety'. Berkeley News. Online: https://news.berkeley.edu/ 2013/ 06/ 25/ anticipate-the-worst/

Asp, K. (2015) 'Lack of Sleep and Depression: Causes and Treatment Options'. The AAST blog: https://www.aastweb .org/blog /the-relationships-between-lack-of-sleep-and-depression. Accessed: 22nd January 2018.

Aurelius, M. (1992). *Meditations.* Trans. by A.S.L. Farquharson. London: Everyman's Library.

Babcock, D.C. (2003) 'The little duck'. Quoted in Josh Baran (ed) *365 Nirvana Here and Now: Living every moment in enlightenment.* London: Element. Page 157.

Baggini, J. and Strangroom, J. (Eds) (2007) *What More Philosophers Think.* London: Continuum.

Ballantyne, C. (2007) 'Fact or Fiction? Vitamin Supplements Improve Your Health'. *Scientific American* (Online): http://www.scientificamerican.com/ article/ fact- or-fiction-vitamin-supplements-improve-health/May 17, 2007. Accessed 26th April 2016.

Bangalore, N.G., and Varambally, S. (2012) Yoga therapy for schizophrenia. *International Journal of Yoga* 2012; **5**(2):85-91. [PUBMED: 22869990]

Baran, J. (ed) (2003) *365 Nirvana: Here and now.* London: HarperCollins/ Element.

Barber, L.K. (2010) 'Sleep consistency and sufficiency: are both necessary for less psychological strain?' Stress & Health blog. Wiley Online Library. https://onlinelibrary.wiley.com/doi/abs/10.1002/smi.1292

Bargh, J.A. and Chartrand, T.L. (1999) 'The unbearable automaticity of being'. *American Psychologist, 54(7):* 462-479.

Behere, R.V, Arasappa, R., Jagannathan, A, et al. (2011). Effect of yoga therapy on facial emotion recognition deficits, symptoms and functioning in patients with schizophrenia. *Acta Psychiatrica Scandinavia, Vol 123 (2);* pp: 147 -53

Boseley, S. (2018) Half of all food bought in UK is ultra-processed. *The Guardian*. Saturday 3rd February 2018. Issue No. 53,323.

Bowell, T. and Kemp, G. (2005) *Critical Thinking: a concise guide.* Second edition. London: Routledge.

Bowlby, J. (2005) *The Making and Breaking of Affectional Bonds.* London: Routledge Classics.

Bretherton, I. (1992) The Origins of Attachment Theory: John Bowlby and Mary Ainsworth. *Developmental Psychology 28:* 759.

Briffa, J. (2005) 'High Anxiety', *Observer Magazine,* 19th June 2005, page 61.

Broderick, J., Knowles, A, Chadwick, J, and Vancampfort D. (2015) 'Yoga versus standard care for schizophrenia'. *Cochrane Database of Systematic Reviews 2015, Issue 10.* Art. No.: CD010554.

Brogan, K. (2016) *A mind of your own: The truth about depression and how women can heal their bodies to reclaim their lives.* London: Thorsons.

Bryant, C.W. (2010) 'Does running fight depression?' Dated 14th July 2010. HowStuffWorks.com. Available online: http://adventure.howstuffworks.com/outdoor-activities/running/health/running-fight-depression.htm. Accessed 16th June 2016.

Byrne, J. (2002) 'Free will and determinism: Am I completely determined by my genes and my environment?' Hebden Bridge: ABC Publications. Available online: http://free-will-assignment.blogspot.com/

Byrne, J. (2010) Fairness, Justice and Morality Issues in REBT and E-CENT. E-CENT Paper No.2(b). Hebden Bridge: The Institute for E-CENT.

Byrne, J. (2011/2013) 'The Innate Good and Bad Aspects of all Human Beings (the Good and Bad Wolf states)'. E-CENT Paper No. 25. Hebden Bridge: The Institute for E-CENT Publications. Available online: https://ecent-institute.org/e-cent-articles-and-papers/

Byrne, J. (2013) *A Wounded Psychotherapist: Albert Ellis's Childhood, and the strengths and limitations of REBT/CBT*. Hebden Bridge: The Institute for CENT Publications/ CreateSpace. Currently out of print.

Byrne, J. (2016) *Holistic Counselling in Practice: An introduction to the theory and practice of Emotive-Cognitive Embodied-Narrative Therapy*. Hebden Bridge. The Institute for E-CENT Publications.

Byrne, J.W. (2018a) *Lifestyle Counselling and Coaching of the Whole Person: Or how to integrate nutritional insights, physical exercise and sleep coaching into talk therapy*. Hebden Bridge: The Institute for E-CENT Publications.

Byrne, J. (2018b) *Daniel O'Beeve's Amazing Journey: From traumatic origins to transcendent love*. Hebden Bridge: The Institute for E-CENT Publications.

Byrne, J. (2018c) *How to Write a New Life for Yourself: Narrative therapy and the writing solution*. Hebden Bridge: The Institute for E-CENT Publications.)

Byrne, J. (2019a) *A Major Critique of REBT: Revealing the many errors in the foundations of Rational Emotive Behaviour Therapy*. Hebden Bridge: The Institute for E-CENT Publications.

Byrne, J. (2019b) *Facing and Defeating your Emotional Dragons: How to process old traumas, and eliminate undigested pain from your past experience*. Hebden Bridge: The Institute for E-CENT Publications.

Byrne, J.W. (2019c) *Holistic Counselling in Practice: An introduction to the theory and practice of Emotive-Cognitive Embodied-Narrative Therapy. Updated edition (2)*. Hebden Bridge: The Institute for E-CENT Publications.

Calm-Clinic (2018) 'How Sleep Debt Causes Serious Anxiety'. Online blog: https://www.calmclinic.com/anxiety/causes/sleep-debt. Accessed: 25th January 2018.

Cameron, J. (1994) *The Artist's Way: a spiritual path to higher creativity*. London: Souvenir Press.

Campbell, T.C. and Campbell, T.M. (2006) *The China Study: The most comprehensive study of nutrition ever conducted and the startling implications for diet, weight loss and long-term health*. Dallas, TX: Benbella Books.

Cardwell, M. (2000) *The Complete A-Z Psychology Handbook*. Second edition. London: Hodder and Stoughton.

Carnegie, D. (1998) *How to Stop Worrying and Start Living.* Berkshire: Random House Books.

Chaitow, L. (2003) *Candida Albicans: The non-drug approach to the treatment of Candida infection*. London: Thorsons.

Cummins, C. (2007) How to Start a Restorative Yoga Practice. *Yoga Journal,* Aug 28, 2007. Available online: http://www.yogajournal.com/article/beginners/restorative-yoga/. Accessed: 17th June 2016.

Deans, E. (2018) Magnesium for Depression: A controlled study of magnesium shows clinically significant improvement. Psychology Today Blog: https://www.psychologytoday.com/ blog/ evolutionary-psychiatry/ 201801/ magnesium-depression. Accessed: 2nd March 2018.

De Bono, E. (1995) *Teach Yourself to Think.* London: Viking/Penguin.

Duhigg, C. (2013) *The Power of Habit: Why we do what we do and how to change.* London: Random House.

Duraiswamy, G., Thirthalli, J, Nagendra, H.R., et al. (2007). 'Yoga therapy as an add-on treatment in the management of patients with schizophrenia – A randomized controlled trial'. *Acta Psychiatrica Scandinavia, 116 (3);* pp: 226-32

Edlund, M. (2011) *The Power of Rest: Why Sleep alone is not enough.* New York: Harper Collins.

Elliott, A.F. (2014) 'Can an Atkins-style diet really fight depression? Research suggests low-carb, high fat foods can drastically improve mental health'. Available online: http://www.dailymail.co.uk/femail/article-2590880/. Down -loaded: 2nd October 2017.

Ellis, A. (1958). Rational Psychotherapy, *Journal of General Psychology,* 59, 35-49.

Ellis A. (1962). *Reason and Emotion in Psychotherapy,* New York, Carol Publishing.

Ellis, A. (1994). *Reason and Emotion in Psychotherapy: revised and updated,* New York, Carol Publishing Group.

Enders, G. (2015) *Gut: The inside story of our body's most under-rated organ.* London: Scribe Publications.

Epictetus (1991) *Enchiridion.* Trans. by George Long. New York: Prometheus Books.

Espie, C. (2018) 'Sleep Basics: Introduction'. Online: https://www.sleepio .com/articles/sleep-basics/sleep-basics-intro/. Accessed: 25th January 2018.

Evans, B. and Julian Reid (2013) 'Dangerously exposed: The life and death of the resilient subject'. *Resilience, Vol. 1, No. 2,* Pages 83-98. Available online: http://www. tandfonline.com/doi/pdf/ 10.1080/ 21693293. 2013. 770703

Friday Editor (2017) 'What are essential fatty acids?' The Fit Day Blog. Available online at: http://www.fitday.com/fitness-articles/ nutrition/ fats/what-are-essential-fatty-acids.html.

Goleman, D. (1996) *Emotional Intelligence: why it can matter more than IQ.* London: Bloomsbury.

Gordon, A.M. (2013) 'Up all night: the effects of sleep loss on mood. Research shows just one bad night of sleep can put a damper on your mood'. *Psychology Today Online.* August 15th 2013. Available here: https://www.psychologytoday.com/ blog/ between-you-and-me/ 201308/all-night-the-effects-sleep-loss-mood. Accessed: 20th January 2018.

Griffin, J. and Tyrrell, I. (2003) *Human Givens: A new approach to emotional health and clear thinking.* Chalvington, East Sussex: HG Publishing.

Hellmich, N. (2013) 'The best preventative medicine? Exercise'. Online: dailycomet.com. Accessed: 18th June 2016

Herbert, W. (2011) 'The midnight ride effect: How imagining a different past increases our appreciation for the present'. *Scientific American Mind,* Jan/Feb, 2011. Pages 66-67.

Hill, D. (2015) *Affect Regulation Theory: A clinical model.* London: W.W. Norton and Company.

Holford, P. (2010) *Optimum Nutrition for the mind.* London: Piatkus.

Howatson, G., Bell, P.G, Tallent, J, et al. (2012) 'Effect of tart cherry juice (Prunus cerasus) on melatonin levels and enhanced sleep quality'. *European Journal of Nutrition. 2012 Dec;51(8)*: 909-16. doi: 10.1007/s00394-011-0263-7. Epub 2011 Oct 30.

Hubbard, B. (2018) 'Not sleeping? Write a to-do list before you go to bed'. *What Doctors Don't Tell You. January 2018.* News.

Irvine, W.B. (2009) *A Guide to the Good Life: The ancient art of Stoic joy*. Oxford: Oxford University Press.

Ismail, N., Taha, W., and Elgzar, I. (2018) The effect of Progressive muscle relaxation on post-caesarean section pain, quality of sleep and physical activities limitation (2018)International Journal of studies in Nursing. Vol 3, No.3 (2018)ISSN (online) DOI: https://doi.org/10.20849/ijsn.v3i3.461

Jacobs, G. (1994) *Candida Albicans: A user's guide to treatment and recovery.* London: Optima.

Jacobson, E. (1963) *Tension Control for Businessmen.* CT. USA: Martino Publishing. (Formerly published by McGraw-Hill Book Co. Inc. New York City. 1963).

Jacobson, E. (1976) *You must Relax: Practical Methods for Reducing the Tensions of Modern Living*. London: Unwin Paperbacks.

Jahnke R. (2002) *The Healing Promise of Qi: Creating Extraordinary Wellness through Qigong and Tai Chi.* Chicago, IL: Contemporary Books.

Jahnke, R. Larkey, L. Rogers, C. Etnier, J. and Lin, F. (2012) A Comprehensive Review of Health Benefits of Qigong and Tai Chi. *American Journal of Health Promotion, Jul-Aug; Vol.24 (6),* Pages e1-e25.

Joines, V. and Stewart, I. (2002) *Personality Adaptations: A new guide to human understanding in psychotherapy and counselling.* Nottingham: Lifespace Publishing.

Just Swim (2016) 'How swimming improves mental health'. An online blog: http://www.swimming.org/justswim/swimming-improves-mental-health/

Koffler, J. (2015) Donald Trump's 16 Biggest Business Failures and Successes. Time Magazine, online: https://time.com/3988970/donald-trump-business/

Kogan, N. (2018) 'The magic of a good night's sleep: Because an exhausted person is never a happy person'. *Happier.* Online: https://www.happier .com/blog/the-magic-of-sleep. Accessed: 25th January 2018.

Koo, M. (2008) It's a wonderful life: Mentally subtracting positive events improves people's affective state, contrary to their affective forecasts. *Journal of Personality and Social Psychology, Vol 95, No.5,* Pages 1217-1224.

Korn, L. (2016). *Nutrition Essentials for Mental Health: A complete guide to the food-mood connection*. New York: W. W. Norton & Company.

Larkey, L., Jahnke, R, Etnier, J, and Gonzalez J. (2009) 'Meditative movement as a category of exercise: Implications for research'. *Journal of Physical Activity & Health. 2009*; Vol.6: Pages 230–238.

Linder, K. and Svardsudd, K. (2006) Qigong has a relieving effect on stress. *Lakartidningen.* (A Swedish Medical Journal) *2006; Vol.103 (24-25):* Pages 1942-1945.

Lopresti, A.L., Hood, S.D, & Drummond, P.D. (2013) 'A review of lifestyle factors that contribute to important pathways associated with major depression: Diet, sleep and exercise'. *Journal of Affective Disorders, Vol.148(1),* Pages 12-27.

Maas, J. (2007) *Sleep Power*. London: HarperCollins.

Marmot, M.G., Davey Smith, G., Stansfeld, S., et al. (1991) 'Health inequalities among British civil servants; The Whitehall II Study'. *The Lancet, 337:* 1387-1393

Mauss, I.B, and Allison S. Troy & Monique K. LeBourgeois (2013) 'Poorer sleep quality is associated with lower emotion-regulation ability in a laboratory paradigm'. *Cognition and Emotion 27 (3):*567-576 (2013)

Meracou, K., Tsoukas, K., Stavrinos, G., et.al. (2019) 'The effect of PMR on emotional competence, depression-anxiety-stress, and sense of coherence, health-related quality of life, and well-being of unemployed people in Greece: An Intervention study'. *EXPLORE, Volume 15, Issue 1,* January–February 2019: Pages 38-46. https://doi.org/10.1016/j.explore.2018.08.001

McGuiness, M. (2013) Poetry: 'Sleep that knits up the ravell'd sleave of care'. Poems and poetry blog. Available online: http://www.mark mcguinness .com/ index.php/ Macbeth-sleep/. Accessed: 22nd January 2018.

Medina, J. (2015) How Yoga is Similar to Existing Mental Health Therapies. Source: Psych Central website: http://psychcentral.com/lib/how-yoga-is-similar-to-existing-therapies/. Accessed: May 2016.

Mozes, A. (2015) 'The Surprising Link Between Carbs and Depression'. Online health blog. Available: http://www.health.com/depression/could-too-many-refined-carbs-make-you-depressed. Accessed: June 2016.

My-Sahana (2012) 'Common Causes for Anger Management Issues'. MySahana blog post. Online: http://mysahana.org/2012/02/common-causes-for-anger-manage-ment-issues/. Accessed: 22nd January 2018.

Nauert, R. (2018) 'Sleep Loss Increases Anxiety – Especially Among Worriers'. PsychCentral blog post. 8th August 2018: Available online: https://psychcentral.com/news/ 2013/ 06/ 27/sleep-loss-increases-anxiety-especially-among-worriers/56531.html

National Sleep Foundation (2018) 'Depression and sleep'. Online blog: https://sleepfoundation.org/sleep-disorders-problems/depression-and-sleep. Accessed: 25th January 2018.

Nota, J.A, and Coles, M.E. (2017) 'Shorter sleep duration and longer sleep onset latency are related to difficulty disengaging attention from negative emotional images in individuals with elevated transdiagnostic repetitive negative thinking'. *Journal of Behaviour Therapy and Experimental Psychiatry*, 2018; 58: 114 DOI: 10.1016/j.jbtep.2017.10.003

O'Connor, P.J., Herring, M.P. and Carvalho, A. (2010). 'Mental health benefits of strength training in adults'. *American Journal of Lifestyle Medicine, 4(5),* Pages 377-396.

Osmun, R. (2015) How sleep balances your mind and emotions. Sonima Blog, Available online: https://www.sonima.com/meditation/sleep-emotions/

Panksepp, J. (1998) *Affective Neuroscience: The foundations of human and animal emotions.* Oxford University Press.

Perlmutter, D. (2015) *Brain Maker: The power of gut microbes to heal and protect your brain – for life.* London: Hodder and Stoughton.

Pilcher, J.J, Morris, D.M, Donnelly J., and Feigl, H.B. (2015) 'Interactions between sleep habits and self-control'. *Frontiers in Human Neuroscience*, 11 May 2015. Online: https://doi.org/10.3389/fnhum.2015.00284

Prochaska, J.O., Norcross, J.C. & DiClemente, C.C. (1998). *Changing for Good.* Reprint edition. New York: Morrow.

Ratey, J. and Hagerman, E. (2010) *Spark! How exercise will improve the performance of your brain.* London: Quercus.

Reder, A. (2007) Unmasking Anger. *Yoga Journal.* August 28th 2007. Available online: http://www.yogajournal.com/article/yoga-101/unmasking-anger/. Accessed: 17th June 2016.

Radhakrishna, S. (2010). Application of integrated yoga therapy to increase imitation skills in children with autism spectrum disorder. *International Journal of Yoga, 3 (1);* pp: 26-30.

Radhakrishna, S, Nagarathna, R. and Nagendra. H.R. (2010). Integrated approach to yoga therapy and autism spectrum disorders. *Journal of Ayurveda and Integrative Medicine, 1 (2);* pp: 120-4.

Sadock, B.J, and Sadock, V.A. (2000). *Kaplan and Sadock's Synopsis of Psychiatry: Behavioural Sciences/Clinical Psychiatry, 7th Edition.* Lippincott Williams & Wilkins. USA.

Santer, M.J. (2015) Why Qigong Is So Effective Against Emotional Illnesses. Source: http://qigong15.com/blog/qigong-exercises/why-qigong-is-so-effective-against-emotional-illnesses/. Accessed May 2015.

Sapolsky R. (2010) *Why Zebras don't get Ulcers.* Third Ed. New York: St Martin's Griffin.

Scullin, M. K., Krueger, M. L., Ballard, H. K., et al. (2018). 'The effects of bedtime writing on difficulty falling asleep: A polysomnographic study comparing to-do lists and completed activity lists. *Journal of Experimental Psychology: General, 147(1),* Pages 139-146.

Seddon, K. (2000) The Stoics on why we should strive to be free of the passions. *Practical Philosophy, Vol.3:3,* Nov 2000. Available online: http://www.wku.edu/ ~jan.garrett/stoa/ seddon2.htm. Accessed: 14th March 2011.

Selye, H. (1956/1975) *The Stress of Life. Revised edition.* New York: McGraw Hill Book Company.

Seneca (1995) On anger. In *Moral and Political Essays.* Trans. John Cooper and P.F. Procoupé. Cambridge: Cambridge University Press.

Shapiro, D., Cook, I.A, Davydov, D.M, et al. (2007). Yoga as a Complementary Treatment of Depression: Effects of Traits and Moods on

Treatment Outcome. *Evidence based complementary and alternative medicine, 4(4),* pp: 493-502.

Sharma, V.K, Das, S, Mondal, S, et al. (2005). Effect of Sahaj Yoga on depressive disorders. *Indian Journal of Physiological Pharmacology,* Oct-Dec, 49(4); pp: 462-8.

Sharma, V.K, Das, S, Mondal, S, et al. (2006). Effect of Sahaj Yoga on neuro-cognitive functions in patients suffering from major depression. *Indian Journal of Physiological Pharmacology,* Oct-Dec, 50(4); pp: 375-83.

Sher, B. (1995) *I Could Do Anything If I Only Knew What It Was: How to Discover What You Really Want and How to Get It.* New York: Dell.

Sherman, N. (2005) *Stoic Warriors: The ancient philosophy behind the military mind.* Oxford: Oxford University Press.

Siegel, D.J. (2015) *The Developing Mind: How relationships and the brain interact to shape who we are.* London: The Guilford Press.

Silberman, B. (2017) *Short life advice from the best in the world.* Boston: in Timothy Ferriss, *Tribe of Mentors:* Houghton Mifflin Harcourt. Page 497.

Smith, R. (2009) 'Sleeping problems such as insomnia linked to suicide attempts'. *The Telegraph,* online: https://www.telegraph.co.uk/news/health/news/5082849/Sleeping-problems-such-as-insomnia-linked-to-suicide-attempts.html

Southwick, S.M. and Dennis S. Charney (2013) *Resilience: The science of mastering life's greatest challenges.* Cambridge: Cambridge University Press.

Stevenson, S. (2016) *Sleep Smarter: 21 Essential strategies to sleep your way to a better body, better health and better success,* London: Hay House.

Strine, T.W. and Chapman, D.P. (2005) Associations of frequent sleep insufficiency with health-related quality of life and health behaviours. *Sleep Medicine, Volume 6, Issue 1,* January 2005, Pages 23-27.

Tartakovsky, M. (2017) Therapists Spill: How To Strengthen Your Resilience. A PsychCentral blog. Available online: https://psychcentral.com/lib/therapists-spill-how-to-strengthen-your-resilience/

Taylor-Byrne, R.E. (2016) Appendix F: Physical Exercise and Emotional Wellbeing. In Byrne, J., *Holistic Counselling in Practice: An introduction to the theory and practice of Emotive-Cognitive Embodied-Narrative Therapy*. Hebden Bridge: The Institute for E-CENT.

Taylor-Byrne, R.E. and Byrne, J.W. (2017) *How to control your anger, anxiety and depression, using nutrition and physical activity.* Hebden Bridge: The Institute for E-CENT Publications.

Taylor-Byrne, R.E. (2019) *Safeguard Your Sleep and Reap the Rewards: Better health, happiness and resilience.* Hebden Bridge: The Institute for E-CENT Publications.

Trowbridge, J.P. and Walker, M. (1989) *The Yeast Syndrome*. London: Bantam Books.

Tse, M. (1995) *Qigong for Health and Vitality*. London: Piatkus.

Turner, M., and Barker, J. (2014) *What Business can learn from Sport Psychology*. Oakamoor, USA: Bennion Kearny Ltd.

Uebelacker LA, Tremont G, Epstein-Lubow G, et al. (2010). Open trial of Vinyasa yoga for persistently depressed individuals: Evidence of feasibility and acceptability. *Behaviour Modification*, May, 34(3); pp: 247-64.

Vancampfort, D., De Hert, M., Knapen, J., et al. (2011). State anxiety, psychological stress and positive well-being responses to yoga and aerobic exercise in people with schizophrenia: A pilot study. *Disability Rehabilitation, 33(8);* pp: 684-9.

Van der Helm, E., & Walker, M. P. (2009) Overnight Therapy? The Role of Sleep in Emotional Brain Processing. *Psychological Bulletin, 135*(5), Pages 731–748.

Van der Helm E., Yao, J, Dutt, S., et al. (2011) 'REM sleep depotentiates amygdala activity to previous emotional experiences'. *Current Biology. 2011 Dec 6;21(23)*: Pages 2029-32. doi: 10.1016/j.cub.2011.10.052.

Wagner, E. (1996) *How to stay out of the doctor's surgery.* Carnell.

Visceglia E and Lewis S (2011). Yoga therapy as an adjunctive treatment for schizophrenia: a randomized, controlled pilot study. *Journal of Alternative and complementary Medicine, 17(7),* pages: 601-7

Walker, M. (2017) *Why We Sleep*. London: Allen Lane.

Wallin, D.A. (2007) *Attachment in Psychotherapy.* New York: Guilford Press.

Weaver, M. (2020) 'Retired NHS staff reluctant to return'. *The Guardian* newspaper. Thursday, 5th March. Page 6.

Wilkinson, R. and Pickett, K. (2010) *The Spirit Level: Why equality is better for everybody.* London: Penguin Books.

Williams, Z. (2020) 'Where did the weekend go?' *The Guardian, 'G2'*. Page 8. Thursday 27th February 2020

Wolpe, J. (1968) *Psychotherapy by Reciprocal Inhibition. Redwood City, Cal: Stanford University Press.*

Women's Running (2015) 'The mental health benefits of running: How running can alleviate symptoms of depression'. Online blog. Available at this url: http://womensrunninguk.co.uk/health/mental-health-benefits-running/. Accessed: 23rd November 2017

Yerkes, R.M. and John D. Dodson (1908) 'The relation of strength of stimulus to rapidity of habit-formation'. *Journal of Comparative Neurology and Psychology. November 1908.* https://doi.org/10.1002/cne.920180503.

~~~
~~~

Appendix A: Zen Tigers and Strawberry Moments

Buddhism teaches us to live in the present moment. But living in the moment is easier said than done. Here's a practical process to support that important aim.

~~~

Let me tell you a story about the philosophy of life of a Zen master. The gender of the Zen master (mistress?) in this story is irrelevant. So you can choose to read the story as if it was about a man or a woman, to suit your preference.

One day, a Zen master/mistress went into the jungle. S/He was enjoying the scenery: trees, vines, flowers; and listening to the sounds of the birds chirping, and various animals moving around and calling to each other. Suddenly s/he saw a tiger. Unfortunately, the tiger also saw the Zen master. S/He ran for his/her life; but s/he ran so fast that s/he ran off the edge of a cliff. Falling, s/he grasped for a tree root which projected from the face of the cliff, and ended up hanging from this root with his/her left hand. The tiger reached the top of the cliff, and stared down hungrily at him/her, but could not reach him/her.

The Zen master looked down to the foot of the cliff, and saw another tiger, looking up hungrily. Then, a couple of feet above his/her left hand, s/he noticed two little mice gnawing through the tree root, and s/he realised that before long s/he would (theoretically) go crashing down to the foot of the cliff, when the root broke. Then s/he noticed, to his/her right, a small strawberry bush, with a large, ripe, wild strawberry. S/He reached out and plucked the strawberry with his/her right hand, and popped it into his/her mouth. It tasted delicious.

~~~

Explanation: A Zen master does not concern themselves with the **past** (the tiger up above); nor with the **future** (the tiger down below). S/He is supremely centred in **the present moment** (the 'strawberry tasting' present moment). The strawberry flavour is intended to communicate the *blissfulness* of being in the present moment, with no distractions from the past or the future.

Clarification: Zen Masters do not ignore things that need to be done. If there is something that can be done (or controlled) about probable future threats or dangers, then s/he does that. If something can be done to clean up a past loss or failure, then she does that. But once controllable actions have been taken, the Zen master returns to the present moment. Why?

Because: "Only in a hut ***built for the moment*** can you be free from fear!"

Or, as the Buddha is said to have said: "One hair's breadth difference between what you want and what you've got and heaven and earth are set apart".

So, we have to focus our mind on the present moment, and accept the things we cannot change, and only try to change the things we can!

~~~

Back to the illustration of the tiger as the threat in the future, and the upset in the past.

Table 1:

The past	**The present moment**	**The future**
The past no longer exists, and therefore cannot harm you. (However, it does still influence you from non-conscious levels of mind!) The 'tiger' is up above, and cannot reach you. (The tiger in the past cannot come into the present and harm you, but your habits from the past come into the present and control	The present moment is a razor-sharp moment of blissful being. (We never experience it. We make up our 'individual moments' from the previous ten seconds or so, and extrapolate from there into the [imagined] near future). There are (normally, or most often!) no 'tigers' in the present moment. So if you can centre yourself in the present moment (as in	The future is difficult and hard to know. It has not arrived yet, and its shape is unknown. (It's good to try to take account of the 'probable future; to plan to protect yourself; and then let your expectations and projections go!) The 'tiger' is down below, and cannot reach you. (No amount of worrying will get rid of all potential tigers
~~~

your current behaviours!)	meditation) then there is nothing to worry about (for the duration of that bout of meditation!)	from the future. Life is difficult, now, and [most likely] in the future; but it can [normally, and most often] be coped with!)

In his book entitled 'How to Stop Worrying and Start Living', Dale Carnegie, also deals with the past, present and future. I have extracted just three of his strategies, and related them to the Zen Tiger story, as follows. They are listed as quotations at the top of each of the three columns in Table 2:

Table 2

The past	**The present**	**The future**
"No use crying (endlessly) over spilled milk". (See clarification about 'Human Tears', below). ~~~ It would be a mistake to say, "I **should not** have gone into the jungle, then I would not be in this mess, hanging from this tree root, with two tigers to worry about!" Why would it be a mistake? Because you cannot change that reality now. You cannot choose your options retrospectively!	***"Live your life in day-tight compartments".*** ~~~ The only time that really exists is now. The past is dead and gone. The future is just a dream. So enjoy the present moment. If you can get your mind out of the past and the future, you will find that the present moment is blissful. Practice daily meditation to get your mind into the present moment. Write about your current problems - your old losses and failures	***"I'll cross that bridge when I come to it".*** (But I'll also do whatever realistic forward planning that I can!) ~~~ If the tiger is there when you fall, it *must* be there when you fall, but you have no way of knowing that it *will* be there, since all kinds of things may have changed by the time the 'future arrives'. The tiger may have gone home for lunch, or a missionary

There is no point lamenting ***this kind*** of reality (and especially endlessly!). Some realities need to be lamented – such as the death of a significant other person; or the loss of a job; or some such highly significant loss or failure). Whatever happened actually did happen, because of all the little steps that had **already** been taken, by you, other people and the world.	from the past; your current worries; and your worries about the future – in your 'Daily pages' – which you should write every morning (or evening. Morning is best!)	might have happened along the lower trail, and the tiger might be busy eating the missionary when you fall. Or you might fall on the tiger, and accidentally break its back – putting it out of action!

~~~

Clarification about Human Tears

By Jim Byrne and Renata Taylor-Byrne, October 2018

The more we try to simplify our philosophy of life, the more we are in danger of over-simplifying it! And an over-simplified philosophy of life – like the extreme Stoicism of Rational Emotive Behaviour Therapy (REBT); or the emotion-denying theory of CBT – will just lead us into misleading others.

Once upon a time, I (Jim) subscribed to the over-simple statement: "There's no use crying over spilled milk!" It came with the territory of having parents who lacked empathy for the suffering of children. And that is where Dale Carnegie and Albert Ellis got it; although it was already there in Greek and Roman philosophy – from a time when you could be taken in slavery to clean the homes of the Athenian ruling class – or thrown to the lions to entertain the bored populace of Rome. Spilled milk seemed supremely unimportant in the context of slavery or death by being savaged by a lion. But in the modern world, we have more sense of entitlement than
~~~

people had in ancient Greece or Rome. (Though we often are no more secure than they were - in a neoliberal world of immoral bankers!)

Anyway, back to human tears:

Extensive research by Dr William Frey (a psychiatric biochemist), in 1949, demonstrated that crying is an essential way of eliminating stress hormones under conditions of sadness and grief. Here's the most relevant point: "Human tears, unlike the tears of any other animal, contain a substance called ACTH, the hormone that actually sets off the stress response and is literally washed away by a good cry".*

*Frey, W. H., Hoffman-Ahern, C., Johnson, R. A., Lykken, D. T., & Tuason, V. B. (1983) Crying behaviour in the human adult. *Integrative Psychiatry, 1,* 94-100.

So there is a very good point to 'crying over spilled milk', or any significant loss or failure, such as the death of a close relative or love object; or the loss of a job, career, or part of your own body, or a valued asset!

Therefore, the quotation should now be amended to this: ***"There is no point crying endlessly over spilled milk - though you should do whatever grieving is necessary to complete your experience of losses and failures, including symbolic losses and failures".***

~~~

More on living in the present

Dale Carnegie teaches many ways to get yourself into the present moment, including this quote from Sir William Osler:

"Our main business is not to see what lies dimly at a distance, but to do what lies clearly at hand".

He is clear that 'living in the past', is a waste of emotional energy. This is his advice:

"Shut off the past! Let the dead past bury its dead ..."

He is also clear that 'living in the future' is an unnecessary burden:

"...the load of tomorrow, added to that of yesterday, carried today, makes the strongest (person) falter. Shut off the future as tightly as the past... The future is today. There is no tomorrow. The day of our salvation is now. ...
~~~

Prepare to cultivate the habit of a life of (living in) 'day-tight compartments'. ..."

If you think of something that needs to be done tomorrow, write it down in your diary, or on an action list, and then return your attention to this moment now. This is the only moment that exists.

If you think of something from that past that worries you, write it out (in your Daily pages); learn what you can from that experience, and then move on.

Once you have trained yourself to live your life in day-tight compartments, then what? Then you are faced with how to live well in the now:

"Think of your life as an hourglass". If you don't know what an hourglass is, it is like a giant egg timer, made of two glass compartments, connected by a narrow tube. Sand flows from one compartment down into the other, and measures the passage of time: three minutes for an egg-timer; one hour for an hourglass.

Dale Carnegie writes: "You know there are thousands of grains of sand in the top of the hourglass; and they all pass slowly and evenly through the narrow neck in the middle. Nothing you or I could do would make more than one grain of sand pass through this narrow neck without impairing the hourglass".

"You and I and everyone else are like this hourglass. When we start in the morning, there are hundreds of tasks which we feel that we must accomplish that day, but if we do not take them one at a time, and let them pass through the day slowly and evenly, as do the grains of sand passing through the narrow neck of the hourglass, then we are bound to break our own physical and mental structure".

Therefore, Dale Carnegie's advice to us all is this:

"One grain of sand at a time... one task at a time". Pace yourself. (If anybody uses the concept of 'multi-tasking' in your presence, call the local mad house and have them dragged away. Multi-tasking is a Big Lie! We must do One Thing at a Time!)

One thing at a time! If we tackle our work life in this way, then we can go on and on, healthily and productively. And if we deal with our personal problems, our worries, in this way, one at a time (in written form – in your journal or notebook – so we can see them clearly, and think about them clearly) – then we can worry constructively (and much more briefly!) To illustrate this point, Dale Carnegie presents this quotation:

'Anyone can carry his/her burden, however, hard, until nightfall. Anyone can do his/her work, however hard, for one day. Anyone can live sweetly, patiently, lovingly, purely, till the sun goes down. And this is all that life really means'. Robert Louis Stevenson.

Don't try to live your life a week or a month at a time:

"Each day is a new life to a wise person".

Don't waste your life dreaming of tomorrow. Live your life today:

"One of the most tragic things I know about human nature is that all of us tend to put off living. We are all dreaming of some magical rose garden over the horizon – instead of enjoying the roses that are blooming outside our windows today". (Dale Carnegie).

Or we are worrying about some dreaded nightmare up ahead, which, despite never arising, drains us of our vitality today, and spoils the only life we have: *this precious moment,* ***Now!***

Live your life in day-tight compartments, and enjoy the moment:

"Most of us are…stewing about yesterday's jam and worrying about tomorrow's jam instead of spreading today's jam thick on our bread right now". Dale Carnegie.

At this point the two stories merge. The Zen master's life was supremely centred in the present moment, and therefore s/he could reach out and pluck the wild strawberry of the present moment. And Dale Carnegie equates this present moment with the sweet taste of jam. If you do not know why the beautiful taste of the strawberry, or the sweetness of jam, is used to describe the present moment, you have never *meditated.* Try it and see. When you come into the present moment, life is beautifully sweet.

March 2020 – Hebden Bridge

~~~
~~~

Appendix B: What is meditation, and how can you do it?

(c) By Renata Taylor-Byrne and Jim Byrne - Updated in November 2019

Meditation involves sitting quietly, 'doing nothing'. It is a simple process of ***paying attention to your breathing***, and letting your thoughts settle down and ***letting your mind become peaceful.*** It's about ***'being in the present moment'***, relaxed, and with ***bare awareness*** to your immediately present environment:

- Meditation is best performed each morning for 10 to 15 minutes. (Twenty or thirty minutes would be even better).
- You don't have to have a special meditation posture (but it can help you to get you into the right frame of mind).

Therapeutic, non-religious meditation, involves focusing the mind on some external thing: (an external object, or internal sensation, like breathing) so our thoughts slow down, in then moves in time with our breathing.

Imagine you and I have a pond in our minds, with lots of silt and debris at the bottom. Our normal daily routines churn up the silt and debris, and this clouds our mind and our vision, and produces stress and strain, and unhappiness, and poor perspectives on life. We often become humourless and constantly worried. Meditation is a process for allowing all the silt and debris to settle down to the bottom of our mind-pond, to restore clarity of vision/perspective, to restore happiness and contentment, and to allow our natural happiness to return.

Simply sitting in one place, quietly counting your breaths, in and out, as they happen, is an amazingly beneficial exercise. This helps your brain, your blood pressure level, your nervous system, your level of physical and mental energy; and it strengthens your immune system, and improves your sense of composure.

Scientific Verification

Science Daily recently reported that: "Mindfulness Meditation Training (which is what meditation consists of) Changes Brain Structure in Eight Weeks".

The *ScienceDaily* report, (Jan. 21, 2011), says: – "Participating in an 8-week mindfulness meditation program appears to make measurable changes in brain regions associated with memory, sense of self, empathy and stress. In a study that will appear in the January 30 issue of Psychiatry Research: Neuroimaging, a team led by Massachusetts General Hospital (MGH) researchers report the results of their study, the first to document meditation-produced changes over time in the brain's grey matter". (See the Britta K. Hölzel et al reference, below).

There are also lots of other reports on the internet on the efficacy of meditation, but this is the first to be able to scientifically link those changes to brain structure changes. (See the recommended reading at the end of this appendix). We can now definitively say that meditation is not just a palliative, not just a cognitive distraction. It changes the brain-mind for the better!

What does meditation do for you?

Why is meditation so good? It reconnects you to the ***real world*** - grounds you in reality - and enables you to slowly separate your wishes, thoughts and fantasies from what is actually going on around you. Regular practice also produces long-term changes in sympathetic nervous system activity", and "quiets down the nervous system". This is a great aid to our resilience when we meet stressful events in our lives.

You reconnect with yourself as a physical and emotional being. You learn to *calmly* watch your mind and its endless activities, and not get pulled into 'working on the past', or emotional fortune-telling and worrying about future events (which haven't happened yet).

If you are very tense and stressed, and cannot imagine what a wonderful state of relaxation would feel like, then try watching a relaxation video on YouTube. It operates differently than meditation, except that they both focus on getting you to reduce and eliminate unnecessary thought.

Our brains are bombarded with information all the time from our social environment and the media. We need time to absorb, digest and sift through all this information in order to sort out the **food** from the **toxic garbage**. And all that is done effortlessly by our brain if we give it the time and space to do its job.

There are very many physical and psychological benefits to the daily practice of meditation. This has now been confirmed in a small but growing number of scientific research studies in the East and the West. And western science has become more and more interested in the benefits of meditation, and of Buddhist philosophy, as potential new aspects of the psychology of wellbeing. You can find this evidence on the internet by conducting your own searches. Try searching these key words: "research on meditation"; "science and meditation"; "meditation and stress". Or take a look at the sources listed in the references below as your starting point.

When we don't take the time to relax, and provide the mental space for information processing (which is maximized by the process of meditation) we experience a build-up of stress. We toss and turn in our beds, trying to deal with problems, creating others, never giving our brain a break, and sleeping fitfully and lightly.

Did you know that when we meditate, it is the only time our brains truly rest? They don't rest when we are sleeping - but we need to sleep for various housekeeping purposes, so do not skip sleep and substitute meditation. That won't work. But a short meditation session can help to top up your sleep. It also reduces the production of cortisol (which is one of the major stress hormones).

The Buddha taught the technique of focusing your awareness on your breathing, while sitting in an alert posture. You can count your breaths in and out - counting 'One' on the inbreath; 'Two' on the outbreath; 'Three' on the inbreath; and, finally, 'Four' on the outbreath.

Then repeat this process, over and over again.

Let your breathing slow down, and allow your bellow to expand on the inbreath, and to go flat again on the outbreath.

Try to feel the inbreath moving upwards through your nostrils. And expand your belly when you breathe in, instead of lifting your rib cage. Always breathe from your belly, like a baby does, and if it helps you, put the palm of one hand flat on top of your belly, and feel it move up and down as you breathe.

Meditation is very simple, but also very effective.

First: the location/setup. You can either sit on a cushion on the floor, with your legs crossed; or you can sit in an armchair, with your back straight. Try resting one hand on the other, in your lap, and allow your thumbs to lightly touch each other. Make sure there are no distracting, avoidable noises, in your environment, such as radio, TV, etc. (Normal 'noises off' can help the meditation, if you just let them come and go). Let your eyelids droop and focus your eyes downwards and straight ahead.

Second: the process. One approach is to count '***One***' on the first in breath, and '***And***' on the out breath. Then count '***Two***' on the second in breath, and '***And***' on the out breath. (Count silently in your mind). Then '***Three***' on the next in breath.. All the way up to '***Four***'... '***And***'. Then back to 'One' again. Try to sit quietly for about fifteen or twenty minutes, preferably every morning. Don't try to ***forcefully*** stop yourself thinking - just ***gently*** *return your attention to your breathing, and counting your breaths again, if you lose track.* Try to focus all your attention on your breathing, your expanding and contracting belly, and the counting of the breaths.

The point is that your mind will wander - that is in the nature of 'monkey mind'. And so your job is to keep bringing it back to a point of concentration, and to keep reminding yourself to breathe, and to pay attention to your counting. As time goes by, you will get better and better at concentrating, but in the beginning you mind is bound to wander.

Once you have the knack of counting your breaths, focus your attention on something simple and still, in front of you, like I use my bedroom slippers.

If you find this hard to do, try **Glenn Harrold's 'Meditation for Relaxation' audio program.**

Or, try attending a meditation class for a while, until you know how to do it on your own. Then do it at home for the rest of your life. It will keep you happy, un-depressed, and de-stressed. It will also help to keep you looking and feeling youthful.

Don't be too influenced by the views of others on meditation. It is a practice that is easy for other people to make fun of. That is their loss! The Buddha suggested that the best way to experience the value of meditation (and everything else in life) was to: "Find out for yourself".

In our (Renata's and Jim's) own personal experience, regular daily meditation will not only improve your physical and mental well-being, it will also improve your efficiency and effectiveness, including your concentration ability. You will find problems much easier to handle and resolve. This is well summed up in the following words by Eckhart Tolle: "Obstacles come all the time. If you get upset that means the ego is back. When obstacles come if you're not upset and you're still present, you will look at whatever the obstacle is with a penetrating gaze of presence, which is stillness also. You look at whatever obstacle arises, you bring this penetrating stillness to it, and that is like a light that shines on it and dissolves the obstacle or shows you a way around it. That's the power of consciousness."

Remember that to feel the full benefits of meditation, you need to develop the habit of doing it every day.

As you build up a daily habit of meditation, you will find that the stillness that existed during your meditation will tend to stay with you throughout the day, and help to calm you in stressful situations.

If you find it hard to get started, begin with just five minutes per day, and gradually build up to 10, 15, 20 minutes.

~~~

Recommended reading:

Britta K. Hölzel, James Carmody, Mark Vangel, Christina Congleton, Sita M. Yerramsetti, Tim Gard, Sara W. Lazar. **Mindfulness practice leads to increases in regional brain gray matter density**. Psychiatry Research: Neuroimaging, 2011; 191 (1): 36 DOI: 10.1016/j.pscychresns.2010.08.006

Brain Longevity, by Dr Dharma Singh Khalsa, with Cameron Stauth (1997), London: Century. (Pages 301-319).

Zen Made Easy, by Timothy Freke, Godsfield Press, 1999. (Pages 62-70).

Watts, A. (1962/1990) *The Way of Zen.* London: Arkana/Penguin. (Pages 174-179).

Zen Mind, Beginners Mind, by Shunryo Suzuki. Random House, 2006.

Everyday Zen, by Charlotte Joko Beck, London: Thorsons, 1999.

'Free your mind', an article from the Sunday Times Magazine, is available here.***

Website: http://www.getsomeheadspace.com/

Meditation, a definition, at Wikipedia.

*How to meditate, **a website with text and video clips.***

How to meditate, a YouTube video clip, is available here.
~~~

On 'the present moment', a YouTube video clip, by Eckhart Tolle.

Science Daily, (2011) Mindfulness meditation training changes brain structures in eight weeks. Available online at: http://www.sciencedaily .com /releases/ 2011/ 01/110121144007.htm. Accessed: 8th February 2011.

~~~
~~~

Appendix C: How to change your habits

By Jim Byrne and Renata Taylor-Byrne

~~~

There are two sections to this appendix: the first by Jim Byrne, and the second by Renata Taylor-Byrne.

Introduction to habit change

By Jim Byrne

In this section, and the next, we intend to give you all the tools you need to implement the behaviour changes which have been recommended in the main body of this book.

1. General theory

In our system of coaching, counselling and therapy (known as the E-CENT[165] perspective), humans are seen as creatures of habit, rather than rational thinkers. (Or, rather, we are ***both***; but the emotional past most often proves to be ***more powerful*** than our present, surface thinking; which is how and why we have survived for so long. We don't have to sit around thinking about how to respond to potential threats. We just automatically do what has kept us safe in the past!) Whatever we did before, you can bet most humans will tend, normally, to repeat in the present - except sometimes. Sometimes we may step outside of our past performances, but ***not** normally*.

In this sense - the sense of being creatures of habit - humans are clearly ***products** of the past*; ***shaped*** by the past; ***driven*** by past experiences; and ***acting out*** scripts and stories which they ***constructed in the past*** in response to 'present time' stimuli which they experience *as if they were a **repetition** of the past*.

Because we humans are ***dominated** by the past* - all our knowledge and skill and habitual behaviour comes to us from our past, which is stored in our body-brain-mind in the present moment. We cannot 'dump the past'; cannot
~~~

step away from the past; or behave as if we do not have a specific, personal, historical past.

We learned to eat from our mothers; and we often copy our parents' attitudes towards exercise and alcohol and smoking, and so on.

So change has to be *gradual,* because it involves the *breaking* of powerful habits. And it requires *self-discipline,* and some kind of *support system.*

~~~

2. The benefits of exercise and dietary self-management skills

Diet is not about weight loss, in the main, but about eating healthily; and not just for physical health, but also for emotional wellbeing. Our guts and our brains communicate constantly, and when we eat the wrong foods, we tend to disrupt our normal gut flora and friendly bacteria, which then produces negative effects upon our brain-mind, and thus upon our moods and emotions, and our ability to think straight. Excess sugar causes stress; gluten damages our guts and disrupts our brains. Caffeine speeds up our nervous systems, by secreting stress hormones. And sedentary lifestyle allows the build-up of stress hormones, and slows down the lymphatic drainage of toxic substances from our bodies.

Exercise is important because it affects the electro-chemical functioning of the whole body-brain-mind, reducing stress hormones, releasing happiness chemicals, and promoting oxygenation of every cell, plus the movement of lymphatic fluid; and thus promoting physical *detoxification* and improving physical health and emotional wellbeing through *stress reduction.*

~~~

3. Our approach to behaviour change

We believe in *gradual* change!

We do not want to encourage you to *overload yourself* with self-change action lists! Or, to put it better: We do not want you to believe that you *have to change* ***everything*** on your self-change list *today, right now,* ***immediately*** and totally!

You cannot do it anyway. Because we are creatures of habit, if we try to change too much too quickly, the deeply emotional, habit-based part of us will panic, and rebel; and not allow it to happen. It's too scary.

So, therefore, change takes time.

Change take effort.

Change takes commitment.

And the best way to proceed is slowly, incrementally, and self-supportingly!

4. A personal example

To make this point well, I (Jim) would like to present an example from my own life:

About fifteen years ago, I found I had lost all my self-discipline in relation to daily physical exercise. I had gone from being a regular exerciser to a regular procrastinator! I could not bring myself to do any exercise whatsoever. So, for a long time I was stuck in this 'pre-contemplation' stage. I was not planning to change anything!

Then, as the weeks and months drifted past, I became more and more annoyed with myself, because I knew I was risking serious damage to my physical health and my emotional wellbeing. At this point I became a 'contemplator'. I was contemplating, or thinking about, change, but I could not quite bring myself to do anything about it. I kept 'planning' to change; or 'trying' to change; but I did not change!

Then one morning I felt so bad about my procrastination, that I became 'determined' to do something about it. This is, obviously, called the 'Determination Stage' of behaviour change. (Prochaska, Norcross and DiClemente, 1998)[166]. That was when I remembered the ***Kaizen*** method of 'gradual improvement'[167]. This system, introduced to Japan by some American teachers, including W. Edwards Deming, at the end of the Second World War, teaches a process of gradual refinement and progress, instead of huge jumps and big goals.

So I decided on the smallest goal I could come up with, which would be acceptable to me. I felt I could run on the spot, right by my armchair, for thirty seconds, and then sit down. I stood up – (this is the Action step) - feeling hopeless, and I did it. I ran on the spot to the count of thirty. That is to say, when my left foot hit the floor, I counted '1'. Then, when my right foot hit the floor, I counted 'And'. When my left foot fell again, I counted '2'. And so on, up to thirty foot falls; like gentle jogging, but on the same spot. Then I sat down. ***I felt great!***

I felt such a sense of self-efficacy – of self-esteem – that I was amazed. Such a small step forward, and such a big reward in terms of how good I felt about myself.

So, the next day, I decided to run on the spot for the count of sixty (foot lifts and falls). When I sat down, I felt even better.

The third morning, I could not stop when I reached 60, or 120, or 240. I was hooked.

I had persuaded the resistant, emotional, non-conscious part of myself that I would not die, or fall apart, if I did my physical exercises; so I went back to doing my old Judo club calisthenics, my Chi Kung, and my press-ups and sit-backs.

And this is the key point: This is how we want you to tackle whatever personal-change goals you come up with, as a result of reading Part 1 and Part 2 of this book.

We do not want you to demoralize yourself, by *aiming too high*, too soon, only to fail; and then to abandon all attempt at personal change. We want you to be *realistic*, and we want you to give yourself the best chance of *succeeding* in making those changes you choose for yourself!

~~~

5. A second example: Using rewards and penalties

The second story I want to tell you follows on from the first.

So, I did my exercises four or five mornings each week, for quite some time, but then I began to skip them, if I was 'too busy'; or if I was 'running late'. So, I remembered another very important principle of behaviour change: rewards and penalties!

So I made this commitment to myself:

"Every morning that I do my exercises, I will give myself permission to read six pages of a novel that I like, as a reward. And if I fail to do my exercises, I will immediately take ***two £1 coins*** (which totals close to $3 US) from my bookcase shelf, and go out into the street, and drop them both down the nearest drain, so they become irretrievably lost!"

Needless to say, I did not skip any exercise sessions from that point onwards!
~~~

~~~

In Section 2 of this, the sixth part of this book, below, Renata presents an even more powerful system of behaviour change, which you can use to make those changes you want to make to your diet and exercise regimes.

~~~

6. The stages of change

So now, we hope, you have an understanding that change has to be *gradual.*

Change begins at the ***Precontemplation*** stage, when you are not planning any change at all. Then it proceeds through ***Contemplation,*** when you are *thinking about* changing something. Then on to becoming ***Determined*** to change something. Then you take ***Action.*** And even after that, you can slip back. So you have to work at ***Maintenance*** of the new habit. When you feel yourself slip back, you have to repeat whatever process you used to make the change. And you have to be vigilant, to make sure you don't slip back too easily.

The important point is this: You cannot make any changes until you reach the ***'determination'*** stage; and it's best to have a system of ***rewards*** and ***penalties*** in place.

One of the best rewards, of course, is the realization that – when you manage your diet and exercise programs well - you are adding years to your life; adding to your physical health and your mental health; and improving your moods and emotions. (And you will also look more attractive, and be more creative, and be more successful in your relationships, at home and in work!)

...

Another approach to changing your negative habits

By Renata Taylor Byrne - Copyright © Renata Taylor-Byrne 2016-2017/2019

~~~

1. The nature of habits

What are habits? Here are two definitions from the Merriam-Webster dictionary:
~~~

(1) Habit is "… (a) *behaviour pattern acquired by frequent repetition or physiologic exposure that shows itself in regularity or increased facility of performance" and/*or:

(2) It's *"…An acquired mode of behaviour that has become nearly or completely involuntary."*

~~~

And here is the viewpoint of one of the fathers of American psychology:

"All our life, so far as it has definite form, is a mass of habits".

William James, 1892

~~~

We are habit-based human beings, and the more we know about how we form habits, the *easier* it will be for us to change old ones that aren't working for us, and to create new ones.

A researcher at Duke University in 2006 discovered that more than 40% of the activities people engaged in every day were habits, and not decisions they had made. And some theorists would say that our habit-based functioning is as high as 95% (Bargh and Chartrand, 1999)[168].

Throughout the animal world, habit based behaviour is the norm. This has served survival well, which is why it is ubiquitous.

Humans have the greatest capacity of all animals to change our habits, but we will never become habit-less.

Our brains have developed the ability to create habits because they allow our brains to save effort, and to function more efficiently without having our minds cluttered with the mechanics of the many basic behaviours we have to follow each day.

2. The structure of a habit

In his book, ***The Power of Habit,*** Charles Duhigg[169] looked very closely at the specific features of what makes up a habit. In his view, a habit is like a loop that has three parts: the cue; the routine; and the reward. Here is a picture of that loop:

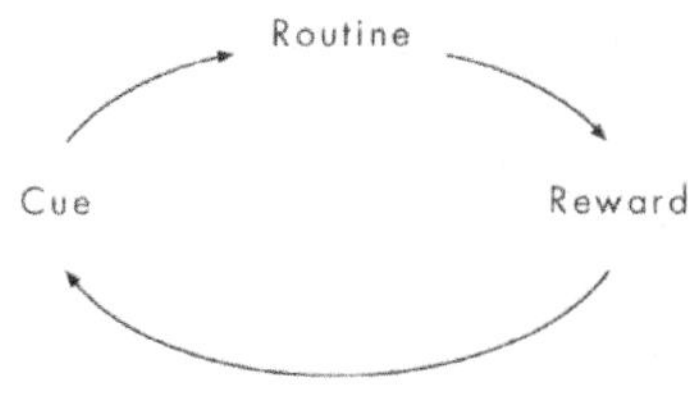

Firstly, there is a ***cue*** (a trigger that starts off a ***routine***: e.g. the sound of the alarm clock in the morning is a cue, which triggers the routine of getting up).

Here's ***an example of a cue*** that I recently found in the ***Sunday Times Magazine,*** in an article by Viv Groscop (who performed her one-woman show at Edinburgh in August this year [2017]). Viv stated that, to make her exercise routine strong, she started keeping her workout clothes and trainers next to her bed, so they were *the first things she saw- the* ***cue!*** *– in the early morning,* as soon as she woke up. (She lost 3 stone [or 42 pounds in weight] in one year through changes in her exercise and nutrition habits).

2. Secondly, this cue is followed by ***a routine***.

A routine is here defined as ***any*** pattern of behaviour. Examples include: eating, going to the pub, watching a TV programme, going to the gym, doing homework, buying clothes, smoking, placing a bet, etc.

3. Finally, there is a ***reward*** – the most important part of the loop.

All habits have a *reward* at the end of them. Here are some examples of rewards:

(1) The feeling of comradeship when drinking at the pub;

(2) the rush of pleasure after you have just done a bout of exercise;

(3) giving yourself a cup of (decaffeinated!) coffee when you've done your daily exercise. And:

(4) seeing the *good, pleasurable results* of any difficult task.

~~~

3. The importance of craving!

For habit change to work you have to ***crave*** *the reward.*
~~~

This is an important alert: You have to *really crave* the reward, or you *won't* have the incentive to change your behaviour. Charles Duhigg describes a research project undertaken by the National Weight Control Agency. The agency examined the ***routines*** for eating food that had been created by people who were successful dieters. They investigated more than 6,000 people's routines.

What was discovered was that *all* the successful dieters eat a breakfast (which was cued by the ***time*** of day). But they also had very real, *very desirable* ***rewards*** in place for themselves if they stuck to their diet plans – and it was the reward that they craved. (For example, being able to fit into new clothes in a smaller size; or having a flatter belly, etc.)

And if they felt themselves *weakening* in their commitment, they ***changed*** *their focus onto the rewards* that they would get if they *kept* to their plans. This visualisation, of the very real rewards they would get, kept them strong in the face of temptation.

Apparently people who started new exercise routines showed that they were more likely to follow an exercise routine if they chose a ***specific cue*** (first thing in the morning, or as soon as they get in from work, or before bedtime).

*So having a cue in place is **crucial** to initiating the new behaviour (or routine).*

The new behaviour (or **routine**) follows from the cue.

Let me give you a personal example: Jim and I get up in the morning, and the first thing we do is to have breakfast, because we ***crave*** the pleasure of raw salad with seeds and nuts, and minor embellishments.

The *end of breakfast* ***cues*** us to meditate, and we crave the rewards of meditation, (a lot of which have to do with stress management, health and happiness, plus creativity).

Then, *the end of meditation* ***cues*** us to begin our physical exercise (Chi Kung [or Qigong], the Plank, some press-ups and sit-backs, and so on]) which we **crave** because of the physical and mental health benefits that we gain.

So, the **reward** is what people crave at the end of their routines. Some of the ***rewards*** mentioned in Duhigg's research were having a (small amount of) beer, or an evening of watching the TV without guilt.

As my own experiment, I (Renata) wanted to establish a daily habit of exercising my arm muscles, to firm them up. Therefore, I set up a **cue** which is the start of the BBC TV programme **'Pointless'**, at 5.15pm every day.

When I hear the theme music for ***Pointless***, I get out our "Powerspin" device - which simulates weight training - and do a pre-planned (recommended) set of exercises.

This exercise **routine** is designed to strengthen my arms and back muscles, and core (stomach); and it is very simple, but involves some physical exertion.

And the **reward** for me (which I *crave* strongly - otherwise it won't work) is the knowledge that my arms and back and core muscles are getting stronger and fitter, and that this will keep me fit and able to carry heavy objects into old age! And so far, so good - I've only missed a few times!

~~~

4. Duhigg's own experiment

Charles Duhigg did a really interesting personal experiment to see if he could change one of his own habits. He was eating too many cookies (or biscuits) and he was starting to put on weight. He did an explanation and a description of his experiment which you can see on YouTube. He broke the habit, by working out what the reward was (and it had nothing to do with cookies/biscuits). Once he knew what the reward was, he found it very easy to substitute a new routine which did not involve eating junk foods! Here is the address of his video clip at YouTube:
https://youtu.be/W1eYrhGeffc

~~~

5. The importance of substitution

What if we have a habit that we want to change? Can we get rid of it?

How do we go about it? Charles Duhigg states that we **can't** get rid of old habits - but what we can do is ***substitute*** new routines for the old ones, and get the same rewards.

He explains that a golden rule of habit change, which has been validated by repeated studies for a long time, is as follows:

"To change a habit, we must keep the old *cue, which delivers the old* *reward, but* ***change the routine.***

"That's the rule: if you use the same cue, and provide the same reward, you can shift the routine and change the habit. Almost any behaviour can be transformed if the cue and reward stay the same". (Page 62)

He gives the example of someone who wants to give up cigarettes. If the person wanting to quit smoking fails to find something else to do (a new routine), when they start to crave nicotine, then they will be unable to stop! It will be ***too hard*** for them. That's why, in Section 1 of Part 6 above, Jim emphasizes substituting stevia for sugar, before giving up the sugar. The reward is the sweetness. The cue may be thirst. But the routine does not have to involve sugar, so long as it involves some sweetness; and stevia is a safer form of sweetness.

6. Stopping addictions

Charles Duhigg states that the organisation called ***'Alcoholics Anonymous'*** (**AA**) is effective in helping people reduce their drinking habits because it examines and shines a very clear light on the **cues** which trigger drinking in people; and the **AA** program deliberately encourages people to **identify** the **cues** and **rewards** that encourages their alcoholic habits, and then ***assists them*** as they try to find new behaviours (or routines).

So the implied question that **AA** asks an alcoholic is: *"What rewards do you get from alcohol?"*

"In order for alcoholics to get the same rewards that they get in a bar, AA has built a system of meetings and ***companionship*** *– (the individual 'Sponsor' that each person works with) – that strives to offer as much escape, distraction and catharsis as a Friday night bender."* (Page 71)

If someone wants to get support from another person, they can receive this by talking to their *sponsor* or by going to a ***group meeting***, rather than "toasting a drinking buddy".

A researcher called J. Scott Tonigan has been looking at the work of *AA* for more than ten years, and he states that if you look at Step 4 of the 12 step program, (which is to make a *'searching and fearless inventory of ourselves and to admit to God, to ourselves* and *another human being the exact nature of our wrongs'*), you will see that something crucial is taking place, which he sums up like this:

"It's not obvious from the way they are written, but to complete those steps, someone has to create a list of ***triggers*** *for all their alcoholic urges. When you make a self-inventory, you're figuring out all the* ***things*** *that make you drink..."* *The* ***cues!***

~~~

7. The rewards of drinking

The *AA* organisation then asks alcoholics (or alcohol dependent individuals) to look really hard for the **rewards** they get from alcohol, and the **cravings** that are behind the behaviour. And what is discovered?

"Alcoholics crave a drink because it offers escape, relaxation, companionship, the blunting of anxieties and an opportunity for emotional release....the ***physical effects*** *of alcohol are one of the least rewarding parts of drinking for addicts."* (Page 71)

So what ***AA*** does is gets you to create *new routines* for your spare time *instead of going out drinking.* You can relax and talk through any worries or concerns you might have at the meetings.

"The triggers (cues) are the same, and the payoffs (rewards) are the same, it's just the ***behaviour*** *that changes,"* states Tonigan.

~~~

8. The result of one experiment

To summarise the value of one particular experiment, Duhigg showed that the former alcoholics in the study only succeeded in eliminating their drinking behaviour because they developed new routines which followed the old *triggers* (or ***cues***), and gave them their comforting ***rewards***.

Apparently the techniques that were developed by the *AA* for changing habits have also been successfully applied to children's temper tantrums, sex addictions and other types of behaviour.

The **AA** is described in Duhigg's book as an organisation which creates techniques to change the habits associated with the use of alcohol:

"AA is in essence a giant machine for changing habit loops and though the habits associated with alcohol consumption are extreme, the lessons AA provides demonstrates how almost any habit - even the most obstinate - can be changed." Charles Duhigg

He makes it clear in his book that overeating, alcoholism, or smoking, are ingrained habits that take real commitment to change. But if you know how your habits are working, this makes it easier to experiment with new behaviours.

~~~

9. Analysing your own habits

If you look very carefully at the **cues** that cause you to avoid physical exercise, or to eat foods that you now know to be bad for your physical and emotional health, and you work out the rewards that you currently get from the *avoidance routine*, or the *consumption routine*, then you can easily identify a new **healthy routine** to substitute for the old unhealthy routine.

It might be best to begin with exercise, because this may help you to find the commitment to change other habits, including some eating habits.

Why is this?

~~~

10. Creating 'keystone habits'

Exercise seems to be a 'keystone habit' that has a beneficial, 'knock-on' effect. When people begin exercising, and it can be as little as once a week, they begin to change other, unconnected habits in their lives. It has been discovered that they reduce their smoking, spend money less, and have more understanding for their family and the people they work with.

"Exercise spills over", stated James Prochaska (a University of Rhode Island researcher). *"There's something about it that makes good habits easier."*

Other studies have revealed that families who are in the habit of having their meals together regularly – which is another 'keystone habit' - raise children with higher school grades, more emotional control, better homework skills and increased confidence.

Apparently making your bed every morning is also a keystone habit, which has a spill over effect. It is correlated with a higher level of happiness, stronger skills at sticking to a budget and a higher level of productivity.

So, by beginning to use the kaizen approach (described in Jim's section above), to get in the habit of doing a few minutes exercise each day, you will be starting a cascade of potential change. Over time, you can learn how to exclude all of the toxic foods; to get on to an exciting, healthy and enlivening diet; and to be happier, healthier and more creative. (But do it slowly, gradually, incrementally. And reward yourself at every step)

~~~

11. Habit reversal

Here is a quote by Nathan Azrin, who was one of the people who developed habit reversal training:

"It seems ridiculously simple, but once you are aware of how your habit works, once you recognise the ***cues*** *and the* ***rewards****, you're half-way to changing it."*

Today, habit reversal is used to treat gambling, depression, smoking, anxiety, procrastination, and sex and alcohol addiction etc. And you can now use it to change your exercise and dietary habits too.

Charles Duhigg makes the point that although the habit process can be simply described, it doesn't mean that it's ***easily*** changed. As Mark Twain argued, a habit cannot be flung out of the window by any person, but has to be coaxed downstairs a step at a time! You cannot eliminate habits that no longer serve, you can only ***replace them*** with new habits that support your goals. You have to be aware of what you want (the implicit reward - the thing that you crave), and work to create new habits (or routines) that will get you what you want.

Charles Duhigg states:

"It's facile to imply that smoking, alcoholism, over-eating or other ingrained patterns can be upended without real effort. Genuine change requires real work and self-understanding of the cravings driving the behaviours. No one will quit smoking because they can sketch a habit loop.

"However, by understanding habits' mechanisms, we gain insights that make new behaviours easier to grasp. Anyone struggling with addiction or destructive behaviours can benefit from help from many quarters, including trained therapists, physicians, social workers and clergy.

"Much of those changes are accomplished because people examine the cues, cravings and rewards that drive their behaviours and then find ways to ***replace*** *their self-destructive* ***routines*** *with healthier alternatives, even if they aren't aware of what they are doing at the time. Understanding the cues and cravings driving your habits*
~~~

won't make them suddenly disappear – but it will give you a way to change the pattern." (Page 77)

It may also help to get you from the 'contemplation stage' of behaviour change to the 'determination stage'.

Once you are determined, you are halfway there. And if you know what the reward will be - and you put secondary rewards and penalties in place - then you are on the home run!

~~~
~~~

Books by the Institute for E-CENT Publications

Distributed by ABC Bookstore Online UK

~~~

How to Resolve Conflict and Unhappiness: Especially during Festive Celebrations:

Coping with and resolving frustrations, disappointments and interpersonal clashes at family celebrations like Christmas, Yuletide, Hanukkah, Eid, and Thanksgiving

Dr Jim Byrne (With Renata Taylor-Byrne)

Conflict can happen in families at any time of year. It just so happens that the first Monday after the Christmas & New Year annual holidays is called 'Divorce Day', because that is when the highest number of divorce petitions is issued. And it seems most likely that the other major family holiday times are the runners up in the divorce stakes. However, what is hidden under these divorce statistics is the mountain of personal and social misery that precedes such drastic 'solutions' to repeated conflict, disappointments and interpersonal clashes.

But there is a better way to deal with these problems. Rather than letting the misery build up over time, you can take control of both your own mind, and the way you communicate within your family and society. You can insulate your social relationships from constant or repeated misery and unhappiness; and learn to have a wonderful life with your family and friends.

The solutions have been assembled by Dr Jim Byrne in this book about how to re-think/re-feel/re-frame your encounters with your significant others; how to communicate so they will listen; how to listen so they can communicate with you; and how to manage your lifestyle for optimum peace, happiness and success in all your relationships.

Paperback (£14.99 GBP) and eBook (£3.99 GBP) on conflict resolution...

Don't let your relationships deteriorate. Get the solution today:

How to Resolve Conflict and Unhappiness

~~~

Anger, resentment and forgiveness:

How to get your inappropriate anger under reasonable control

By Dr Jim Byrne

This book is based on twenty years' experience by the author of providing anger management counselling and coaching to hundreds of individuals.

It includes a unique chapter on the processes required to achieve forgiveness, and a rationale for doing so. And it contains lots of insights into the philosophy and biology of anger management.

Price: £14.75 from Amazon.

Safeguard Your Sleep and Reap the Rewards:

Better health, happiness and resilience

By Renata Taylor-Byrne

A detailed review of the science of sleep, and what this tells us about the importance of sleep for a happy, successful life.

Now you can begin to understand why you need sleep; how much you need; how to optimize your chances of getting a good night's sleep; and what to do if you experience sleep disturbance. You will also learn how to defend your sleep against modern sleep-distractions.

Price: £14.99 (GBP)

How to Quickly Fix your Couple Relationship:

A brief DIY handbook for serious lovers

By Dr Jim Byrne

This book has been specially designed to provide some quick relief up front. That means that, right at the start of the book, I share with you some of the most powerful insights into how to have a happy relationships. I then help you to complete a couple of exercises that take five minutes per day, and which will begin to change your relationship situation almost at once.

Kindle: £5.02

Paperback: £12.10

How to Write a New Life for Yourself:

Narrative therapy and the writing solution.

By Dr Jim Byrne, with Renata Taylor-Byrne

Prices: from £4.22 GBP (Kindle) to £13.27 (paperback)

This book contains more than twenty exercises to help you to get more of what you want from your life.

Journal writing, and various forms of writing therapy, and reflective writing are included, with specific exercises for specific purposes.

How to Have a Wonderful, Loving Relationship:

Helpful insights for couples and lovers

By Jim Byrne (with Renata Taylor-Byrne)

~~~

Originally published with the title, ***Top secrets for Building a Successful Relationship***, in 2018. Reissued with a new title and minor changes in November 2019.

~~~

Do you sometimes feel that you are just reliving your parents' relationship? The unworkable, misery-inducing pattern that you witnessed in childhood? If so, you are probably right. That is most often how relationships turn out, unless you wake up and begin to change your unconscious pattern of relating.

Most human beings long to be engaged in a loving relationship with another person who they like and admire, and who likes, admires, loves and respects them in turn.

But most people have no idea how to bring this about.

A few lucky people will automatically 'know' what to do, non-consciously, because they had parents who openly demonstrated their love for each other.

If your parents did not love, like, respect and/or care for each other; or they failed to demonstrate active love for you; then you are going to have to learn from scratch. But do not despair. The answers to your problem can be found in this book...

PAPERBACK BOOK ON RELATIONSHIP AND COMMUNICATION SKILLS...

Find out how to reprogram yourself for a loving, joyful, peaceful relationship that enriches your life, instead of making you miserable and disappointed.

Prices from £6.65 GBP (Kindle) to £19.48 GBP (paperback)

How to Control Your Anger, Anxiety and Depression:

Using nutrition and physical activity.

By Renata Taylor-Byrne, and Jim Byrne

Changing your philosophy of life will not control your emotions, unless you also attend to your diet and exercise needs.

It is now increasingly being argued, by cutting edge scientists, that the root cause of physical and mental health problems is inflammation in the body, especially in the guts. The concept of leaky gut giving rise to leaky brain is increasingly being verified; and very often the causes of anxiety, depression and anger are to be found in the client's diet; or their lack of physical exercise.

By Renata Taylor-Byrne and Jim Byrne

Prices: from £3.10 (Kindle) to £9.93 GBP (paperback)

Lifestyle Counselling and Coaching for the Whole Person:

Or how to integrate nutritional insights, exercise and sleep coaching into talk therapy.

By Dr Jim Byrne, with Renata Taylor-Byrne

Because diet, exercise and sleep are increasingly seen to be important determinants of mental health and emotional well-being, it is now necessary to rethink our models of counselling and therapy. This book will show counsellors how to incorporate lifestyle coaching and counselling into their system of talk therapy. It will also help self-help enthusiasts to take better care of their own mental and physical health, and emotional well-being.

Prices: from £4.26 GBP (Kindle) to £12.64 (paperback)

~~~

~~~

Facing and Defeating your Emotional Dragons:

How to process old traumas, and eliminate undigested pain from your past experience

By Jim Byrne, Doctor of Counselling

This book presents two processes that are necessary for the digestion of old, traumatic or stress-inducing experiences.

The first looks at how to re-think or re-frame your traumatic memory; and the second is about how to digest it, so it can disappear.

Prices from: £6.16p (Kindle) and £13.63 GBP (Paperback)

Holistic Counselling in Practice:

An introduction to the theory and practice of Emotive-Cognitive Embodied-Narrative Therapy

By Jim Byrne DCoun FISPC

With Renata Taylor-Byrne BSc (Hons) Psychol

This book was the original introduction to Emotive-Cognitive Embodied Narrative Therapy (E-CENT), which was created by Dr Jim Byrne in the period 2009-2014, building upon earlier work from 2003. It is of historic importance, but it has been superseded by Lifestyle Counselling and Coaching for the Whole Persson, above.

Prices from: £5.83p GBP (Kindle) and £15.18p (Paperback)

A counsellor reflects upon models of mind

Integrating the psychological models of Plato, Freud, Berne and Ellis

By Dr Jim Byrne

Prices from: £5.99 (Kindle) and £14.99 GBP (Paperback)

Every counsellor needs to think long and hard about their perceptions of their clients. Are they based on 'common sense', or have they been subjected to the discipline of considering the theories of great minds that preceded us, like Plato, Freud, Berne and Ellis. (Ellis, of course, *oversimplified* the SOR model of mind into the simple ABC model, but he is still important because of his impact on the whole CBT theory, which currently dominates the field of counselling and therapy in the US, UK and elsewhere).

A Major Critique of REBT:

Revealing the many errors in the foundations of Rational Emotive Behaviour Therapy

There was a need to clarify the bottom line of Dr Byrne's critique of REBT, and that has been done in a 22 page Preface to the reissued, 2019 edition.

Also, we have added a reference to the research which shows that emotional pain and physical pain are both mediated and processed through significantly overlapping neural networks, which contradicts Dr Ellis's claim that *nobody could **hurt you**, except with a baseball bat.*

This is a comprehensive and devastating critique of the foundations of Rational Emotive Behaviour Therapy, as developed by Dr Albert Ellis.

Price: £23.58 GBP

If you want to know the essence of our critique of REBT, but you don't want to have to read 500+ pages, then this 150 page summary should appeal to you:

Discounting Our Bodies:

A brief, critical review of REBT's flaws

By Dr Jim Byrne

This book is a brief, summary critique of the main errors contained in the foundations of Rational Emotive Behaviour Therapy (REBT) theory. And especially the invalidity of the ABC model, which asserts that *nothing other than **beliefs*** intervenes between a negative experience and an emotional-behavioural reaction. (The body is ignored!)

Paperback only (at the moment). Price £9.50 GBP

The Amoralism of Rational Emotive Behaviour Therapy (REBT):

The mishandling of self-acceptance and unfairness issues by Albert Ellis

By Dr Jim Byrne

This book is an extensive, detailed critique of two of the central ideas of REBT:

(1) The concept of 'unconditional self-acceptance'; and

(2) The idea that life *is fundamentally unfair*, and that it should be accepted as such, and *never complained about.*

In the process we also deal with Albert Ellis's idea that people should *never be blamed* for anything; that praise and blame are bad; that guilt and shame are to be eliminated, and never taken to be indicators that we've done something wrong. Along the way we have a debate with Dr Michael Edelstein about the role of fairness in couple relationships.

~~~

Albert Ellis and the Unhappy Golfer:

A critique of the simplistic ABC model of REBT

By Dr Jim Byrne

This is a book of reflections upon a case study, presented by Dr Ellis in his 1962 book about the theory of Rational Therapy.

The 'unhappy golfer' is in Dr Albert Ellis's office, in New York City, somewhere around the end of the 1950's. He tells Dr Ellis that he feels terribly unhappy about being rejected by his golfing peers, and Dr Ellis tells him: ***This is something you are doing to yourself!***

Ellis uses the unhappy golfer to introduce his readers to his simple ABC model of Rational (REB) Therapy, which claims – in those places that matter most – that a person cannot be upset emotionally in any way other than by their own beliefs!

This book sets out to refute this simplistic idea.

Albert Ellis and the Unhappy Golfer.

Paperback: £15.71 GBP
~~~

Daniel O'Beeve's Amazing Journey: From traumatic origins to transcendent love

The memoir of Daniel O'Beeve: a strong-willed seeker after personal liberation: 1945-1985

Transcribed by Jim Byrne

It is rare that any of us gets a chance to peer inside of the life of a troubled individual, from a dysfunctional family, and to have our lives enriched by their struggles for freedom and self-understanding. And their quest for love in a cold world can motivate us to keep trying to achieve our own emotional development.

~~~

Available in Kindle eBook for £5.54 GBP

And in paperback for £27.38 GBP:

The Relentless Flow of Fate

By Kurt Llama Byron

An Inspector Glasheen Mystery

This novel introduces the enigmatic Inspector Glasheen in his forty-eighth year of life, and his twenty-first year as a detective in the Gardai, in Dublin. A series of murders awaits him at his new posting. And one in particular, the death of a sixteen year old youth, in his bed, at home, is destined to bring up Glasheen's own demons, from a very disturbed childhood.

Paperback only at the moment, for £11.95 GBP

Fiction is a great vehicle for teaching and learning about social relationships, psychological problems, and the law of karma.

~~~

The Bamboo Paradox:

The limits of human flexibility in a cruel world – and how to protect, defend and strengthen yourself

By Dr Jim Byrne; With Renata Taylor-Byrne

At the age of thirty-four years, I woke up. Woke up for the first time. Became conscious of the fact that I was living a life that did not really work for me – which had never really worked in a fully satisfactory way. At that point, I began to seek wisdom – to examine my life – and to explore better ways of living a fuller, more satisfying life.

In this book, I want to share some of the fruits of my journey towards wisdom, happiness and health.

This is a book about how to take care of yourself in a difficult world; so you can be happy and healthy, and realistically successful and wealthy. Your physical height, weight, muscle bulk and so on, are not the most important determinants of your ability to be *strong* in the face of life's difficult challenges. Nor is your flexibility alone. And misunderstood flexibility can destroy your future chances of happiness and health.

~~~
~~~

Endnotes

[1] Joines, V. and Stewart, I. (2002) *Personality Adaptations: A new guide to human understanding in psychotherapy and counselling.* Nottingham: Lifespace Publishing.

[2] Source: https://exploringyourmind.com/be-like-bamboo-patient-strong-flexible/

[3] Source: https://www.presentationzen.com/presentationzen/2010/07/be-like-the-bamboo-trees-lessons-from-the-japanese-forest.html

[4] Babcock, D.C (2003) 'The little duck'. Quoted in Josh Baran (ed) *365 Nirvana Here and Now: Living every moment in enlightenment.* London: Element. Page 157.

[5] Joines, V. and Stewart, I. (2002) *Personality Adaptations: A new guide to human understanding in psychotherapy and counselling.* Nottingham: Lifespace Publishing.

[6] Taylor-Byrne, R.E. and Byrne, J.W. (2017) *How to control your anger, anxiety and depression, using nutrition and physical activity.* Hebden Bridge: The Institute for E-CENT Publications.

[7] Byrne, J. (2019a) *A Major Critique of REBT: Revealing the many errors in the foundations of Rational Emotive Behaviour Therapy*. Hebden Bridge: The Institute for E-CENT Publications.

[8] Bowell, T. and Kemp, G. (2005) *Critical Thinking: a concise guide.* Second edition. London: Routledge.

[9] Baggini, J. and Strangroom, J. (Eds) (2007) *What More Philosophers Think*. London: Continuum.

[10] Irvine, W.B. (2009) *A Guide to the Good Life: The ancient art of Stoic joy*. Oxford: Oxford University Press.

[11] Dichotomy refers to 'separation' or 'contrast' between **two** events or objects, or concepts, etc.

[12] Byrne, J. (2002) 'Free will and determinism: Am I completely determined by my genes and my environment?' Diploma in Counselling Psychology and Psychotherapy – Assignment 5(c) - submitted to Rusland College, Bath. Hebden Bridge: ABC Publications. Available online: http://free-will-assignment.blogspot.com/

[13] Byrne, J. (2010) Fairness, Justice and Morality Issues in REBT and E-CENT. E-CENT Paper No.2(b). Hebden Bridge: The Institute for E-CENT.

[14] Herbert, W. (2011) The midnight ride effect: How imagining a different past increases our appreciation for the present. *Scientific American Mind*, Jan/Feb, 2011. Pages 66-67.

[15] Koo, M. (2008) It's a wonderful life: Mentally subtracting positive events improves people's affective state, contrary to their affective forecasts. *Journal of Personality and Social Psychology, Vol 95, No.5,* Pages 1217-1224.

[16] Carnegie, D. (1998) *How to Stop Worrying and Start Living.* Berkshire: Random House Books.

[17] Seneca (1995) On anger. In *Moral and Political Essays.* Trans. John Cooper and P.F. Procoupé. Cambridge: Cambridge University Press.

[18] Aurelius, Marcus (1992. *Meditations.* Trans. by A.S.L. Farquharson. London: Everyman's Library.

[19] Epictetus (1991) *Enchiridion.* Trans. by George Long. New York: Prometheus Books.

[20] Irvine, W.B. (2009) *A Guide to the Good Life: the ancient art of Stoic joy*. Oxford: Oxford University Press.

[21] BCE = Before Current Era (which used to be 'BC', in the Christian system of dating events before or after Christ).

[22] Seddon, K. (2000) The Stoics on why we should strive to be free of the passions. *Practical Philosophy, Vol.3:3,* November 2000. Available online: http://www.wku.edu/~jan.garrett/stoa/seddon2.htm. Accessed: 14th March 2011.

[23] *Opinions* here are equivalent to *perceptions, judgements*, and *evaluations*.

[24] Griffin, J. and Tyrrell, I. (2003) *Human Givens: A new approach to emotional health and clear thinking.* Chalvington, East Sussex: HG Publishing.

[25] Ellis, A. (1958). Rational Psychotherapy, *Journal of General Psychology,* 59, 35-49.

Ellis A. (1962). *Reason and Emotion in Psychotherapy,* New York, Carol Publishing.

Ellis, A. (1994). *Reason and Emotion in Psychotherapy: revised and updated,* New York, Carol Publishing Group.

[26] Irvine, W. (2009) *A Guide to the Good Life: The ancient art of stoic joy.* Oxford: Oxford University Press.

[27] Bowlby, J. (2005) *The Making and Breaking of Affectional Bonds.* London: Routledge Classics.

[28] Byrne, J. (2018b) *Daniel O'Beeve's Amazing Journey: From traumatic origins to transcendent love*. Hebden Bridge: The Institute for E-CENT Publications.

[29] Byrne, J. (2016) *Holistic Counselling in Practice: An introduction to the theory and practice of Emotive-Cognitive Embodied-Narrative Therapy*. Hebden Bridge. The Institute for E-CENT Publications.

[30] For an understanding of the process of 'completing your experience' of difficult life circumstances, please see my book on 'Facing and defeating your emotional dragons': Byrne, J. (2019b) *Facing and Defeating your Emotional Dragons: How to process old traumas, and eliminate undigested pain from your past experience.* Hebden Bridge: The Institute for E-CENT Publications.

[31] Dr John Briffa, 'High Anxiety', *Observer Magazine,* 19th June 2005, page 61.

[32] Taylor-Byrne, R.E. (2016a) Appendix F: Physical Exercise and Emotional Wellbeing. In Byrne, J., *Holistic Counselling in Practice: An introduction to the theory and practice of Emotive-Cognitive Embodied-Narrative Therapy*. Hebden Bridge: The Institute for E-CENT.

[33] Byrne, J. (2018b) *Daniel O'Beeve's Amazing Journey: From traumatic origins to transcendent love*. Hebden Bridge: The Institute for E-CENT Publications.

[34] Byrne, J. (2013) *A Wounded Psychotherapist: Albert Ellis's Childhood, and the strengths and limitations of REBT/CBT*. Hebden Bridge: The Institute for CENT Publications/CreateSpace.

[35] Rees, D.A. (1960) In the Introduction to *'Meditations', the book* by Marcus Aurelius (1946/1992) above. Page vii.

[36] Epictetus (1991) *The Enchiridion*. New York: Prometheus Books.

[37] Goleman, D. (1996) *Emotional Intelligence: why it can matter more than IQ*. London: Bloomsbury.

[38] Panksepp, J. (1998) *Affective Neuroscience: The foundations of human and animal emotions.* Oxford University Press.

[39] Siegel, D.J. (2015) *The Developing Mind: How relationships and the brain interact to shape who we are*. London: The Guilford Press.

[40] Hill, D. (2015) *Affect Regulation Theory: A clinical model*. London: W.W. Norton and Company.

~~~

[41] See William Glasser's concept of 'quality world pictures', in his system of Reality Therapy. (Page 173 of Nelson-Jones, 2001).
~~~

[42] Byrne, J. (2011d/2013) The Innate Good and Bad Aspects of all Human Beings (the Good and Bad Wolf states). E-CENT Paper No. 25. Hebden Bridge: The Institute for E-CENT Publications. Available online: https://ecent-institute.org/e-cent-articles-and-papers/

[43] Aurelius, M. (1946/1992) *Meditations*. Trans. A.S.L. Farquharson. London: Everyman's Library.

[44] Sherman, N. (2005) *Stoic Warriors: The ancient philosophy behind the military mind.* Oxford: Oxford University Press. Page 9.

[45] Irvine, W. (2009) *A Guide to the Good Life: the ancient art of Stoic joy.* Oxford: Oxford University Press. Page 30.

[46] As Evans and Reid (2013) write, in the Abstract of their article: "What does it mean to live dangerously? This is not just a philosophical question or ethical call to reflect upon our own individual recklessness. It is a deeply political question being asked by ideologues and policy makers who want us to abandon the dream of ever achieving security and embrace danger as a condition of possibility for life in the future. As this article demonstrates, this belief in the necessity and positivity of human exposure to danger is fundamental to the new doctrine of 'resilience'. Resilience demands our disavowal of any belief in the possibility to secure ourselves and accept that life is a permanent process of continual adaptation to dangers said to be outside our control. The resilient subject is a subject which must permanently struggle to accommodate itself to the world, and not a subject which can conceive of changing the world, its structure and conditions of possibility. However, it is a subject which accepts the dangerousness of the world it lives in as a condition for partaking of that world and which accepts the necessity of the injunction to change itself in correspondence with threats now presupposed as endemic. This is less than acceptable. Not only is it politically catastrophic, it is fundamentally nihilistic. Identifying resilience as a nihilism that forces the subject to wilfully abandon the political, we argue for a wholesale rethinking of the question of what a politics of life is and can be."

[47] Evans, B. and Julian Reid (2013) 'Dangerously exposed: The life and death of the resilient subject'. *Resilience, Vol. 1, No. 2,* Pages 83-98. Available online: http://www. tandfonline.com/doi/pdf/10.1080/21693293.2013.770703

[48] Tartakovsky, M. (2017) Therapists Sp'ill: How To Strengthen Your Resilience. A PsychCentral blog. Available online: https://psychcentral.com/lib/therapists-spill-how-to-strengthen-your-resilience/

[49] Southwick, S.M. and Dennis S. Charney (2013) *Resilience: The science of mastering life's greatest challenges.* Cambridge: Cambridge University Press.

[50] *The Dhammapada* (1973/2015)

[51] See page 245 of Cardwell, M. (2000) *The Complete A-Z Psychology Handbook.* Second edition. London: Hodder and Stoughton.

[52] Bretherton, I. (1992) The Origins of Attachment Theory: John Bowlby and Mary Ainsworth. *Developmental Psychology 28:* 759.

[53] Ayya Khema quotation taken from: Josh Baran (ed) (2003) *365 Nirvana: Here and now.* London: HarperCollins/Element.

[54] Byrne, J. (2019b) *Facing and Defeating your Emotional Dragons: How to process old traumas, and eliminate undigested pain from your past experience.* Hebden Bridge: The Institute for E-CENT Publications.

[55] Epictetus (1991) *The Enchiridion.* New York: Prometheus Books.

[56] Aurelius, M. (1946/1992) *Meditations.* Trans. A.S.L. Farquharson. London: Everyman's Library.

[57] Selye, H. (1956/1975) The Stress of Life. Revised edition. New York: McGraw Hill Book Company. Pages 370-371.

[58] CoRT Tools. This range of thinking tools is described in De Bono (1995: 49-52). CoRT-1 tools are 'attention directors', and are as follows:

- PMI: Plus, Minus and Interesting. Direct your attention to the Plus points, then the Minus points and finally the Interesting points (of any decision you wish to consider making). The result is a quick assessment scan. (You can then decide to ask yourself, "In the light of this PMI, what action should I now take?" Or you could defer that question until you have also applied the following six CoRT tools):
- CAF: Consider All Factors. What should we take into account when we are thinking about something? What are the factors involved here?
- C&S: This tool directs attention to the 'Consequences and Sequels' of the action under consideration. The request is for a forward look at what will happen later. Different time scales can be requested.
- AGO: What are the Aims, Goals and Objectives? What are we trying to do? What are we trying to achieve? Where are we going?
- FIP: First Important Priorities: Direct attention to those things which really matter. Not everything is of equal importance. What are the priorities?
- APC: Alternatives, Possibilities and Choices. Create new alternatives? What are the possibilities? What are the choices?

- OPV: Direct attention to Other People's Views. Who are the other people involved? What are their views?

"The tools are used explicitly and directly. They are a formal way of directing perceptual attention in a defined direction". (Page 51 of De Bono, 1995).

De Bono, E. (1995) *Teach Yourself to Think.* London: Viking/Penguin.

~~~

[59] Byrne, J.W. (2018a) *Lifestyle Counselling and Coaching of the Whole Person: Or how to integrate nutritional insights, physical exercise and sleep coaching into talk therapy.* Hebden Bridge: The Institute for E-CENT Publications.

[60] Taylor-Byrne, R.E. (2019) *Safeguard Your Sleep and Reap the Rewards: Better health, happiness and resilience.* Hebden Bridge: The Institute for E-CENT Publications.

[61] Maas, J. (2007) *Sleep Power*. London: HarperCollins.

[62] Stevenson, S. (2016) *Sleep Smarter: 21 Essential strategies to sleep your way to a better body, better health and better success,* London: Hay House.

[63] Walker, M. (2017) *Why We Sleep*. London: Allen Lane.

[64] Taylor-Byrne, R.E. and Byrne, J.W. (2017) *How to control your anger, anxiety and depression, using nutrition and physical activity.* Hebden Bridge: The Institute for E-CENT Publications.

[65] Lopresti, A.L., and Sean D. Hood, and Peter D. Drummond (2013) A review of lifestyle factors that contribute to important pathways associated with major depression: Diet, sleep and exercise. *Journal of Affective Disorders, Vol.148(1),* Pages 12-27.

[66] Professor Colin Espie: Online: https://www.sleepio.com/articles/sleep-basics/sleep-basics-intro/. Accessed: 25th January 2018).

[67] McGuiness, M. (2013) Poetry: "Sleep that knits up the ravell'd sleave of care". Poems and poetry blog. Available online: http://www.markmcguinness.com/index.php/macbeth-sleep/. Accessed: 22nd January 2018.

[68] Mauss, I.B, and Allison S. Troy & Monique K. LeBourgeois (2013) Poorer sleep quality is associated with lower emotion-regulation ability in a laboratory paradigm. Cognition and Emotion 27 (3):567-576 (2013)

[69] Strine, T.W. and Chapman, D.P. (2005) Associations of frequent sleep insufficiency with health-related quality of life and health behaviours. *Sleep Medicine, Volume 6, Issue 1,* January 2005, Pages 23-27.
~~~

[70] Walker (2017) conducted an experiment in his sleep lab, to show how the lack of sleep affects people's emotional intelligence. He took two groups of people and placed them under two different experimental conditions. One group had a full night's sleep, and then were shown a range of pictures of individual human faces, which displayed a wide range of emotions, varying from friendliness through to intense dislike and anger. The participants had to individually assess this range of facial expressions, to decide if they were displaying threatening or friendly messages. While they were engaged in this activity, their brains were being scanned in a Magnetic Resonance Imaging (MRI) machine. (The following night, this group was deprived of sleep, particularly rapid eye movement (REM) sleep).

The second groups in Walker's research had the sleep deprivation condition first, and then examined the pictures, and had to assess the emotions on display. (They had a full night's sleep the following night, and did a similar visual assessment the following day).

The results of Walker's experiments were as follows: If participants had had a good night's sleep beforehand, then they had no difficulty in distinguishing facial expressions ranging from hostility through to benevolence. Their assessments (spoken, and neurological, confirmed by the MRI scans) – unlike those of the sleep deprived condition - were accurate, showing that the quality of their sleep had helped them in their reading of facial expressions.

But in the sleep deprived condition, participants found it much harder to differentiate between the facial expressions displayed on in the range of pictures shown to them. Their ability to quickly spot and decipher facial expressions accurately had deserted them. And their errors were far from minor. For example, they perceived facial expressions of kindliness and welcome as hostile and menacing. According to Walker (2017):

"Reality and perceived reality were no longer the same in the 'eyes' of the sleepless brain. By removing REM sleep we had, quitter literally, removed participants' level-headed ability to read the social world around them". (Page 217).

For an illustration of why this kind of loss of emotional intelligence might be very serious indeed, it is the kind of ability to read social signals which has to be used by police officers in situations of social conflict, to decide whether or not to use gunfire, or to use a lesser form of response. And it is crucial in making judgements in sales and negotiation situations; and in managing personal and professional relationships. Thus lack of adequate sleep is clearly a very costly form of poor self-management!

~~~
~~~

[71] Gordon, A.M. (2013) Up all night: the effects of sleep loss on mood. Research shows just one bad night of sleep can put a damper on your mood. *Psychology Today Online.* August 15th 2013. Available here: https://www.psychology today.com/ blog/ between-you-and-me/201308/all-night-the-effects-sleep-loss-mood. Accessed: 20th January 2018.

[72] Asp, K. (2015) Lack of Sleep and Depression: Causes and Treatment Options. The AAST blog: https://www.aastweb.org/blog /the-relationships-between-lack-of-sleep-and-depression. Accessed: 22nd January 2018.

[73] Jacob A. Nota, Meredith E. Coles. Shorter sleep duration and longer sleep onset latency are related to difficulty disengaging attention from negative emotional images in individuals with elevated transdiagnostic repetitive negative thinking. *Journal of Behaviour Therapy and Experimental Psychiatry*, 2018; 58: 114 DOI: 10.1016/j.jbtep.2017.10.003

[74] Nauert, R. (2018) 'Sleep Loss Increases Anxiety — Especially Among Worriers'. PsychCentral blog post. 8th August 2018: Available online: https://psychcentral.com/news/2013/06/27/sleep-loss-increases-anxiety-especially-among-worriers/56531.html

[75] Anwar, Y. (2013) 'Tired and edgy? Sleep deprivation boosts anticipatory anxiety'. Berkeley News. Online: https://news.berkeley.edu/2013/06/25/anticipate-the-worst/

[76] Gordon, A.M. (2013) Up all night: the effects of sleep loss on mood. Research shows just one bad night of sleep can put a damper on your mood. *Psychology Today Online.* August 15th 2013. Available here: https://www.psychology today.com/ blog/ between-you-and-me/201308/all-night-the-effects-sleep-loss-mood. Accessed: 20th January 2018.

[77] My-Sahana (2012) 'Common Causes for Anger Management Issues'. MySahana blog post. Online: http://mysahana.org/2012/02/common-causes-for-anger-manage-ment-issues/. Accessed: 22nd January 2018.

[78] According to the NHS Choices (UK) website, lack of sleep affects physical health as much as emotional wellbeing: "Many effects of a lack of sleep, such as feeling grumpy and not working at your best, are well known. But did you know that sleep deprivation can also have profound consequences on your physical health?"

The bottom line of this statement was this: "Regular poor sleep puts you at risk of serious medical conditions, including obesity, heart disease and diabetes – and it shortens your life expectancy." (See NHS Choices, 2015).

"One in three of us suffers from poor sleep, with stress, computers and taking work home often blamed.

"However, the cost of all those sleepless nights is more than just bad moods and a lack of focus.

"Regular poor sleep puts you at risk of serious medical conditions, including obesity, heart disease and diabetes – and it shortens your life expectancy."

"It's now clear that a solid night's sleep is essential for a long and healthy life." Available online: https://www.nhs.uk/Livewell/tiredness-and-fatigue/Pages/lack-of-sleep-health-risks.aspx. Accessed: 25th January 2018.

~~~

[79] Smith, R. (2009) Sleeping problems such as insomnia linked to suicide attempts. The Telegraph, online: https://www.telegraph.co.uk/news/ health/news/ 5082849/ Sleeping-problems-such-as-insomnia-linked-to-suicide-attempts.html

[80] Koffler, J. (2015) Donald Trump's 16 Biggest Business Failures and Successes. Time Magazine, online: https://time.com/3988970/donald-trump-business/

[81] Barber, L.K. (2010) 'Sleep consistency and sufficiency: are both necessary for less psychological strain?' Stress & Health blog. Wiley Online Library. https://onlinelibrary.wiley.com/doi/abs/10.1002/smi.1292

[82] van der Helm E1, Yao J, Dutt S, Rao V, Saletin JM, Walker MP. (2011) 'REM sleep depotentiates amygdala activity to previous emotional experiences'. *Current Biology. 2011 Dec 6;21(23)*: Pages 2029-32. doi: 10.1016/j.cub.2011.10.052.

[83] Osmun, R. (2015) How sleep balances your mind and emotions. Sonima Blog, Available online: https://www.sonima.com/meditation/sleep-emotions/

[84] Van der Helm, E., & Walker, M. P. (2009) Overnight Therapy? The Role of Sleep in Emotional Brain Processing. *Psychological Bulletin*, *135*(5), Pages 731–748.

[85] June J. Pilcher, Drew M. Morris, Janet Donnelly and Hayley B. Feigl (2015) Interactions between sleep habits and self-control. Frontiers in Human Neuroscience, 11 May 2015. Online: https://doi.org/10.3389/fnhum.2015.00284

[86] Calm-Clinic (2018) How Sleep Debt Causes Serious Anxiety. Online blog: https://www.calmclinic.com/anxiety/causes/sleep-debt. Accessed: 25th January 2018.

[87] NSF (2018) Depression and sleep. Online blog: https://sleepfoundation.org/sleep-disorders-problems/depression-and-sleep. Accessed: 25th January 2018.
~~~

[88] Kogan, N. (2018) The magic of a good night's sleep: Because an exhausted person is never a happy person. Happier. Online: https://www.happier.com/blog/the-magic-of-sleep. Accessed: 25th January 2018.

~~~

[89] Wagner, E. (1996) *How to stay out of the doctor's surgery*. Carnell.

[90] ***The effects of physical exercise on insomnia.*** There is scientific research evidence, from the Journal of Clinical Sleep Medicine – Cited in Stevenson, (2016); pages 88-89 - to support the conclusion that ***"consistent exercise" will produce the following positive effects upon sleep***:

1. A 55% improvement in sleep onset latency. (This means the study participants fell asleep faster, or sooner than normal, when they had exercised their bodies).

2. An 18% increase in total sleep time during the test nights.

3. A 13% increase in sleep efficiency (which means an improvement of the quality of sleep. [The quality of sleep is measured by how refreshed you feel the following day]).

The research participants in this study were all said to be suffering from 'primary insomnia', which is a psychiatric term for serious sleep problems described as: "difficulty initiating or maintaining sleep, or suffering from non-restorative sleep, for at least 1 month" before the study began.

And in our view, an adequate definition of 'consistent exercise regime' could be as little as 30 minutes of brisk walking, in an enjoyable context, at least five days per week.

~~~

[91] Hubbard, B. (2018) Not sleeping? Write a to-do list before you go to bed. *What Doctors Don't Tell You. January 2018*. News.

[92] Scullin, M. K., Krueger, M. L., Ballard, H. K., Pruett, N., & Bliwise, D. L. (2018). The effects of bedtime writing on difficulty falling asleep: A polysomnographic study comparing to-do lists and completed activity lists. *Journal of Experimental Psychology: General, 147(1),* Pages 139-146.

[93] Howatson G1, Bell PG, Tallent J, Middleton B, McHugh MP, Ellis J. (2012) 'Effect of tart cherry juice (Prunus cerasus) on melatonin levels and enhanced sleep quality'. European Journal of Nutrition. 2012 Dec;51(8):909-16. doi: 10.1007/s00394-011-0263-7. Epub 2011 Oct 30.

~~~
~~~

[94] Taylor-Byrne, R.E. and Byrne, J.W. (2017) *How to control your anger, anxiety and depression, using nutrition and physical activity.* Hebden Bridge: The Institute for E-CENT Publications.

[95] Campbell, T.C. and Campbell, T.M. (2006) *The China Study: The most comprehensive study of nutrition ever conducted and the startling implications for diet, weight loss and long-term health.* Dallas, TX: Benbella Books.

[96] Elliott, A.F. (2014) 'Can an Atkins-style diet really fight depression? Research suggests low-carb, high fat foods can drastically improve mental health'. Available online: http://www.dailymail.co.uk/ femail/ article-2590880/Can-Atkins-style-diet-really-fight-depression-Research-suggests-low-carb-high-fat-foods-drastically-improve-mental-health.html Downloaded: 2nd October 2017.

[97] Mozes, A. (2015) The Surprising Link Between Carbs and Depression. Online health blog. Available: http://www.health.com/depression/could-too-many-refined-carbs-make-you-depressed. Accessed: June 2016.

[98] Boseley, S. (2018) Half of all food bought in UK is ultra-processed. *The Guardian.* Saturday 3rd February 2018. Issue No. 53,323.

[99] Brogan, K. (2016) *A mind of your own: The truth about depression and how women can heal their bodies to reclaim their lives.* London: Thorsons.

[100] Perlmutter, D. (2015) *Brain Maker: The power of gut microbes to heal and protect your brain – for life.* London: Hodder and Stoughton.

[101] Holford, P. (2010) *Optimum Nutrition for the mind*. London: Piatkus.

[102] Korn, L. (2016). *Nutrition Essentials for Mental Health: A complete guide to the food-mood connection.* New York: W. W. Norton & Company.

[103] Watch the movie: 'All Jacked Up': The explosive junk food documentary the food companies hope you never see; by Mike Adams, 2008: https://www.naturalnews.com/022510.html

[104] And see also Morgan Spurlock's documentary - ('Super Size Me', 2004) - about trying to live on McDonald's burgers for 30 days, and the medically confirmed negative impact on his physical and mental health! Source: http://watchdocumentaries.com/super-size-me/. Accessed: 21st November 2017.

[105] Coenzyme Q10 may be important for general health. According to the Mayo Clinic: "Coenzyme Q10 (CoQ10) is an antioxidant that your body produces naturally. Your cells use CoQ10 for growth and maintenance.

"Levels of CoQ10 in your body decrease as you age. CoQ10 levels have also been found to be lower in people with certain conditions, such as heart disease.

"CoQ10 is found in meat, fish and whole grains. The amount of CoQ10 found in these dietary sources, however, isn't enough to significantly increase CoQ10 levels in your body.

"As a supplement, CoQ10 supplement is available as capsules, tablets and by IV. CoQ10 might help treat certain heart conditions, as well as migraines and Parkinson's disease." Source: https://www.mayoclinic.org/ drugs-supplements-coenzyme-q10/ art-20362602. Accessed: 30th October 2017.

~~~

[106] According to NHS choices: "Probiotics (like Acidophilus) are live bacteria and yeasts promoted as having various health benefits. They're usually added to yoghurts or taken as food supplements, and are often described as 'good' or 'friendly' bacteria.

"Probiotics are thought to help restore the natural balance of bacteria in your gut (including your stomach and intestines) when it has been disrupted by an illness or treatment." (Source: https://www.nhs.uk/Conditions/probiotics/Pages/ Introduction.aspx. Accessed: 30th October 2017.

According to Enders (2015) changing the variety of live bacteria in the guts of lab mice can change their behaviour so radically that it is thought they could change character and temperament (in human terms)." And gut bacteria have been shown to be involved in communication between the gut and the brain in humans. (Enders, 2015).

[107] Enders, G. (2015) *Gut: The inside story of our body's most under-rated organ*. London: Scribe Publications.

[108] "Essential fatty acids are, as they sound, fats that are necessary within the human body. Though you've probably often heard the word "fats" and associated it with bad health, there are some essential fatty acids that are necessary for your survival. Without them, you could cause serious damage to different systems within the body. However, essential fatty acids are also not usually produced naturally within the body. This means that you have to obtain essential fatty acids by adding them to your diet. There are two basic types of essential fatty acids": Omega-3 and Omega-6. And it is argued that we need more of the 3's than the 6's; or, at least, we have to get the balance right (which could be as low as 1:1). Too much omega-6 seems to be bad for our health (and western diets currently include too much omega-6). Sources: Friday Editor (2017) 'What are essential fatty acids?' The Fit Day
~~~

Blog. Available online at: http://www.fitday.com/fitness-articles/ nutrition/ fats/what-are-essential-fatty-acids.html. And, Dr Michael Greger (2016).

[109] Akbaraly TN, Brunner EJ, Ferrie JE, et al. (2009) Dietary pattern and depressive symptoms in middle age. *The British Journal of Psychiatry, 2009 Nov;195(5):* 408-413. doi: 10.1192/bjp.bp.108.058925.

[110] Ballantyne, C. (2007) Fact or Fiction? Vitamin Supplements Improve Your Health. *Scientific American* (Online): http://www.scientificamerican.com/ article/ fact- or-fiction-vitamin-supplements-improve-health/May 17, 2007. Accessed 26th April 2016.

[111] Deans, E. (2018) Magnesium for Depression: A controlled study of magnesium shows clinically significant improvement. Psychology Today Blog: https://www.psychologytoday.com/ blog/ evolutionary-psychiatry/ 201801/ magnesium-depression. Accessed: 2nd March 2018.

[112] Chaitow, L. (2003) *Candida Albicans: The non-drug approach to the treatment of Candida infection*. London: Thorsons.

[113] Jacobs, G. (1994) *Candida Albicans: A user's guide to treatment and recovery*. London: Optima.

[114] Trowbridge, J.P. and Walker, M. (1989) *The Yeast Syndrome*. London: Bantam Books.

[115] Silberman, B. (2017) in Timothy Ferriss, *Tribe of Mentors: Short life advice from the best in the world*. Boston: Houghton Mifflin Harcourt. Page 497.

[116] Hellmich, N. (2013) The best preventative medicine? Exercise. Online: dailycomet.com. Accessed: 18th June 2016

[117] Atkinson (2007), page 355.

[118] Source: Just Swim (2016) 'How swimming improves mental health'. An online blog: http://www.swimming.org/justswim/swimming-improves-mental-health/

[119] Source: Women's Running (2015) 'The mental health benefits of running: How running can alleviate symptoms of depression'. Online blog. Available at this url: http://womensrunninguk.co.uk/health/mental-health-benefits-running/. Accessed: 23rd November 2017

[120] Source: O'Connor, P.J., Herring, M.P. and Carvalho, A. (2010). 'Mental health benefits of strength training in adults'. *American Journal of Lifestyle Medicine, 4(5),* Pages 377-396.

[121] Here are some of the sources:

(a) Broderick J, Knowles A, Chadwick J, Vancampfort D. (2015) Yoga versus standard care for schizophrenia. Cochrane Database of Systematic Reviews 2015, Issue 10. Art. No.: CD010554. DOI: 10.1002/14651858.CD010554.pub2 - (Further research is required).

(b) Bangalore NG, Varambally S. (2012) Yoga therapy for schizophrenia. *International Journal of Yoga* 2012; **5**(2):85-91. [PUBMED: 22869990]

(c) Behere RV, Arasappa R, Jagannathan A, Varambally S, Venkatasubramanian G, Thirthalli J, Subbakrishna DK, Nagendra HR, Gangadhar BN (2011). Effect of yoga therapy on facial emotion recognition deficits, symptoms and functioning in patients with schizophrenia. Acta Psychiatrica Scandinavia, Vol 123 (2); pp: 147 -53

(d) Duraiswamy G, Thirthalli J, Nagendra HR and Gangadhar BN (2007). Yoga therapy as an add-on treatment in the management of patients with schizophrenia – a randomized controlled trial. Acta Psychiatrica Scandinavia, 116 (3); pp: 226-32

(e) Radhakrishna S (2010). Application of integrated yoga therapy to increase imitation skills in children with autism spectrum disorder. *International Journal of Yoga, 3 (1);* pp: 26-30.

(f) Radhakrishna S, Nagarathna R and Nagendra HR (2010). Integrated approach to yoga therapy and autism spectrum disorders. Journal of Ayurveda and *Integrative Medicine, 1 (2);* pp: 120-4.

(g) Sadock BJ and Sadock VA (2000). *Kaplan and Sadock's Synopsis of Psychiatry: Behavioural Sciences/Clinical Psychiatry, 7th Edition*. Lippincott Williams & Wilkins. USA

(h) Shapiro D, Cook IA, Davydov DM, Ottaviani C, Leuchter AF and Abrams M (2007). Yoga as a Complementary Treatment of Depression: Effects of Traits and Moods on Treatment Outcome. *Evidence based complementary and alternative medicine, 4(4),* pp: 493-502.

(i) Sharma VK, Das S, Mondal S, Goswami U and Gandhi A, (2006). Effect of Sahaj Yoga on neuro-cognitive functions in patients suffering from major depression. Indian *Journal of Physiological Pharmacology*, Oct-Dec, 50(4); pp: 375-83.

(j) Sharma VK, Das S, Mondal S, Goswami U and Gandhi A (2005). Effect of Sahaj Yoga on depressive disorders. Indian *Journal of Physiological Pharmacology*, Oct-Dec, 49(4); pp: 462-8.

(k) Uebelacker LA, Tremont G, Epstein-Lubow G, Gaudiano BA, Gillette T, Kalibatseva Z and Miller IW (2010). Open trial of Vinyasa yoga for persistently depressed individuals: evidence of feasibility and acceptability. *Behaviour Modification*, May, 34(3); pp: 247-64.

(l) Vancampfort D, De Hert M, Knapen J, Wampers M, Demunter H, Deckx S, Maurissen K and Probst M (2011). State anxiety, psychological stress and positive well-being responses to yoga and aerobic exercise in people with schizophrenia: a pilot study. *Disability Rehabilitation, 33(8);* pp: 684-9.

(m) Visceglia E and Lewis S (2011). Yoga therapy as an adjunctive treatment for schizophrenia: a randomized, controlled pilot study. *Journal of Alternative and complementary Medicine, 17(7),* pages: 601-7

~~~

[122] **Definition**: Restorative postures are basically supported reposes, like the Death Pose. 'Let's face it: Some yoga poses taste a little bit sweeter than others. And if yoga were a smorgasbord, restorative postures would most definitely be at the dessert table. These...

These soothing and well-supported poses offer us the opportunity to linger quietly for a few moments and savor the simple sweetness of life.' (Claudia Cummins, (2007) How to Start a Restorative Yoga Practice. *Yoga Journal,* Aug 28, 2007. Available online: http://www.yogajournal.com/ article/beginners/restorative-yoga/. Accessed: 17th June 2016.

[123] Reder, A. (2007) Unmasking Anger. *Yoga Journal*. August 28th 2007. Available online: http://www.yogajournal.com/article/yoga-101/unmasking-anger/. Accessed: 17th June 2016.

[124] Medina, J. (2015) How Yoga is Similar to Existing Mental Health Therapies. Source: Psych Central website: http://psychcentral.com/lib/how-yoga-is-similar-to-existing-therapies/. Accessed: May 2016.

[125] Santer, M.J. Why Qigong Is So Effective Against Emotional Illnesses. Source: http://qigong15.com/blog/qigong-exercises/why-qigong-is-so-effective-against-emotional-illnesses/. Accessed May 2015.

[126] Tse, M. (1995) *Qigong for Health and Vitality*. London: Piatkus.

[127] Linder *and colleagues* conducted a randomized controlled trial to assess the ability of Qi Gong to relieve stress. See: Linder K. and Svardsudd, K. (2006) Qigong has a relieving effect on stress. *Lakartidningen.* (A Swedish Medical Journal) *2006; Vol.103 (24-25):* Pages 1942-1945.

[128] Jahnke, R. Larkey, L. Rogers, C. Etnier, J. and Lin, F. (2012) A Comprehensive Review of Health Benefits of Qigong and Tai Chi. *American Journal of Health Promotion, Jul-Aug; Vol.24 (6),* Pages e1-e25.

[129] Larkey L, Jahnke R, Etnier J, Gonzalez J. (2009) Meditative movement as a category of exercise: Implications for research. *Journal of Physical Activity & Health. 2009*; Vol.6: Pages 230–238.
~~~

[130] Jahnke R. (2002) *The Healing Promise of Qi: Creating Extraordinary Wellness through Qigong and Tai Chi*. Chicago, IL: Contemporary Books.

[131] Ratey, J. and Hagerman, E. (2010) *Spark! How exercise will improve the performance of your brain.* London: Quercus.

[132] Sapolsky R. (2010) *Why Zebras don't get Ulcers.* Third Ed. New York: St Martin's Griffin.

[133] Bryant, C.W. (2010) Does running fight depression? 14th July 2010. HowStuffWorks.com. Available online: http://adventure. howstuffworks.com/ outdoor-activities/ running/health/running-fight-depression.htm. Accessed 16th June 2016.

~~~

[134] Jacobson, E. (1976) *You must Relax: Practical Methods for Reducing the Tensions of Modern Living*. London: Unwin Paperbacks.

[135] Jacobson, E. (1963) *Tension Control for Businessmen.* CT. USA: Martino Publishing. (Formerly published by McGraw-Hill Book Co. Inc. New York City. 1963).

[136] Jacobson, E. (1963) *Tension Control for Businessmen.* CT.USA: Martino Publishing. (Formerly published by McGraw-Hill Book Co. Inc. New York City. 1963).

[137] Jacobson, E. (1976) *You must Relax: Practical Methods for Reducing the Tensions of Modern Living*. London: Unwin Paperbacks.

[138] Edlund, M. (2011) *The Power of Rest: Why Sleep alone is not enough*. New York: Harper Collins.

[139] Turner, M., and Barker, J. (2014) *What Business can learn from Sport Psychology.* Oakamoor, USA: Bennion Kearny Ltd.

[140] Meracou, K., Tsoukas, K., Stavrinos, G., et.al. (2019) The effect of PMR on emotional competence, depression-anxiety-stress, and sense of coherence, health-related quality of life, and well-being of unemployed people in Greece: An Intervention study. *EXPLORE, Volume 15, Issue 1*, January–February 2019: Pages 38-46. https://doi.org/10.1016/j.explore.2018.08.001

[141] Ismail,N.,Taha, W., and Elgzar, I. (2018) The effect of Progressive muscle relaxation on Post-caesarean section pain, quality of sleep and physical activities limitation (2018)International Journal of studies in Nursing. Vol 3, No.3 (2018)ISSN (online) DOI: https://doi.org/10.20849/ijsn.v3i3.461.
~~~

[142] Wolpe, J. (1968) *Psychotherapy by Reciprocal Inhibition. Redwood City, Cal: Stanford University Press.*

[143] Byrne, J.W. (2019c) *Holistic Counselling in Practice: An introduction to the theory and practice of Emotive-Cognitive Embodied-Narrative Therapy. Updated edition (2).* Hebden Bridge: The Institute for E-CENT Publications.

[144] 'Unifying principles' – as defined by *Charles R. Hobbs (1991) 'Insight on Time Management', Audio tape program* – are statements of **principle** which hold together your **values** and your **actions**. They help to keep you in **integrity**: living from your deepest commitments and values.

[145] **CoRT Tools**. This range of thinking tools is described in De Bono (1995: 49-52). CoRT-1 tools are 'attention directors', and are as follows:

- PMI: Plus, Minus and Interesting. Direct your attention to the Plus points, then the Minus points and finally the Interesting points (of any decision you wish to consider making). The result is a quick assessment scan. (You can then decide to ask yourself, "In the light of this PMI, what action should I now take?" Or you could defer that question until you have also applied the following six CoRT tools):
- CAF: Consider All Factors. What should we take into account when we are thinking about something? What are the factors involved here?
- C&S: This tool directs attention to the 'Consequences and Sequels' of the action under consideration. The request is for a forward look at what will happen later. Different time scales can be requested.
- AGO: What are the Aims, Goals and Objectives? What are we trying to do? What are we trying to achieve? Where are we going?
- FIP: First Important Priorities: Direct attention to those things which really matter. Not everything is of equal importance. What are the priorities?
- APC: Alternatives, Possibilities and Choices. Create new alternatives? What are the possibilities? What are the choices?
- OPV: Direct attention to Other People's Views. Who are the other people involved? What are their views?

"The tools are used explicitly and directly. They are a formal way of directing perceptual attention in a defined direction". (Page 51 of De Bono, 1995).

De Bono, E. (1995) *Teach Yourself to Think.* London: Viking/Penguin.

~~~
~~~

146 Part of the process of the normal socialization of every child involves ensuring that the new person mainly develops their 'good side' - (or what the Native American Cherokee people call the 'good wolf') - through the moral teachings of their parents, teachers and others; and that their 'bad wolf' (or evil or anti-social tendency) is constrained and contained. (It cannot ever be totally or permanently eliminated. We each contain the capacity for significant levels of evil to the end of our days!) See Byrne (2011/2013):

Byrne, J. (2011-2013) The Innate Good and Bad Aspects of all Human Beings (the Good and Bad Wolf states). E-CENT Paper No.25: Hebden Bridge: The Institute for E-CENT Publications. Available online: https://ecent-institute.org/e-cent-articles-and-papers/

~~~

147 The spiritual roots of E-CENT: See our web page outlining the E-CENT position: web.archive.org/web/20150316101014/web.archive.org/web/*/http://abc-counselling.com/id434.html

148 In her work on therapeutic writing, Julia Cameron (1992) uses several metaphors and similes to try to communicate what her readers and students can gain from using her system of therapeutic writing. The one I like the most is this:

"Writing in your journal, about the trials and tribulations of your life, is like ***building a bridge into a better future for you!"*** (See ...

Byrne, J. (2018c) *How to Write a New Life for Yourself: Narrative therapy and the writing solution*. Hebden Bridge: The Institute for E-CENT Publications.)

149 Cameron, J. (1994) *The Artist's Way: a spiritual path to higher creativity.* London: Souvenir Press.

150 Byrne, J.W. (2019c) *Holistic Counselling in Practice: An introduction to the theory and practice of Emotive-Cognitive Embodied-Narrative Therapy. Updated edition (2).* Hebden Bridge: The Institute for E-CENT Publications.

151 For example, you can use the WDEP model to explore the following questions:

W = What do you want?

D = What are you doing to get what you want?

E = Let's evaluate how well your D (Doing) serves your W (Want or goal).

P = Plan or re-Plan. (Very often, there is a mismatch between the W and the D which, once understood, resolves the problem).
~~~

[152] Sher, B. (1995) *I Could Do Anything If I Only Knew What It Was: How to Discover What You Really Want and How to Get It.* New York: Dell.

[153] Wallin, D.A. (2007) *Attachment in Psychotherapy.* New York: Guilford Press.

[154] Bowell, T. and Kemp, G. (2005) *Critical Thinking: A concise guide. Second edition.* London: Routledge.

[155] Robert M. Yerkes and John D. Dodson (1908) 'The relation of strength of stimulus to rapidity of habit-formation'. *Journal of Comparative Neurology and Psychology. November 1908.* https://doi.org/10.1002/cne.920180503.

[156] Marmot, M.G., Davey Smith, G., Stansfeld, S., et al. (1991) 'Health inequalities among British civil servants; the Whitehall II Study'. *The Lancet, 337:* 1387-1393

[157] CE = Current era, which was previous expressed as AD (or Ano Domini)).

[158] Epictetus (1991) *Enchiridion*, New York, Prometheus Books.

[159] Wilkinson, R. and Pickett, K. (2010) *The Spirit Level: Why equality is better for everybody.* London: Penguin Books.

[160] Weaver, M. (2020) 'Retired NHS staff reluctant to return'. *The Guardian* newspaper. Thursday, 5th March. Page 6.

[161] Williams, Z. (2020) 'Where did the weekend go?' *The Guardian, 'G2'.* Page 8. Thursday 27th February 2020

[162] Ratey, J., and Hagerman, E. (2009) *Spark: The revolutionary new science of exercise and the brain.* London: Quercus.

[163] Orfeu Buxton, Professor of behavioural health at Penn State University. Quoted in: Huffington, A. (2017) The Sleep Revolution: Transforming your life one night at a time. London: W.H. Allan.

[164] Southwick, S.M. and Dennis S. Charney (2013) *Resilience: The science of mastering life's greatest challenges.* Cambridge: Cambridge University Press.

[165] **E-CENT** stands for Emotive-Cognitive Embodied Narrative therapy. The ***emotive*** component of the human being, and of our approach to counselling, is emphasized, by being given first place, because humans are ***primarily*** emotional beings. ***Cognition*** (which includes attention, perception, language, and thinking), is in second place, because language and thinking are products of our socialization, rather than being innate or fixed. ***Embodiment*** is the physical stratum which underpins and sustains our innate feelings and our socialized language/thinking. ***Narrative*** is next, because we create our narratives (or stories of our experience) out of our socialized language and socially shaped thinking. And ***therapy*** is what we do with these insights into the social individual.

[166] Prochaska, J.O., Norcross, J.C. & DiClemente, C.C. (1998). *Changing for Good*. Reprint edition. New York: Morrow.

[167] Kaizen: A philosophy of continuous improvement, often in very small steps. In E-CENT we emphasize the importance of *gradual* change through *small* steps in personal habit change, because attempts at big steps often backfire, because the habit-based part of us rebels against the challenge of dramatic change.

[168] Bargh, J.A. and Chartrand, T.L. (1999) 'The unbearable automaticity of being'. *American Psychologist, 54(7):* 462-479.

[169] Duhigg, C. (2013) *The Power of Habit: Why we do what we do and how to change*. London: Random House.

~~~
~~~

Printed in Great Britain
by Amazon